YOU and
the United States

Clarence Samford   Professor in College of Education, Southern Illinois University

Edith McCall   Former Reading Supervisor, La Grange, Illinois

Floyd F. Cunningham   Professor in Department of Geography, Southern Illinois University

Benefic Press   Publishing Division of Beckley-Cardy Company
CHICAGO   Atlanta   Dallas   Long Beach   Portland

Learning for Living in Today's World

YOU ARE HERE

YOU AND THE NEIGHBORHOOD

YOU AND THE COMMUNITY

YOU AND REGIONS NEAR AND FAR

YOU AND THE UNITED STATES

YOU AND THE AMERICAS

YOU AND THE WORLD

Library of Congress
Number 64-16998

Illustrations by:

James Teason   75-115, 169, 170, 173, 174, 176, 205, 210, 211, 214-216, 219, 221

Berthold Tiedemann 30, 32-35, 38-41, 51, 54, 58, 59, 62, 64, 72, 73, 120, 122-125, 128, 131, 132, 134-137,
                    151, 154, 156, 178, 179, 183, 187-189, 192-198, 202, 203, 206, 208, 209, 212

William Tanis   11, 20, 26-27, 28, 36, 37, 46, 47, 52, 53, 56, 57, 60, 61, 67, 68, 116-119, 127, 139, 140,
                    141, 142, 143, 144, 147-149, 152, 153, 155, 158-159, 160-167, 175, 190-191, 199, 200,
                    207, 230-233, 235, 242-243, 254, 259, 260-263, 368-369

George Rohrer   8-9, 226-227, 239, 248, 249, 282, 288, 300-301, 310, 316-317, 328, 346, 364

Theodore Street   12, 13, 14, 15, 272, 318, 370

Patricia Jackson   17, 18, 19, 25, 223, 224, 228, 240, 251, 276, 277, 281, 311, 338, 365, 371, 372, 375

Robert Friedl   48-49, 77, 79, 81, 88, 89, 92, 98, 129, 171, 176, 227, 234-235, 253, 275, 280, 304, 314,
                    332, 350, 354, 356, 357

Gregory Orloff   218, 229, 258, 294, 303, 305, 320-321, 322, 325, 334, 351

Contents

THE COLONIES BECOME A NATION

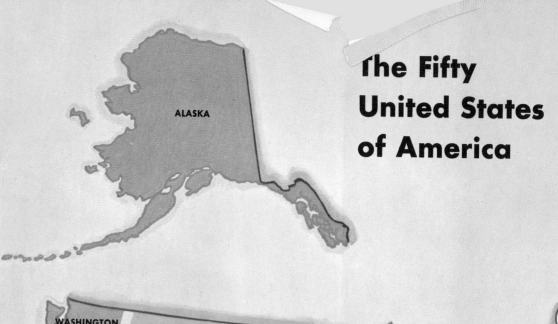

The Fifty
United States
of America

ALASKA

WASHINGTON

MONTANA

NORTH DAKOTA

MINNESOTA

OREGON

IDAHO

WYOMING

SOUTH DAKOTA

WISCONSIN

MICHIGAN

MAINE

VT.
N. H.
MASS.

NEW YORK

NEVADA

UTAH

NEBRASKA

IOWA

ILLINOIS

INDIANA

OHIO

PENN

R. I.
CONN.

NEW JERSEY

CALIFORNIA

COLORADO

KANSAS

MISSOURI

KENTUCKY

WEST VIRGINIA

MD.

DEL.

VIRGINIA

ARIZONA

NEW MEXICO

OKLAHOMA

TENNESSEE

NORTH CAROLINA

ARKANSAS

SOUTH CAROLINA

TEXAS

LOUISIANA

MISSISSIPPI

ALABAMA

GEORGIA

FLORIDA

HAWAII

Indian

Explorer

Settler

Pioneer

Patriot

Soldier

Business Leader

Soldier — W. W. I

Soldier — W. W. II

Working Man

Spaceman

Using Tools for Learning

The book you are about to read is the story of how your country was changed from a wilderness into the richest land in the world. It is a story of adventure and of hardship, of plain folks and of heroes, of good times and hard. It is perhaps the most interesting story in the history of the world.

More than words are needed to tell this story. Drawings, photographs, and maps help unfold it for you, but there are other ways of making ideas clear, too. There are charts and special kinds of drawings used throughout the book, which may be new tools of learning for you. Using them well will make clearer the story of *You and the United States.*

The story of You and the United States is the story of many people working to build a free nation in a new land.

A globe gives an accurate picture of the land and water regions of the earth. The lines of latitude and longitude can be used to tell the location of any point on the globe.

What can you learn from a globe?

You have already learned to use a *globe*, which is one kind of picture of the earth. Because it is roughly the same shape as the earth, it is best for comparing sizes and distances between the earth's many land and water forms.

Take time now to recall the ways in which this learning tool can help you. With a globe in your hands, show the tilt of the earth on its axis, the way it turns on its axis, and the way it travels around the sun. Can you explain how these facts of the earth's movements bring night and day and the change of seasons?

Look at the way the globe is marked with lines. Find the equator, the Tropics of Cancer and Capricorn, and the Arctic and Antarctic Circles. How do they roughly tell about the climate on the earth? Which state of the United States lies south of the Tropic of Cancer? Which continent is crossed by the equator and by both the Tropics?

There are other lines, too, going around the earth on the globe. They are numbered in degrees. You may remember that the lines marking *longitude* are numbered east and west of a place in England. Can you find where the numbering begins?

Lines of longitude are usually numbered along the equator on a globe. They draw closer together to the north and to the south, until they all come together at the poles.

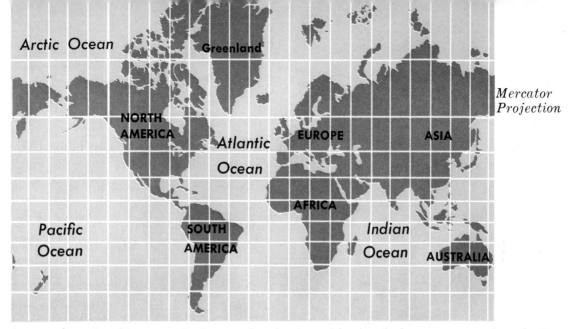

Arctic Ocean

Greenland

NORTH AMERICA

Atlantic Ocean

EUROPE

ASIA

Mercator Projection

AFRICA

Pacific Ocean

SOUTH AMERICA

Indian Ocean

AUSTRALIA

A mapmaker using this map projection stretches the sizes of land and water areas near the poles in order to show the earth on a flat surface.

The lines going around the globe north and south of the equator are lines of *latitude*. The poles are at 90 degrees north latitude and 90 degrees south latitude. The equator is at 0 degrees.

What do maps teach us?

A *map* is a drawing of land and water areas on a flat surface. Since the earth is round, land and water areas lie on a curved surface. Trying to show a curved area on a flat surface is a problem every mapmaker faces.

Many different methods of mapmaking have been worked out. These methods are called *projections*. For each projection, there is a special system for drawing lines of latitude and lines of longitude.

The map on this page is drawn according to one of the first projections ever worked out. You can see that the distance between the lines of longitude remains the same for the whole map. The lines of latitude, however, grow farther apart as they approach the poles. The land and water bodies near the poles are drawn larger than they really are in relation to the other areas of the earth.

This projection is easy to draw, and it shows the correct shapes of land and water bodies. It is also easy to find directions on this map. Other projections may show correct sizes and shapes for certain portions of the earth but give a false idea about distances and directions.

Although maps cannot give as true a likeness of the earth as a globe can, they are still very useful. A map can give you a much better understanding of a small area than a globe can. A globe would have to be huge to show your community in detail.

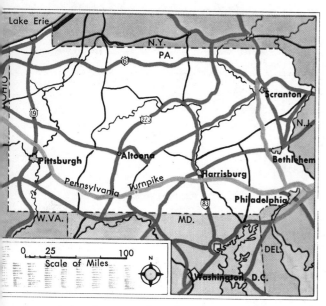

Road maps such as this one can give the traveler much useful information.

Areas as large as states are often shown on maps. On automobile trips, perhaps you and your family have used road maps such as this one.

Both of these maps take up about the same amount of space on the page. There is a great deal of difference in the amount of space they show of the earth's surface. Yet both of these maps are correct because the scale for each map is different. The *scale* of a map tells how much of the earth's surface is shown by a certain measure on the map. For example, on the map of Pennsylvania, one inch stands for ninety miles. You can measure these distances on the map with your ruler.

Maps can help you find direction. On most maps, north is at the top. On some maps, however, north may not be at the top. You must look at the *compass*, or direction finder, to be sure which direction is meant for each side of the map.

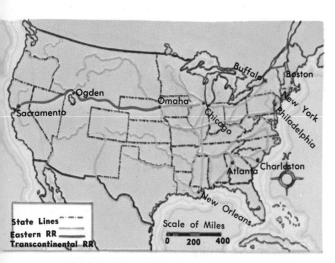

Each inch stands for a great many miles when a small map is used for a large area.

A large area such as the United States can be shown on a map.

The mapmaker could give a better picture of this area by not placing north at the top of the map.

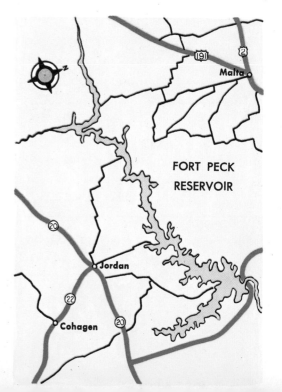

Many maps show the kind of land found in a certain area of the earth's surface. There are a number of ways this can be done. The map on this page uses colors and symbols to show mountains, deserts, plains, plateaus, lowlands, and frozen regions of North America. Read the names of some of these special areas in the United States.

Land Surfaces
Of North America

High Mts.
Low Mts. and
Plateaus
High Plains
and Prairies
Lowlands

0   500   1000
Scale of Miles

Equal Area Projection

13

This map uses symbols and colors to show the types of plant life found in different areas throughout the North American continent.

ICELAND

GREENLAND

ALASKA

CANADA

Natural Plant Life Of North America

Equal Area Projection

UNITED STATES

0   500
Scale of Miles

Needle-leaved Evergreen Trees

Broad-leaved Evergreen Trees

Broad-leaved Deciduous Trees

Mixed Evergreen and Deciduous Trees

Shrub Trees

Grasslands

Desert Plants

Barren or Almost Barren

Tundra

MEXICO

WEST INDIES

CENTRAL AMERICA

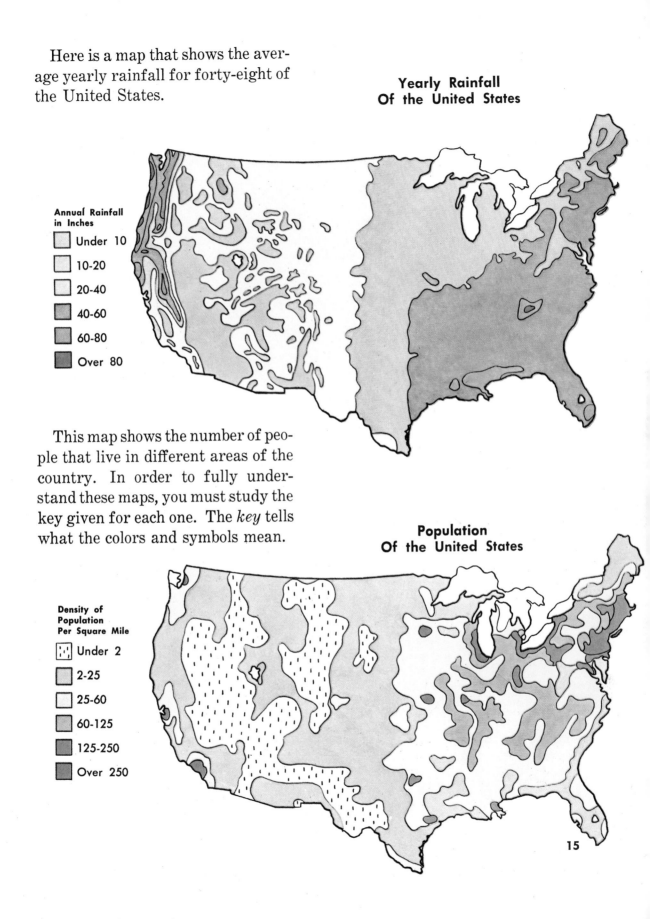

Here is a map that shows the average yearly rainfall for forty-eight of the United States.

Yearly Rainfall Of the United States

Annual Rainfall in Inches

Under 10

10-20

20-40

40-60

60-80

Over 80

This map shows the number of people that live in different areas of the country. In order to fully understand these maps, you must study the key given for each one. The *key* tells what the colors and symbols mean.

Population Of the United States

Density of Population Per Square Mile

Under 2

2-25

25-60

60-125

125-250

Over 250

15

What can be shown on a chart?

A chart is a very helpful kind of study tool. A *chart* sorts information and puts it into special order. Charts are read both across and up and down the page.

Name	Abbre-viation	Population	Capital	Area in Square Miles	Year Admitted to Union
Alabama	Ala.	3,266,740	Montgomery	51,609	1819
Alaska	Alaska	226,167	Juneau	586,400	1959
Arizona	Ariz.	1,302,161	Phoenix	113,909	1912
Arkansas	Ark.	1,786,272	Little Rock	53,104	1836
California	Calif.	15,717,204	Sacramento	158,693	1850
Colorado	Colo.	1,753,947	Denver	104,247	1876
Connecticut	Conn.	2,535,234	Hartford	5,009	1788
Delaware	Del.	446,292	Dover	2,057	1787
Florida	Fla.	4,951,560	Tallahassee	58,560	1845
Georgia	Ga.	3,943,116	Atlanta	58,876	1788
Hawaii	Hawaii	632,772	Honolulu	6,424	1959
Idaho	Ida.	667,191	Boise	83,557	1890
Illinois	Ill.	10,081,158	Springfield	56,400	1818
Indiana	Ind.	4,662,498	Indianapolis	36,291	1816
Iowa	Ia.	2,757,537	Des Moines	56,290	1846
Kansas	Kans.	2,178,611	Topeka	82,264	1861
Kentucky	Ky.	3,038,156	Frankfort	40,395	1792
Louisiana	La.	3,257,022	Baton Rouge	48,523	1812
Maine	Me.	969,265	Augusta	33,215	1820
Maryland	Md.	3,100,689	Annapolis	10,577	1788
Massachusetts	Mass.	5,148,578	Boston	8,257	1788
Michigan	Mich.	7,823,194	Lansing	58,216	1837
Minnesota	Minn.	3,413,864	St. Paul	84,068	1858
Mississippi	Miss.	2,178,141	Jackson	47,716	1817
Missouri	Mo.	4,319,813	Jefferson City	69,686	1821
Montana	Mont.	674,767	Helena	147,138	1889
Nebraska	Nebr.	1,411,330	Lincoln	77,227	1867
Nevada	Nev.	285,278	Carson City	110,540	1864
New Hampshire	N.H.	606,921	Concord	9,304	1788
New Jersey	N.J.	6,066,782	Trenton	7,836	1787
New Mexico	N. Mex.	951,023	Santa Fe	121,666	1912
New York	N.Y.	16,782,304	Albany	49,576	1788
North Carolina	N.C.	4,556,155	Raleigh	52,712	1789
North Dakota	N. Dak.	632,446	Bismarck	70,665	1889
Ohio	Ohio	9,706,397	Columbus	41,222	1803
Oklahoma	Okla.	2,328,284	Oklahoma City	69,919	1907
Oregon	Ore.	1,768,687	Salem	96,981	1859
Pennsylvania	Pa.	11,319,366	Harrisburg	45,333	1787
Rhode Island	R.I.	859,488	Providence	1,214	1790
South Carolina	S.C.	2,382,594	Columbia	31,055	1788
South Dakota	S. Dak.	680,514	Pierre	77,047	1889
Tennessee	Tenn.	3,567,089	Nashville	42,244	1796
Texas	Tex.	9,579,677	Austin	267,339	1845
Utah	Ut.	890,627	Salt Lake City	84,916	1896
Vermont	Vt.	389,881	Montpelier	9,609	1791
Virginia	Va.	3,966,949	Richmond	40,815	1788
Washington	Wash.	2,853,214	Olympia	68,192	1889
West Virginia	W. Va.	1,860,421	Charleston	24,181	1863
Wisconsin	Wis.	3,951,777	Madison	56,154	1848
Wyoming	Wyo.	330,066	Cheyenne	97,914	1890

What is a graph?

A *graph* is somewhat like a chart in that it sorts and presents information in a certain order. Very often the information given on a graph will answer questions that begin with the words "how much" or "how many."

On this page are two sets of graphs. Each set has four graphs, each of which shows the same information. One graph uses picture symbols, two graphs use bars, and another graph uses lines and squared paper. The numbers stay the same.

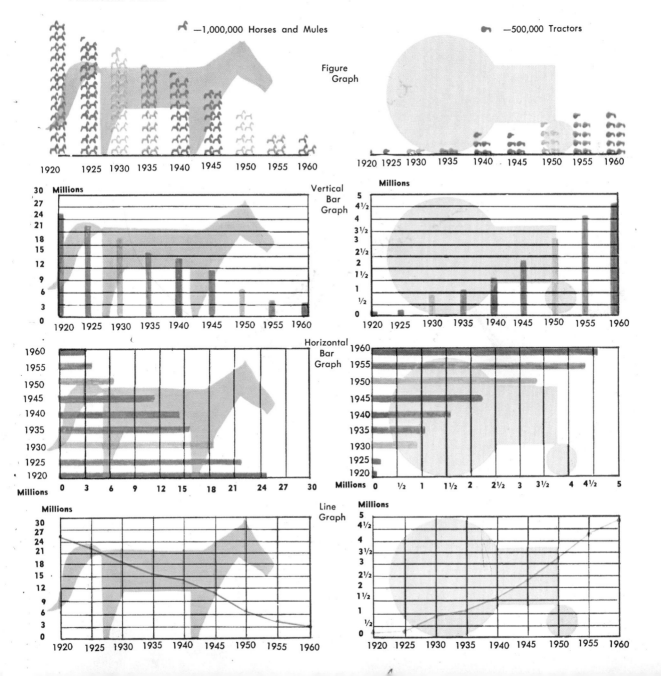

Decreasing Number of Horses and Mules on American Farms

Increasing Number of Tractors on American Farms

—1,000,000 Horses and Mules

—500,000 Tractors

Figure Graph

Vertical Bar Graph

Horizontal Bar Graph

Line Graph

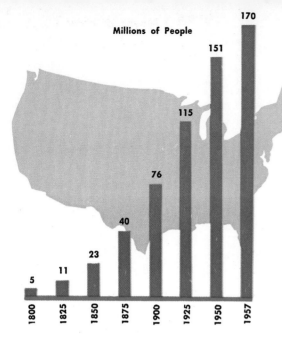

Growth of American Population

World Production of Wool and Cotton

This graph compares the number of people living in the United States at different years throughout the history of this country. A graph can clearly show the pattern of America's growth. The number of Americans has grown steadily since the early days of our country.

The graphs on the right-hand side of this page, are circle graphs. A circle graph is often used to show how the whole of something is divided or how parts of one thing are used.

The first graph here stands for all the cotton grown in the world. Each section of the circle pictures how much of the world's cotton comes from certain countries. The second graph gives the same kind of information for wool.

Cross Section of United States Land Forms

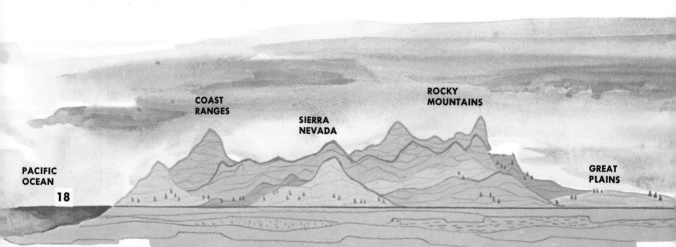

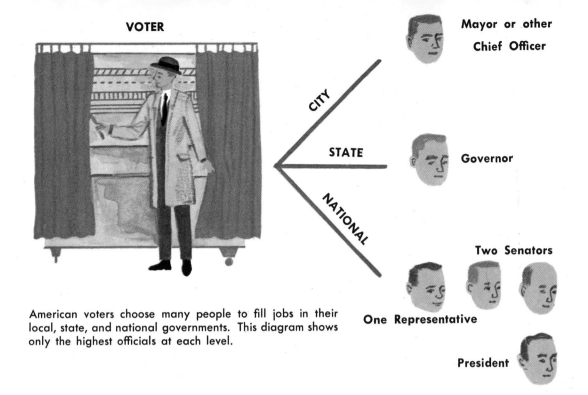

VOTER

CITY — Mayor or other Chief Officer

STATE — Governor

NATIONAL — Two Senators / One Representative / President

American voters choose many people to fill jobs in their local, state, and national governments. This diagram shows only the highest officials at each level.

What is a diagram?

A *diagram* is a drawing that may show any number of things, including how something is made, how a machine works, or even how people work together under one government. One of the maps you studied earlier in this unit showed the different kinds of land in the United States. The diagram at the bottom of this page shows how these land areas would look if you could slice the United States through the center and then look at the edge.

Diagrams can be used to show how the American voter helps in the government of his community, state, and nation. Neither of these ideas could be told as clearly or in as little space if words alone were used.

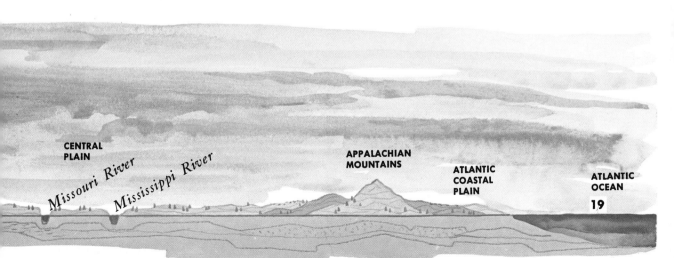

CENTRAL PLAIN — Missouri River — Mississippi River — APPALACHIAN MOUNTAINS — ATLANTIC COASTAL PLAIN — ATLANTIC OCEAN

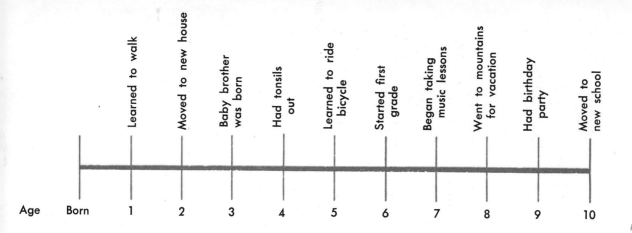

Age | Born | 1 | 2 | 3 | 4 | 5 | 6 | 7 | 8 | 9 | 10

Learned to walk · Moved to new house · Baby brother was born · Had tonsils out · Learned to ride bicycle · Started first grade · Began taking music lessons · Went to mountains for vacation · Had birthday party · Moved to new school

How are time lines used?

You are about to begin a study of American history. You will learn of important events in the order in which they took place. Often one event was the cause of another. Sometimes these events can be shown through the use of a time line.

At the top of this page is a time line that a ten-year-old girl made to show the important events in her life. She began by marking off ten equal spaces along a straight line. Each space stands for one year in her life. She thought of what she felt were the most important events in her life and placed them in the proper spaces on the line.

A line marked off in the same way could show another person's lifetime.

Stages of Life before the Appearance of Man in North America

500 Million Years Ago
All creatures are believed to have lived in the sea. They are called invertebrates because they had no backbones.

420 Million Years Ago
Creatures began to develop backbones and jaws, but continued to live in the sea.

20

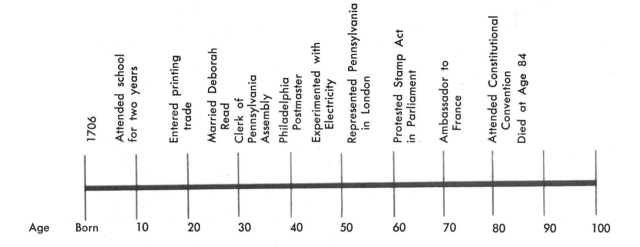

1706
Attended school for two years
Entered printing trade
Married Deborah Read
Clerk of Pennsylvania Assembly
Philadelphia Postmaster
Experimented with Electricity
Represented Pennsylvania in London
Protested Stamp Act in Parliament
Ambassador to France
Attended Constitutional Convention
Died at Age 84

Age Born 10 20 30 40 50 60 70 80 90 100

To do this, however, you would need to change the *scale*, or the amount of time each space on the line stands for. Each space on the time line on this page stands for ten years in the life of Benjamin Franklin.

When you begin your study of America in Unit Two, you will go back five hundred years in the story of our country. Most of the events you study will be those that have taken place within the last five hundred years.

You will also learn something of what was happening in North America much earlier than five hundred years ago. The time line at the bottom of these pages shows some of these things, and gives you an idea of when they took place.

290 Million Years Ago
Some creatures developed the ability to live out of water as well as in it. They are called amphibians.

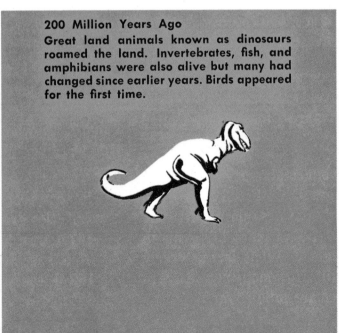

200 Million Years Ago
Great land animals known as dinosaurs roamed the land. Invertebrates, fish, and amphibians were also alive but many had changed since earlier years. Birds appeared for the first time.

60 Million Years Ago
First mammals resembling those of today appeared.

500,000 Years Ago
Man appears on earth.

Words to Know

chart (chärt) 16

compass (kŭm′pȧs) 12

diagram (dī′ȧ grăm) 19

globe (glōb) 10

graph (grȧf) 17

key. (kē) 15

latitude (lăt′ĭ tūd) 11

longitude (lŏn′jĭ tūd) 10

map (măp) 11

projection (prō jĕk′shŭn) 11

scale (skāl) 12

Questions

1. Why is a globe the best kind of picture of the earth?

2. Use your globe to find and name the five oceans of the world. Which three touch the United States?

3. Find your community on the maps on pages 13, 14, and 15. What kind of land area do you live in? What types of plant life grow in the region? What is the yearly rainfall? How many people live in each square mile of land?

4. Find your state and the states that touch it on the chart on page 16. Which three states have been part of the United States for the longest time? Which is the largest state? Which state has the smallest number of people?

5. What does the circle stand for on a circle graph?

6. Look at the diagram of United States land shown on pages 18 and 19. Find the highest point. Find the lowest point. Which are higher, the Appalachian Mountains or the Rocky Mountains? What kind of land stretches across the center regions of our country?

7. At what point in time will you begin your study of our country in Unit Two?

You See for Yourself

Bring to class a road map for your own state. What is the scale of miles for this map? How many miles is it from your school to the nearest large city? Is there a compass on the map? In what section of the state do you live? What states lie next to yours?

Read a globe or map to find out what cities are in these locations:
157 d. west long., 22 d. north lat.
87 d. east long., 22 d. north lat.
152 d. east long., 33 d. south lat.
88 d. west long., 43 d. north lat.

Now You Know

The story of *You and the United States* is told with the help of a number of study tools, including maps, charts, graphs, diagrams, and time lines. These aids are used because they often give the writer a way to tell something more clearly and in less space than he could with words.

The surface of the earth can be pictured on both maps and globes. A globe is round, like the earth, and so gives us a more nearly correct picture of the earth than a map does. Maps are flat, so land and water areas have to be changed somewhat in order to show them on a flat surface.

Maps can show any number of different things, such as rainfall or the kind of land in a region. In order to understand them, you must read the key. The scale and the compass show size and direction on the map.

Charts and graphs sort information and present it in an orderly way. Both can be very useful in comparing facts and ideas.

A diagram is especially helpful in explaining how something looks on the inside or how something works.

Time lines show events in the order in which they happened. The scale shows the amount of time they cover.

You Talk It Over

Study the map on page 15 which shows where the most and the fewest people live in forty-eight of the United States. Find the regions in which the most people live on both the rainfall map (page 15) and the land regions map (page 13). Do you think the kind of land and the amount of rainfall have something to do with where people choose to live? Explain your answer.

Discuss "time" and words that deal with time with your classmates. When do you think "long ago" was? When do you think "a short time ago" was? Do your classmates have different ideas about these questions? Make a list of all the words you know that tell about time and tell how much time they mean to you. The list may include "lately," "in the future," "last night."

Puzzlers

A fifth-grade boy made a list of the important events during the school year. The list is shown on this page. Along the left side of the page is a time line of the school year with the correct number of marks on it to show the events from the list. Match the letter of each mark with the number of the correct event from the list.

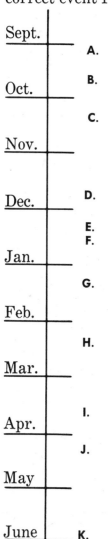

1. Memorial Day Program—May 30

2. Decorating of school Christmas tree—Dec. 10

3. Band Concert—Sept. 18

4. Class Indian play—Oct. 13

5. Thanksgiving parade—Nov. 22

6. First day of school—Sept. 5

7. Spring chorus concert—March 20.

8. Valentine party—Feb. 14

9. Semester tests—Jan. 12

10. Christmas program—Dec. 16

11. School picnic—June 2

12. Yearly tests—June 3

13. Clean-up Week—April 10

Unit Activities

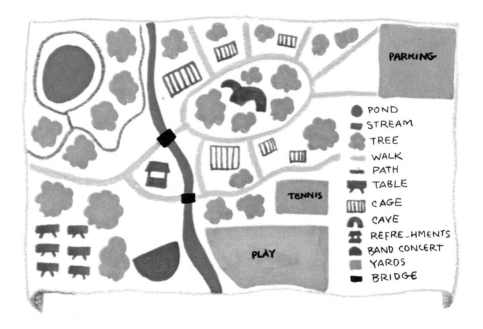

You make a chart

With the help of your teacher, make a large chart of your class schedule for the week. Use a large piece of poster board that can be hung on the wall and read by everyone in the room. Write the names of days of the week down the left-hand side of the chart. Across the top of the chart, write the periods of each day and the times at which they begin and end. Fill in the correct subject or activity for each period of every day.

You use map symbols

Draw a map of an imaginary park which has all the things listed at the end of this paragraph. Make a key for your map, explaining the symbols you have chosen to show each of these things.

Pond

Woods with paths
  for hiking

Playground

Sidewalks

Animal cages

Stream

Cave

Picnic area

Tennis courts

Parking lot

Refreshment stand

Band concert stage

25

Two Worlds

The story of *You and the United States* begins over five hundred years ago. Then, as now, the earth made its yearly trip around the sun. It turned the land of America toward the bright sunlight each day and into the darkness of space each night.

Five hundred years ago, the Indians were the only Americans. As they saw the sun set on their own world each evening, they did not know that it was bringing day to a very different "world" on the other side of the earth. Nor did the people on that side of the earth know anything of the Indians' world. The two worlds were vastly different from each other. They were separated from each other by two great oceans.

Indians of the Eastern Woodlands little dreamed of the ships that would bring men from a strange land to the shores of their homeland.

The World of the Indian

It is true that people of both worlds told stories and poems about faraway places. Some of the Indians knew stories of golden-haired warriors from another world. Yet, five hundred years ago, no one had left any written record of journeys across the oceans to faraway lands.

How had America changed?

The America that the Indians knew five hundred years ago had not always been the way it was then. Several million years ago, only plants and animals lived in North America. Scientists who learn of past life by digging into buried layers of rock and earth tell us that dinosaurs, large elephant-like animals, called *mammoths*, and strange birds and insects once lived in North America.

About one million years ago, the Ice Age began. The *Ice Age* was a long period of time in which four great glaciers pushed southward to cover almost all of the upper half of North America, except Alaska, and then melted away. Each *glacier* was a thick sheet of ice and snow that spread out from a center near what is now Hudson Bay, in Canada. The winters were long, and the cool summers were too short to melt much of the ice and snow. The ever-growing sheet built up to a thickness of two miles at its center.

Strange birds and beasts once roamed the lands of North America.

A number of glaciers, such as this one in Alaska, can be found still today in parts of North America.

As all glaciers do, these great glaciers slid. They pushed down giant trees in their paths, scraped the earth bare of soil, and scooped out great hollows in level lowlands. Many animals moved farther south to escape. Others stayed and were destroyed.

When winters of little snow came, the summer suns cut into the edges of the ice sheets. As the glaciers melted, rocks, soil, and anything else that had mixed with the ice and snow was left. New hills, lakes and rivers were formed.

The last of the great glaciers began its melting and shrinking about eleven thousand years ago. Its melting formed the Great Lakes. These lakes are today little changed from their early sizes and shapes. The largest of the North American river systems was also influenced by the glaciers. This is the Mississippi-Missouri-Ohio system.

The Mississippi, Missouri, and Ohio rivers were miles wide at first. Through the years, they settled into their present *channels*, or big grooves in the earth. Trees and other plants grew again, and new animals came.

When did the Indians arrive?

No one is quite sure when men first began to live in North America or where they came from. There were some here as the last glacier melted, and perhaps even before that.

There were people living in Alaska during the Ice Age. It is believed that they came from Asia across the Bering Strait, which separates North America from Asia by less than sixty miles at one point.

29

In those thousands of years between the melting of the last glacier and the time our story opens, a number of Indian tribes had lived and then died out. Other tribes lived on. A *tribe* could be large or small. Often all the people in the tribe belonged to one big family. But the tribe could also be made up of a group of different families.

Some tribes advanced until the people had learned to cut stone and use it to build great temples. They made and decorated fine pottery, wove fibers into cloth, and shaped copper, gold, and silver into beautiful and useful objects. Most of these Indians were to the south, in the lands of Mexico, Central America, and South America.

In the land that would someday be the United States of America, there were once some Indian tribes who did fine work with copper, bone, shell, and pottery. These people built great earthen mounds as part of their religious life and for burying their dead. There was trading among different tribes. Some of the traders may have journeyed far. Although their mounds may still be seen in some places today, these people had vanished by the time our story opens.

The Arrival of People in North America

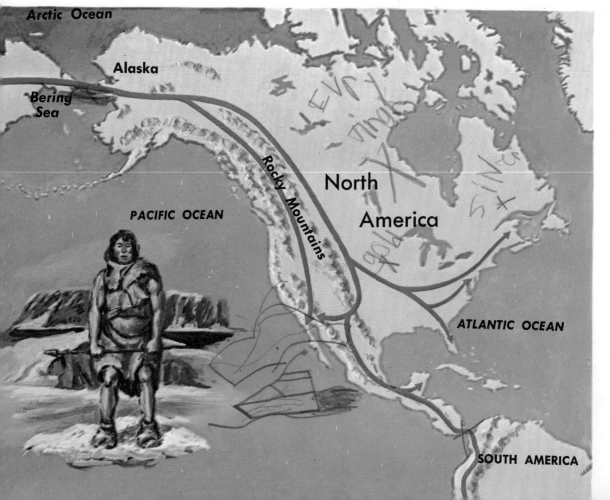

Other tribes arrived to take the places of the earlier ones. From the Mississippi River eastward to the Atlantic Ocean, forests covered most of the land. But here and there, Indian villages stood in the clearings.

There were many miles of open prairie and grasslands reaching westward from the Mississippi to the foothills of the Rocky Mountains. Tribes were scattered throughout this region, too, mostly near the Missouri and Mississippi rivers. There were still more tribes in the warm, dry southwest, and in the forests along the Pacific Coast.

The people of each tribe took the food they needed from the earth, the waters, and the animals of the great lands around them. They sheltered themselves from the weather and their enemies as they felt the need. Yet just as nature differed from one part of the country to another, so the tribes differed from one another.

How did the Indians of the Eastern Woodlands live?

Five hundred years ago, the Indian tribes throughout the Eastern Woodlands all lived in much the same manner. The men were hunters and fishermen. The women worked the gardens and did most of the other work necessary for living.

The people lived in villages. Some of the tribes built walls around their villages by setting poles upright into the ground.

The houses of some tribes were shaped like large loaves of bread. Each was built of poles set firmly into the ground to form arches. Cross poles strengthened the walls, and sheets of bark made a shaggy covering. All the parts were tied together with wild grapevine. At the end of each house was a doorway. Such homes were called *long houses*.

Inside the houses, the women cared for the fires. A large house might have four fires in it; a small one would have only one or two. Each fire served more than one family, and some houses were home for six or seven families. In the longer houses, the fires were in a row down the center, with a hole in the roof above each fire for the smoke to escape.

Along the walls were the sleeping spaces for the families. They spread out their mats there each night. Pottery jars for holding water and food, clothing, weapons, and tools that belonged to a family were also stored along the walls. Each family stayed within its own space.

Many tribes had small houses that were almost round in shape. They often were home to only one family. These were called lodges or *wigwams*.

The first warm months of spring brought planting time to the village. Outside the village, the women went to work in the cleared field, breaking up lumps of earth with crude hoes. These were made by tying a piece of flat bone or wood to a wooden handle.

Corn, beans, and squash were foods usually grown by these Indians. The crops were divided among all the families of the village. The women also gathered wild berries and roots in the summer and dried them for use during the winter months.

The tools the women used and the weapons the men used were made from bone, wood, stone, or shell. They had not learned to use iron for making things.

The men could most often be found away from the village in the woods. Two or three might be seen together as they waited silently in the shadows near a stream or brook. Holding their bows and arrows ready, they watched for the woodland animals that came to the water to drink.

Perhaps the hunters would bring down a bear, whose fur would make warm robes for winter. They might shoot a deer that would provide meat for their families. The skin of the deer would provide clothing, and its bones could be made into tools.

The leggings, moccasins, belts, and other clothing worn by these Indians were all made of deerskin. The men rubbed red and black dyes into the skin of their backs, arms, chests, and faces to complete their dress.

Each man's hair was shaved off, except for a thick brush of it running from the forehead to the unshaved back hair, which was drawn together and braided. Around their heads, they wore headbands orna-

mented with bright bits of copper, shell, pearl, and porcupine quill. The brush of hair above the headband was rubbed with bear fat to make it shine. This hair was also decorated with the stiffer hairs of deerskin dyed bright red.

The Indian children might be found playing in or near the village. The older boys often played a game by tossing small bones onto the bare ground. They also knew a team game in which each team tried to get a ball past the other by hitting it with rackets. They sometimes tried their skill at throwing a spear through a rolling hoop.

Indians of the Eastern Woodlands took much of their living from the forests around their villages. The men spent much of their time hunting in the woods. Women stayed in the villages, tending the homes and gardens.

The older girls spent their time helping their mothers with weaving, rubbing fat into deerskin to make it soft, or cooking. At mealtime, they helped the women grind corn into meal for corncakes.

The younger girls had time to play. They sometimes played kickball with a ball made of deerskin stuffed with corn husks.

Some villages of the Eastern Woodland Indians had many buildings; others had only a few. Some houses were large and some were small. Some had rounded roofs and

others had peaked roofs and straight walls. All were made from the materials found in the forests—slender tree trunks, vines for binding, and broad leaves, grasses, or bark.

The largest Indian towns were in the south, where the growing season was long and the soil was good for farming. The villages of the northern Indians were sometimes rather small. The houses could be taken apart and moved, for the people lived more by hunting than by farming. They had to move from time to time to new hunting grounds.

33

Chiefs from many villages would meet with the tribal chief at the great council.

Each village had its chief, but the chief did not usually rule the village by himself. He met with his *braves*, the tribe's soldiers, when there were important questions to be settled.

Now and then the chiefs from all the villages of one tribe would journey to meet with the great chief of the whole tribe. Such a meeting was the *great council*. At the council, the chiefs might decide to go to war against another tribe or to hold a great festival to please their gods.

Each tribe was a branch of a great family of tribes that had come from the same beginnings. Their spoken languages within the great family were much alike. They were different from those used by tribes that lived in other places.

The largest language group in the woodlands was the *Algonkian*. Among the Algonkian family were the *Shawnee, Sauk, Chippewa, Delaware, Mohican,* and *Powhatan* tribes. Most of the woodland Indians to the south were members of the *Muskogean* family. They were mainly *Chickasaw* tribes. The *Osage* and *Santee* were members of the *Sioux* language group to the south.

Sioux, Muskogean, and Algonkian all feared the warlike tribes of the *Iroquois* group. The Iroquois lived mostly around Lake Ontario, Lake Erie, and in what is today the state of New York.

The tribes of the Iroquois often worked together. Many an Algonkian village was wiped out when the Iroquois went on the warpath. Five Iroquois tribes especially, worked together, for they lived near each other. These were the *Seneca*, the *Cayuga*, the *Onondaga*, the *Oneida*, and the *Mohawk* tribes.

There was plenty of room for all the tribes in the woodlands, and the living was generally easy. The woods supplied meat and fruit, materials for clothing and shelter. Plenty of rain and sunshine helped the seeds sprout almost as quickly as they were put into the ground. There were many streams, so each village had a ready water supply. Wars were usually not very serious except when the Iroquois tribes banded together against the other Indians.

How did the Plains Indians live?

West of the Mississippi River lived most of the tribes of the Sioux language family. The Sioux lived in the land where the woodland gave way to the open prairie. The prairie lands, also called the plains, were those lands in the center of the country that stretched westward and were covered with grass. Here the forests gave way to only groves of trees, and finally, farther west, to only thin bands of cottonwoods and willows found near the rivers and the lakes.

This was buffalo country. Great herds of these buffalo fed in the rich grasslands all through the year. Winter found them moving into the region of the *Rio Grande* River in today's Texas. As the spring rains turned the red-brown stubble to green grass, the buffalo would move northward by the thousands.

Most of these buffalo had never seen a man, for the Indians of the plains were far fewer in number five hundred years ago than they were in later years. Most of them lived not far west of the Mississippi River.

Indian villages were widely scattered across the plains. Farthest south were the *Quapaw*, the Osage and the *Kansa* tribes. On the plains north of the Missouri River lived the Missouri, *Oto*, Iowa, *Mandan*, Dakota, and Crow tribes, all members of the Sioux language family.

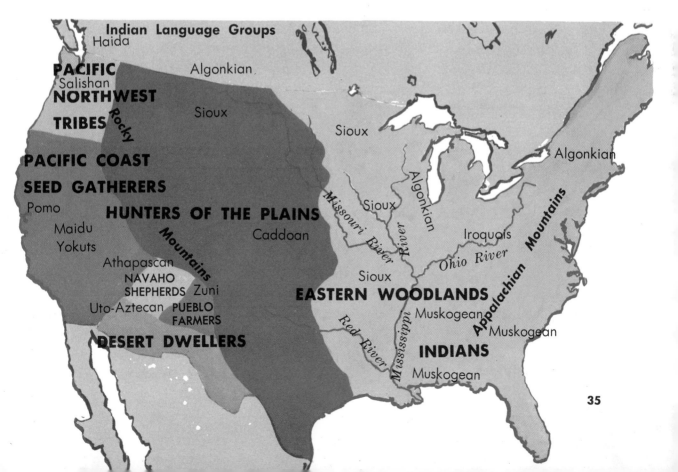

Indian Language Groups

The buffalo provided the living for the Plains Indians, who did little farming. They did not build houses as did the Eastern Woodland Indians, for they were likely to move several times a year.

Buffalo meat was their main food. Buffalo hides were made into clothing, and buffalo bones supplied the material for simple tools.

The boys practiced running so that they could run swiftly in the buffalo chase. In those days, the Indians had no horses. The Indian would often creep as close as he could to a buffalo herd, hiding himself under the skin of a wolf or a coyote. He held arrows and spears ready for the moment when he would drop the animal skin and swiftly follow the herd.

During the winter months, when the buffalo left the hunting ground of the northern tribes, the Indians used their fur for warmth. Moccasins, worn with the furry side in, were made of buffalo fur. The snowshoes the Indians strapped to their moccasins were also made from parts of the buffalo.

The *squaws*, or Indian women, used buffalo hide for making leggings, shirts, and dresses. The hides used for clothing were scraped free of hair and then rubbed with a chunk of fat. Such hides were also used to make bags for holding water or dried meat.

A boat could be made by bending and crossing the limbs of a willow tree and tying them together with buffalo hide. This made a round frame that was covered with the hide of a big bull buffalo. Perhaps the shoulder blade or hipbone of the same animal made the paddle for the boat.

Buffalo bones were used for tools, arrowheads, and ornaments. The horns made spoons, and other parts of the animal could be used for strong thread. The hair, after it was scraped off, could be twisted together to make rope. Even the needles used in the sewing were made from buffalo bone. Hides could be sewed together, and placed over poles to make a house that could be quickly taken down and moved to a new hunting ground. The Indians called these houses *tepees*.

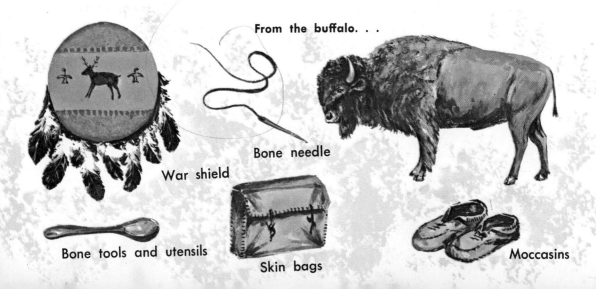

From the buffalo. . .

War shield

Bone needle

Bone tools and utensils

Skin bags

Moccasins

Prairie chickens and other large birds were hunted for their meat and for their feathers. Many of the Sioux tribesmen liked to use feathers in their headdresses. The chiefs wore *war bonnets*, long headdresses with many feathers.

Hunting and fighting took up most of the men's time. Bravery among the men was very important. Each boy, as he grew to manhood, had to prove his courage. Sometimes men and boys of the Sioux tribes caused themselves great pain and suffering to show that they were brave.

Most of these tribes owned and trained dogs to be very useful to them. Dogs helped the men in hunting. They were also useful around the villages. They were always on guard against wild animals or attacking enemy tribes. When moving day came, a pair of tepee poles was strapped to each dog's sides. The folded tepee covering and other buffalo hide was hung between the two poles. The dog pulled the load to the new home of his Indian owner.

South and west of the Sioux country was the land of the *Caddo* language family. This was where the *Pawnee*, the *Arikara*, the *Wichita*, and the Caddo tribes lived. These tribes were more likely to live in villages and to build more solid homes than the Sioux. They often used logs and *sod*, chunks of earth and grass cut from the ground, to build homes.

The houses were round, perhaps forty feet across and about twelve feet high at the center. There was a hole in the roof for smoke to escape from the big fire that was kept burning in the center of the house.

The floor of the house was just the bare ground. The walls were divided into rooms with buffalo hides hung from poles. Each family had one or more of these rooms. These were used for sleeping and for storing household goods and supplies. Several families shared each house, with perhaps two dozen or more people in each one.

The Caddo tribes usually did some farming, raising corn, beans, and squash. They usually built their villages near a river to have a water supply. The Caddo men hunted the buffalo, too, but they were more settled than the Sioux tribes.

Tepee

Rope

Bull boat

Snow shoes

The adobe pueblos of the Southwest Indians were the first American apartment buildings.

What Indians lived in the desert?

Still standing today are some of the homes of the Southwest Indians of five hundred years ago. These homes are much like great apartment houses, built of stone and sun-baked adobe. *Adobe* is a kind of clay found in many desert regions.

Some of these houses are cut out of the faces of cliffs, and skillfully planned. Others are built entirely of blocks of cut stone held together with adobe. Some houses had more than five hundred rooms. They were called *pueblos*, the Spanish word for villages. They were the homes of the most settled of all the Indians who lived five hundred years ago in what is now the United States of America.

The roof of one apartment made a kind of porch, or *terrace*, for the apartment above it. Each story was set back a little from the others in stair-step fashion. The pueblos were from one to five stories high. To go from one story to another, the Indians kept ladders on the terraces.

The largest pueblo known was big enough so that about one thousand people could live in it. Each family's rooms were entered through a doorway on the terrace. In the doorway usually hung a skin or cloth curtain. One room of the apartment had a fireplace where the cooking was done. A hole in the ceiling let the smoke rise to the terrace above.

The main Pueblo people of five hundred years ago were the *Hopi* and the *Zuni*. They lived in the northern part of the present-day states of Arizona and New Mexico.

These people were different from most other American Indians, not only in the building of their homes, but also in their ways of living. They were peaceful farmers to whom hunting was not nearly as important as seeing that their crops grew well.

The men worked in the fields. They dug ditches to let water flow from nearby creeks into their gardens. Watering of crops in this manner is called *irrigation*. Farmers in dry regions still carry on irrigation in much the same manner as these Indians did.

The Pueblo women took clay from the riverbanks and shaped it into jars and bowls and decorated them beautifully. They also made fine baskets and wove fibers into cloth.

The Pueblo people also made use of the turquoise found near their homes as they decorated everyday things or made jewelry. *Turquoise* is a kind of stone that has a blue-green color and can be polished to a high shine.

The Pueblo people ate less meat than the other tribes, but they hunted jack rabbit and other small game. The meat was made into stew with dried beans to make it filling. It was almost always eaten with some kind of cornbread, a flat, thin cake baked on hot stones. The family sat on the floor to eat the meal, remembering to give thanks to their gods by scattering a bit of cornmeal in each direction before they ate.

The *pinion pine* was a valuable tree for these people. Its small branches were fuel for the cooking fire. The nuts it bore as seeds in its cones were food for the people.

Religion was an important part of the lives of the Pueblo Indians. There was almost always one or more circular rooms, called *kivas*, hollowed out of the ground in front of the living spaces. Here the men met to carry out many religious practices. They taught the young boys stories, dances, and passed on to them the secrets of their religion. There were great religious dances and festivals above ground, too. For the festivals, the people wore their best clothing and jewelry, bright feathers, turquoise, and perhaps some trimmings of fur from a skunk or a fox.

The Hopi and Zuni may have learned many of their skills from the Indians of Mexico and those farther south. The Mexican Indians put up many fine buildings, worked with gold and silver, and had cities that were truly beautiful. These Mexican Indians were the *Aztec* tribe.

Pueblo Indians sometimes irrigated their gardens by carrying water to the plants in handmade earthen jars.

39

Living all around the peaceful Pueblo people were tribes of the *Athapascan* language family. Among these were the *Apache* and the *Navaho*. These were hunting tribes that moved around a great deal. Sometimes they built winter houses of timber and earth, but they were not settled as were the Hopi and Zuni. Other Athapascans lived in Canada and Alaska.

There were other wandering tribes in the southwest, too. Most of them lived by hunting and by gathering their food from wild plants. They valued the nuts of the pinion pine, most of all for food but they also dug up roots and picked the berries they found growing wild in the mountainous country through which they roamed. Many of these tribes were warlike. They had not learned the skills of weaving and pottery-making as their Pueblo neighbors had. Most spoke a *Ute* language.

Who were the Pacific Coast Indians?

Several tribes, such as the *Maida*, the *Pomo* and the *Yokut*, lived west of the Rocky Mountains. These people hunted and fished for a living and gathered what they could from plants growing in the region. In California, many of them gathered acorns. The women hulled the acorns and pounded them into meal.

The acorns were bitter in taste, but the women had a way of removing the acid that caused the bitterness. They mixed the meal with water to make a kind of paste, or dough. Then they dug a hole in the sandy earth and lined the hole with the dough. They poured hot water into the hole. As it seeped through the dough, it took out the bitterness. They did this several times.

Their way of heating water was slow. They filled some of the tightly woven baskets they made with water. They dropped stones that had been heated in fire into the water. These Indians had not learned how to make pottery, so they had no bowls or jars that could be placed directly over a flame. Baskets would burn if they were put over a fire. The women used the heated stones to carry the heat to whatever they wished to warm or cook.

Pacific Coast Indians gathered plant seeds for much of their food.

The Indians of the Northwest Coast wore beautifully carved masks and fancy dress for a potlatch.

Up in the northwest, near *Puget Sound*, the tribes such as the *Shuswap* lived most of the year on the salmon they caught when the fish went upstream. They kept the fish for a long time by drying it.

These Northwest Coast Indians, most of the *Salishan* language family, had plenty of woodland nearby. They used the wood to make good solid houses, often of planks and with pointed roofs. Their door posts were skillfully carved, as were many of their religious objects such as face masks. They made big canoes from hollowed-out logs.

In their spare time, these Indians made smaller wooden items and wove fine baskets of cedar bark and bear grass, often with fancy designs.

Some of these tribes were well known for the *potlatch*, which was a feast given to celebrate almost anything that they felt needed celebrating. Fine gifts were given to the guests. The person giving the party tried to make his gifts as fancy and valuable as he possibly could. It was expected, however, that all of the guests would later give parties of their own at which even bigger and more valuable gifts would be given.

INDIANS OF NORTH AMERICA

Name	Language	Region	States Today Occupying Region
1. Apache	Athapascan	Plains & Southwest	Arizona, New Mexico
2. Arikara	Caddoan	Plains	North Dakota
3. Aztec	Uto-Aztecan	Central America	Mexico (country)
4. Caddo	Caddoan	Plains	Arkansas, Louisiana, Texas
5. Cayuga	Iroquois	Eastern Woodlands (N.)	New York
6. Chickasaw	Muskogean	Eastern Woodlands (S.)	Mississippi
7. Chippewa	Algonkian	Eastern Woodlands (N.)	Wisconsin, Minnesota, North Dakota
8. Choctaw	Muskogean	Eastern Woodlands (S.)	Mississippi, Alabama
9. Creek	Muskogean	Eastern Woodlands (S.)	Alabama, Georgia
10. Crow	Sioux	Plains	Montana, Wyoming
11. Dakota	Sioux	Plains	Minnesota, N. Dakota, S. Dakota
12. Delaware	Algonkian	Eastern Woodlands (N.)	New Jersey, Pennsylvania
13. Haida	Haida	Northwest Coast	Alaska, Canada (country)
14. Hopewell (Mound Builders)			Ohio River Valley
15. Hopi (Pueblo)	Uto-Aztecan	Southwest (desert)	Arizona
16. Iowa	Sioux	Plains	Iowa
17. Kansa	Sioux	Plains	Kansas
18. Maidu	Maidu	California Intermountain	California
19. Mandan	Sioux	Plains	N. Dakota & S. Dakota
20. Maya	Mayan	Central America	Guatemala, Honduras, El Savador, & Mexico (countries)
21. Missouri	Sioux	Plains	Missouri
22. Mohawk	Iroquois	Eastern Woodlands (N.)	New York
23. Mohican	Algonkian	Eastern Woodlands (N.)	New York
24. Navajo or Navaho	Athapascan	Southwest (desert)	New Mexico & Arizona
25. Oneida	Iroquois	Eastern Woodlands (N.)	New York
26. Onondoga	Iroquois	Eastern Woodlands (N.)	New York
27. Osage	Sioux	Plains	Arkansas, Missouri, Oklahoma, Kansas
28. Oto	Sioux	Plains	Nebraska
29. Pawnee	Caddoan	Plains	Kansas & Nebraska
30. Pomo	Pomo	California Intermountain	California
31. Quapaw	Sioux	Plains & Eastern Woodlands	Arkansas
32. Santee	Sioux	Eastern Woodlands (N.)	Minnesota, Wisconsin
33. Sauk	Algonkian	Eastern Woodlands (N.)	Illinois, Iowa, Wisconsin
34. Seminole	Muskogean	Eastern Woodlands (S.)	Alabama, Georgia
35. Seneca	Iroquois	Eastern Woodlands (N.)	New York
36. Shawnee	Algonkian	Eastern Woodlands (N.)	Ohio, Pennsylvania, W. Virginia, Tennessee, Kentucky
37. Shoshone	Uto-Aztecan	California Intermountain	Idaho, Nevada, Utah
38. Shuswap	Salishan	Northwest	British Columbia, Canada
39. Wichita	Caddoan	Plains	Kansas, Oklahoma
40. Yokuts	Yokuts	California Intermountain	California
41. Zuni (Pueblo)	Zuniai	Southwest (desert)	New Mexico

INDIANS OF NORTH AMERICA

Type of Home	Additional Information
1. Simple huts of brush & matting	Followed buffalo herds—Used stone tools
2. Earthen lodges	Raised corn—Hunted buffalo in autumn and winter
3. Wattle-and-daub huts	Built magnificent temples and halls of stone
4. Grass houses	Grew corn and other crops—Made useful pottery
5. Long houses of bark and branches	Lived settled life in villages—Built bark canoes
6. Sturdy log huts	Brave, warlike tribe—Fought De Soto in 1541
7. Round wigwams of trees and bark	Excellent fishermen—Made fine birch bark canoes
8. Small log huts	Could raise large army in time of war
9. Log huts	Looked to farming for living—Did corn dances
10. Tall, roomy tepees	Did much farming—Crossed Rocky Mts. to trade
11. Tepees	Hunted buffalo for their living
12. Rectangular, bark-covered houses	Had advanced culture—Signed treaties with William Penn
13. Large wooden houses	Fished, hunted, gathered berries—Skilled wood carvers
14. Unknown	Made earth pyramids, probably for religious reasons
15. Large dwelling of clay or stone	Highly skilled in crafts of weaving, silver work
16. Bark or mat-covered wigwams	Had ample food supply—Developed advanced culture
17. Bark or mat-covered wigwams	Grew corn and other crops—Hunted buffalo
18. Round huts of reeds and grass	Gathered nuts and seeds—Built sweat houses for steam baths
19. Earthen lodges	Work done mostly by women—Tanned leather, made pottery
20. Thatched huts	Nobles, priests spent life in ceremonies and war
21. Bark or mat-covered wigwams	
22. Long, bark-covered lodges	Led in the organizing of the Five Nations of the Iroquois
23. Round huts of bark and branches	Powerful tribe—Chief Uncas friendly to white settlers
24. Made "hogans" of stone, logs	Were hunters before white man—Became shepherds
25. Long houses of branches, bark	Member of Five Nations—Sided with Americans against English
26. Long houses of branches, bark	Members of Five Nations—Sided with English against Americans
27. Earth lodges and tepees	Grew corn—Hunted buffalo
28. Earth lodges and tepees	Peaceful farmers and hunters
29. Earth lodges	Raised corn in fields
30. Windbreaks & huts of rushes	Gathered seeds and roots for food
31. Bark and mat-covered wigwams	Also called Arkansas Indians—Met De Soto's expedition
32. Dome-shaped wigwams	Skilled craftsman—Grew corn and vegetables
33. Long lodges covered with elm bark	Close relation of Fox Indians
34. Unwalled sheds and thatched roofs	Independent and warlike—Fought white man longer than other tribes
35. Long houses covered with bark	Member of Five Nations
36. Wigwams of leaves, bark, mud	Wandered in groups—Lived separate and apart from other Indians
37. Movable desert dwellings	Lived in small groups—Moved around searching for food
38. Timber and plant houses	Skilled fishermen—Advanced social system
39. Grass houses	Grew corn and other crops—Made pottery cookware
40. Rough shelters, mat roofs	Spent much time just finding food—Made fine baskets
41. Large adobe apartment dwellings	Built dams for use in irrigation—Skilled weavers

This was the Indian's world. He lived in a way that he had learned from his fathers before him, and he was satisfied with his world most of the time. If the land in which he lived could satisfy his needs for food, shelter, and clothing, he built up a community and left it only to go to war or on hunting trips. If the land could not supply his needs throughout the year, he moved about, as did the tribes of the plains.

Horses were not to be found in North America five hundred years ago. Nor had the Indian learned to use the wheel. Traveling was done on foot or in boats. The dog was the only animal the Indian had trained to help him.

The Indian did not write, as we think of writing. Sometimes he used pictures to pass along a message or as a form of art. But his stories, his songs, and his beliefs were passed from parent to child by word of mouth. His religion and government could be very simple or not so simple. Almost always his religion stemmed from a worship of nature. Often his government was quite democratic, or one in which all the people were allowed to say what they thought.

Five hundred years ago, the Indian had no idea that 2500 miles away there lay another world, much different from his own. He could not know that this other world would soon break into the world that he knew.

Words to Know

adobe (ȧ dō′bĭ) 38
Algonkian (ăl gŏng′kĭ ăn) 34
Apache (ȧ păch′ė̇) 40
Arikara (ȧ rē′kȧ rȧ) 37
Athapascan (ăth ȧ păs′kăn) 40
Aztec (ăz′těk) 39

braves (brāvz) 34

Caddo (kä′dō) 37
Cayuga (kȧ ōō′gȧ) 34
channels (chăn′ĕlz) 29
Chickasaw (chĭk′ȧ sô) 34
Chippewa (chĭp′ė̇ wä) 34

Delaware (dĕl′ȧ wâr) 34

glacier (glā′shēr) 28
great council (koun′sĭl) 34

Hopi (hō′pė̇) 38

Ice Age (īs āj) 28
Iroquois (ĭr′ō kwoi) 34
irrigation (ĭr ĭ gā′shŭn) 38

Kansa (kăn′sô) 35
kivas (kē′vȧz) 39

long houses (lŏng houz′ĕz) 31

Maida (mā dȧ) 40
mammoths (măm′ŭths) 28
Mandan (măn′dăn) 35
Mohawk (mō′hôk) 34
Mohican (mȯ hē′kăn) 34
Muskogean (mŭs kō′gė̇ ăn) 34

Navaho (năv′ȧ hō) 40

Questions

1. How did the great glaciers of the Ice Age help to shape the land that is North America?

2. From where is it believed that the first Indians came to North America? What route did they follow?

3. How did the homes of the Eastern Woodland Indians differ from the homes of the Plains Indians? The homes of the Southwest Indians? Why were they different?

4. How did the Indians of the Eastern Woodlands make their living?

5. In what ways was the buffalo the "living" of the Plains Indians?

6. Tell how the Southwest Indians were able to grow crops in the desert regions.

7. How did the Pacific Coast Indians make bitter acorns good to eat?

8. What was the leader of an Indian village or tribe usually called? Did this person rule by himself? Explain your answer.

You See for Yourself

This chapter tells how the Indians of North America lived *about* five hundred years ago. Subtract 500 from this year to find out *exactly* what year this chapter could have described.

Look in an encyclopedia or other book to find patterns of moccasins and other things Indians made.

The World of the European

If the Algonkian Indians could have looked across the Atlantic Ocean and seen what was happening on August 13, 1476, they probably would have been amazed and a little frightened. On that day, something that would change the history of the world was happening just off the southwestern tip of Portugal. Two groups of ships, with deck guns booming, were meeting in a kind of battle unknown to the Indians. Some of the ships were sinking or burning. On the decks of others, men were fighting the men of an enemy ship with swords. The battle went on all day. When it was over, almost all of the ships had gone down.

Why was this a special battle?

The nations of Europe had many wars. In most ways, this battle was not much different from others that had taken place. Yet on one of the ships was a young sailor who was not just another sailor.

In the darkness, this sailor clung to one of the long oars from his sunken ship. Although he was wounded, he somehow stayed afloat. The next morning he was lying on the beach in the country of Portugal.

The ordinary sailor might have been interested only in staying alive in this foreign country until he could find another ship on which to sail. But this was no ordinary sailor. This young man was Christopher Columbus, a sailor from the city of *Genoa* in Italy. Columbus stayed in Portugal and there began his life's work.

Young Christopher Columbus was shipwrecked off the coast of Portugal in 1476.

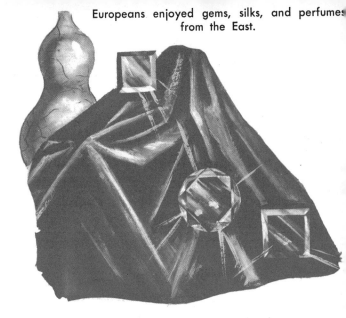

Why was trade important to the Europeans of five hundred years ago?

Columbus's home city of Genoa, Italy, had once been a great trading center. Most of the European trading goods once poured through Italian ports on their way to markets at the eastern end of the Mediterranean Sea. At these markets, Europeans traded their goods for the spices, silks, and other fine goods brought from China, Japan, and India. The Europeans called these Asian countries and their offshore islands the Far East. Far Eastern goods were brought to the eastern Mediterranean markets by traders who packed the goods on camels and traveled overland with them. The traders usually had long trains of camels called camel *caravans*.

The Turks, however, who were enemies of the Europeans, captured the lands at the eastern end of the Mediterranean Sea and closed the markets. The Europeans, unwilling to give up the things they had been getting from these markets, began to look for another way to trade for the goods of the Far East. Portugal especially was trying to find a way for ships to sail all the way to the Far East. Prince Henry, the son of the Portuguese king, set up schools for the study of *navigation*, or the art of sailing and charting a course.

The main part of every meal in those days was meat. The meat usually was not fresh and juicy, but dry, tough, and tasteless. The animals may have been butchered months before. Salt was needed to keep meat, packed into barrels, from spoiling. The people had few vegetables, so if the meat did not taste good, the meal was poor. They needed pepper and cloves from the *Indies*, islands near Asia, to make their meat enjoyable. The plants producing these spices as well as cinnamon, nutmeg, and ginger could not be grown in Europe.

The Europeans also needed perfume from the Far East. They used it both for medicine and for overcoming bad odors. The people themselves had little to help them keep clean. They often used perfume to hide odors. They did not know about germs. They had no idea that the rotting garbage in their cities brought rats and insects that carried many diseases. But they did know that the *benzoin*, *cassia* bark, and herbs and roots of the Far East sometimes helped cure the diseases.

47

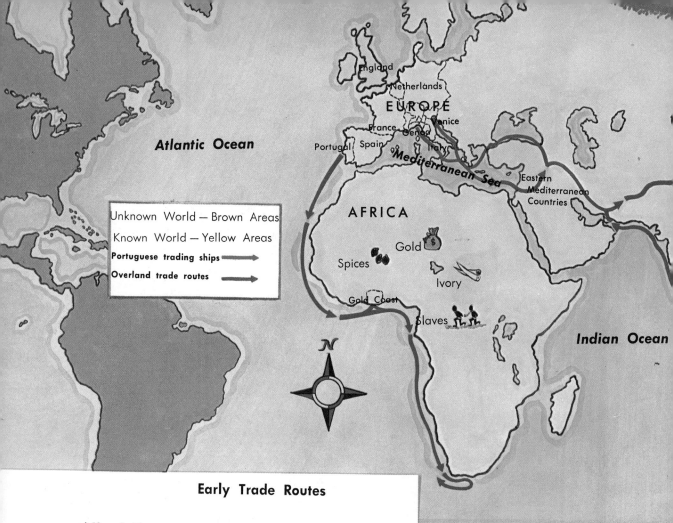

Early Trade Routes

All of Europe was interested in finding a sea route to the Far East. Early in the 1400's, Prince Henry began sending his sea captains south along the coast of Africa. He was sure that if they could find the way around Africa, his ships could sail straight to India. No Portuguese ship had yet reached the southern tip of Africa by 1460, the year of Henry's death. Still the Portuguese continued his work, and each year the Portuguese captains sailed a little farther south along the coast of Africa. Portuguese mapmakers recorded the African coastline mile after mile.

The work of the sea captains was the biggest news in Portugal. There was even a new idea that a few people were beginning to talk about. These people were saying that it might be possible to reach the Far East by sailing west across the Atlantic Ocean. Some people said this was impossible because the world was flat and ships would fall off if they came too close to the edge. But in all the universities, men were being taught that the earth was round. It seemed sensible that a ship going westward from Europe could sail around the earth to Asia.

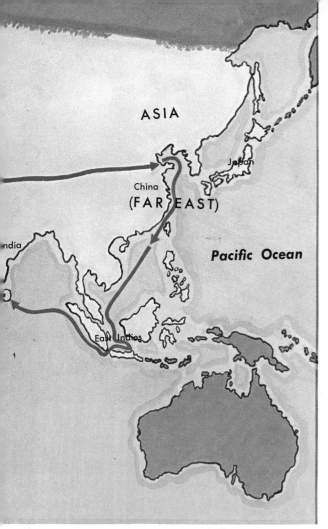

ASIA

Japan

China
(FAR EAST)

Pacific Ocean

India

East Indies

The boys did not go to school. Only those few young men who were going to be priests or who were very rich were taught to read and write. Books were still very scarce, for the printing press was not invented until Columbus was five years old.

Young Christopher and Bartholomew went down to the waterfront whenever they could. Both longed to sail on one of the many ships they saw at the docks in Genoa.

Columbus first went to sea while he was in his teens. During these years, he learned much about ships and sailing. During his early sailing days, he also noticed how the high points of mountains came into view before the low shoulders of the hills could be seen. "That is because the world is round," he thought.

Columbus made many journeys in the Mediterranean Sea. The ship which was wrecked in 1476 was the first one on which he had sailed into the Atlantic Ocean. This was the same year that Bartholomew also came to Portugal to study the map-making trade in the city of Lisbon. Christopher stayed for some months with his brother in Lisbon.

Columbus would learn of the work being carried on by the Portuguese sea captains during the years he was to spend in Portugal.

What did Columbus do as a boy?

Columbus was twenty-five years old the year he landed in Portugal. Until then, he had spent most of his life in Genoa. There, his father had a weaver's shop. Christopher and his brother Bartholomew, who was about two years younger, often worked at carding wool for their mother to spin into yarn. Their father used the yarn in his weaving.

Biography Outline

Christopher Columbus

1451-1506

Italian

Discoverer

One of the greatest navigators and seamen in history. His search to reach the Indies by sailing west led to the discovery of America in 1492.

What did Columbus do in Lisbon?

While in Lisbon, Columbus spent his time studying maps and learning to read and write in both Portuguese and Latin. Most of the books written before the invention of the printing press were in Latin.

Columbus saw the first Portuguese ships that came back from the African "Gold Coast" dock at Lisbon. The Portuguese had found that some of the same goods that came from the Far East could also be found in Africa, particularly along the Gold Coast. The ships brought back bags of pepper, gold dust, and stacks of elephant tusks. They also brought something else: dark-skinned men, women, and children who were led onto the piers with their ankles bound and chained. The slave trade was just beginning.

Columbus continued his life as a sailor, joining the crew of a different ship from time to time. Yet he always returned to Lisbon to study and to help his brother in the mapmaking business. He married the daughter of one of Prince Henry's sea captains. He was given the captain's maps and charts to help him in his studies. He began planning a sea trip, or *voyage*, to the Indies by sailing west. In 1484, Columbus felt that he was ready to make this voyage.

How did Columbus get men and ships?

Columbus went first to the king of Portugal to ask for the ships, men, and supplies he needed for his voyage. He showed the king on maps he had made how he planned to sail west until he reached Japan. "It is about 2,400 miles from Portugal," he said. "Three weeks of sailing should bring land in sight, given good winds to help us."

The distance from Portugal to Japan, if one could sail straight through North America, is really almost 11,000 miles. Columbus either believed the world to be much smaller than it is or else he told the king it was that small in order to make him more willing to back the voyage.

The Portuguese king was interested, but he felt that he could not afford to pay for such a trip. Portugal was at war, and wars cost money. Next, Columbus went to Spain, but Spain, too, had a war to pay for. When Columbus returned to Portugal in 1488, he learned that *Bartholomeu Diaz*, a Portuguese captain, had just returned from a trip to the tip of Africa. King John II of Portugal named the point the Cape of Good Hope. All Portugal was excited.

When Columbus again spoke with the Portuguese king, he was told, "Portugal has a sea route to India now. It would be foolish for me to send more ships with you when we are certain that we have already found a way to Asia."

The king did not know that it would take Portuguese captains another ten years to find the way to India from the Cape of Good Hope.

50

Columbus went back again to Spain. This time Queen Isabella seemed interested, but King Ferdinand did not. Columbus asked for three ships stocked with trading goods, seamen, a title of nobility for himself and his family, and promotion to the rank of "Great Admiral of the Ocean." He also wanted to be governor of any islands that he might find on the way to Japan and one-tenth of the money that would come from trading.

"The price is too high," said King Ferdinand.

Columbus left Spain and started for France, where he planned to speak with the French king. On the way, however, a messenger from Spain caught up with him. The messenger said that the King and Queen had changed their minds. The "Keeper of the Purse" in Spain had gone to Isabella and told her that Spain was foolish to let this chance for glory slip by for the cost of three sailing ships. Isabella agreed with this officer and offered her crown jewels as a guarantee for the loan of the money Columbus needed. The jewels did not have to be used, and finally King Ferdinand, too, saw the wisdom of helping Columbus.

What was the first voyage like?

After fourteen years of waiting, Columbus set sail from Palos, Spain, on August 3, 1492. He had three ships: the *Santa Maria*, on which he

Columbus explained his maps and charts to a number of European rulers.

himself sailed, the *Pinta*, and the *Nina*, both smaller ships. The ships were stocked with a year's supply of food, as well as glass beads, brass bells, bright red caps, lengths of colorful cloth, and other things for trading. Forty men sailed on the *Santa Maria*, twenty-six on the *Pinta*, and twenty-four on the *Nina*.

After nine days at sea, the three ships stopped at the Canary Islands.

The little fleet set sail again on September 7. On September 9, the crews sighted the last land they were to see until they were across the Atlantic. This was the land of another island in the Canary group.

Columbus had no map that showed anything beyond the Canary Islands. He was the first to sail that far west. He had a simple compass to help him tell direction. A ship's boy was given the duty of turning the sand glass each half hour to keep track of time, but sometimes the boy forgot.

To try to judge where he was on the earth, Columbus had a simple tool called a *quadrant*. He used the quadrant to sight a star and then looked at the marking on the wood to tell where he was.

The northeast winds and the ocean currents probably helped to guide the ships as much as anything else. In finding these paths, Columbus was lucky. Without the help of currents and winds, his voyage might have ended much differently.

All went well at first. On September 16, the sailors saw greenish-yellow seaweed covering the water. It frightened them, for they remembered old tales of ships being held captive on the sea by weeds or by sea monsters that hid beneath them. But the weeds were only an inch or two thick, and the ships went through them. On September 25, the sailors thought they saw land ahead, but they were mistaken.

After three more weeks of sailing, Japan still was not in sight. The ships' officers told Columbus that they wanted to go back. Columbus said, "We should reach land any day. It would be foolish to turn back when we are so near Japan. Sail on!"

On October 7, the men thought they saw land. Again they were mistaken. That evening, as Columbus stood by the rail of the ship, he saw a flight of land birds coming from the southwest. He remembered that the Portuguese sailors had found the *Azores Islands* by going in the direction from which birds had come. He ordered his ships to sail southwest.

Three days later, the ships' officers again told Columbus that the men would go no farther. They feared the ocean was endless and that the winds would keep them from ever reaching Spain again. Columbus promised to turn back if land was not in sight at the end of two more days.

The First Voyage of Columbus

The men agreed to go on, mainly because they were seeing more signs of land. They saw branches of trees floating in the water and more flocks of land birds.

On October 12, at two in the morning, the lookout on the *Pinta* was sure that the dark ridge just ahead must be land. "Land ahoy!" he shouted, and as daylight came, the ships dropped anchor just off the shore of a small island.

The world of the European met the world of the Indian. The island onto which Columbus stepped, with the royal banner of Spain in his hand, was the island of San Salvador in the West Indies. Columbus thought the brown-skinned people were Asian people. Since the Europeans spoke of all western Asia as the "Indies," he called these people "Indians."

Later, these islands were called the West Indies, and the islands of Asia were called the East Indies.

The Indians saw the beautiful colors of the flags and the fine silks that Columbus and his captains wore. The size of the Spanish ships amazed them. The swords gleaming in the sunlight and all the finery of the Spaniards delighted the Indians. When Columbus opened the chest and gave them some of the colored beads, red caps, and little brass bells, they were greatly pleased. They became the friends of the Spanish at once and were willing to help them in any way they could.

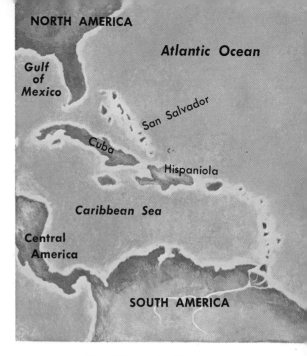

The West Indies

In the following weeks, Columbus sailed from island to island. He was puzzled to find no cities of ivory and gold. Instead of people wearing silks and satins, he found only brown-skinned people who wore hardly any clothing and lived in grass huts. The Indians could tell him nothing about gold, silks, or spices.

The men found some plants that were something like pepper and cinnamon. There were other plants, too, that were new to them. There were sweet potatoes, beans, corn, cotton, and a plant whose leaves the Indians rolled together. They lit one end, and placed the other in one nostril. As the Indians blew smoke out through the other nostril, the sailors watched in amazement. They tried smoking the new plant, tobacco, themselves and put some of it on the ships to take back to Europe.

The Indians of the West Indies taught Columbus' men how to smoke tobacco.

Columbus could not know the amount of business the tobacco plant would bring. Smoking became very popular in Europe soon after the first tobacco was brought there. In later years, tobacco-growing brought more money than all the gold the Spanish found.

Columbus and his men went on looking for gold for two more months. At last, they found little gold nuggets in a river on the island they called *Hispaniola*.

While the men were building a fort on Hispaniola and gathering gold dust, the *Santa Maria* was wrecked. There was not enough room for her crew on the other two ships. It was decided that thirty-nine men would stay on Hispaniola and live in the fort until Columbus returned.

Columbus and the rest of his men left for Spain on January 16, 1493, in the *Pinta* and the *Nina*. They took samples of things they had found in the islands, including several Indians. They reached Spain in March.

King Ferdinand and Queen Isabella welcomed Columbus warmly. They gave him all the honors he had asked, and ordered him to prepare for a second voyage.

Columbus returned to Hispaniola in November of 1493. He found that the fort and all thirty-nine of his men had disappeared. The men probably had made the Indians angry and had been attacked.

Columbus made two more trips across the Atlantic. He explored the coasts of Central America and northern South America. He realized that he had not reached the Far East.

People today think of Columbus as a great man. Yet, he himself was a disappointed and unhappy man. He was disappointed in not finding the Far East and in not finding gold or riches in the islands. The Spaniards who came to live in the islands soon after Columbus's discovery did not get along with each other or with the Indians. Many of these Spaniards blamed Columbus for their troubles.

Although Columbus was made governor of the islands as Ferdinand and Isabella had promised, his governorship was taken away from him because of the things the Spaniards said about him. After his fourth and last voyage, Columbus was no longer received by the royal court of Spain. Queen Isabella was dead and King Ferdinand refused to have anything to do with him. When he died in 1506, Columbus had no idea of the importance his discoveries held for Spain and for the whole world.

Words to Know

Azores Islands (á zōrz′ ī lăndz′) 52

Bartholomeu Diaz (bàr′tōō lōō mā′ ŏŏ dā′ásh) 50

benzoin (bĕn′zŏ ĭn) 47

caravans (kăr′á vănz) 47

cassia bark (kăsh á bärk) 47

Genoa (jĕn′ŏ á) 46

Hispaniola (hĭs′păn yō′lá) 54

Indies (ĭn′dĭz) 47

navigation (năv′ĭ gā′shŭn) 47

Nina (nē′nyä) 51

Pinta (pēn′tá) 51

quadrant (kwŏd′rănt) 52

Santa Maria (săn′tá mä rē′á) 51

voyage (voi′ĭj) 50

Questions

1. Tell two things that Columbus did as a young man that helped to prepare him for his work in navigation.

2. Name three things the Europeans bought from the Far East. How were these things used?

3. By what route were the Portuguese trying to reach the Far East? How far had they gone by the year 1488?

4. What is the name of the island on which Columbus landed? Where is this island on the map? Where did Columbus think he was?

5. Why didn't Columbus take all his men back to Spain with him?

6. In what country was Columbus born? For what country did he sail?

You See for Yourself

The island of Hispaniola became very important to the Spanish as they explored and settled America. Find this island on a present-day map or globe. What two countries are now found on this island?

The Meeting of the Two Worlds

What English captain looked for a sea route?

After Columbus returned from his first voyage, he and other people of Europe believed that he had found some islands just off the coast of Asia. All of Europe was excited about the possibility of finding a sea route to Asia across the Atlantic.

In England, the king listened with interest to Captain *John Cabot*, another seaman from Genoa. Captain Cabot had wanted for many years to look for a sea route to the Indies.

Cabot, with the help of the English king, set out in the ship *Mathew* in 1497. After sailing eight weeks, he dropped anchor off the shore of what is now southeastern Canada, near the mouth of the St. Lawrence River.

John Cabot was the first English explorer to visit the shores of North America. He also discovered and named the island of Newfoundland on his return trip to England.

Cabot did not know it at the time, but he was near the same place where other European sailors had landed almost five hundred years earlier. About the year 1000, bold seamen from the north of Europe, known as the *vikings* visited North America. They were led by the viking known as *Leif Ericson*. The vikings did not spread the word of their discovery, and no Europeans came to live in North America because of their trips. The people of southern Europe had never learned of the vikings' voyages. For these reasons, Columbus, rather than Leif Ericson, is said to have discovered America.

Cabot's men looked for the gold and other riches they hoped to find in the Far East, but they found none. The land was cold, and as the ships moved along the coast, heading northward, floating ice threatened to crush the wooden boats. Disappointed, Cabot ordered the return trip to England. On the way, he noticed that there were many fish off the coasts of *Newfoundland*, as he named the island. Before many years passed, English fishermen were visiting these fishing waters, bringing back the biggest catches ever known to them.

The English king sent Cabot back the next year with a fleet of six ships. This time, Cabot headed southward, turning his ship into harbors he found along the coast. He went as far south as North Carolina.

Vikings from northern Europe visited North America many years before Columbus sailed.

Cabot and the king of England were again disappointed not to have found the Indies. They were sure that the Indies could not be much farther away, but Cabot had not found a way around this large body of land. They and other Europeans felt that there must be a water route around or through North America that would lead to the Indies. They even called the route they hoped to find the "Northwest Passage."

Biography Outline
John Cabot
1450-1498
Italian
Navigator
Made the first English voyage to North America—gave England claim to North America and prepared the way for the first English colonies on the continent.

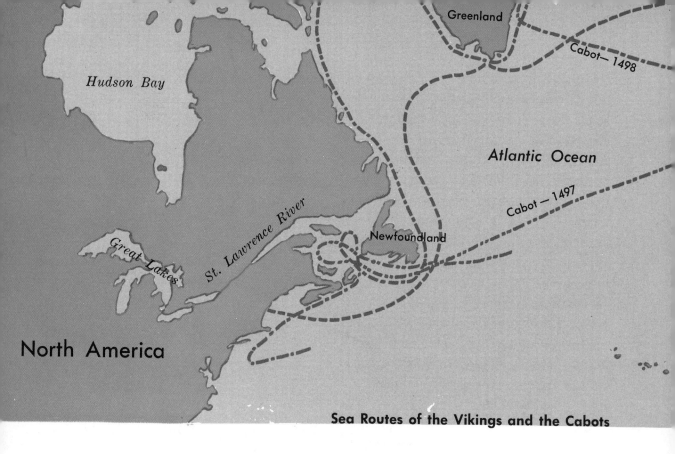

Sea Routes of the Vikings and the Cabots

Sebastian Cabot, the son of John Cabot, sailed into a passage of water that would later be named Hudson Strait. He saw the broad waters of Hudson Bay ahead. He thought China must be on the other side of this sea, and then hurried back to England to tell the king that he had found the Northwest Passage. But there was a new king on the English throne, and he was not interested in Cabot's report.

England lost interest in America and the Northwest Passage for a long time after the voyages of the Cabots. But in later years, their discoveries were very important to the English. Because of them, one hundred years later England claimed the right to the land along the Atlantic Coast of North America.

Words to Know

John Cabot (jŏn kăb′ŭt) 56

Leif Ericson (lāv ĕr′ĭk s′n) 57

Newfoundland (nū′fŭn[d] lănd′) 57

vikings (vī′kĭngz) 57

Questions

1. What important discovery did John Cabot make for the English?

2. What is meant by the Northwest Passage?

3. What large body of water did Sebastian Cabot discover? What did he think he had found?

You See for Yourself

In an encyclopedia or other book, read about the Northmen, or Norsemen as they were also called. These were the people who have become known as the vikings. Find out from what countries in Europe the vikings came. Learn about the settlement the vikings made in North America.

Using the globe, trace with your finger the route that a ship would have to follow in going from England to Japan if it sailed around North America. Why would this be a difficult trip? Would the distance be less or greater if it sailed around South America?

The Spanish and Portuguese Learn More

The Spanish and Portuguese did not give up their search for the Far East so easily. They knew that they had been mistaken, that they had found a "New World" and not Asia and its offshore islands. But they continued sending ships for two reasons. They wanted to find out if there were any gold and riches in the New World, and they wanted to find a way around or through this block in the path to Asia.

Spanish and Portuguese ships were sent out in great numbers. The two countries decided that all the trading rights in any newly discovered lands should be theirs, but they quarreled over which one had rights in each new place. To settle the argument, they had the Pope in Rome draw a line on the world map, dividing the world into two parts. Most of the New World was in Spain's half, while Africa and the route to Asia around it was in Portugal's half. Portugal sent most of her sailing ships around Africa from then on, while Spain kept on sending ships across the Atlantic Ocean. Spain claimed all rights to the New World.

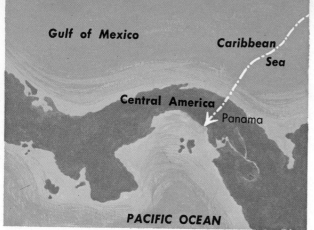

Balboa's Route to the Pacific

How did America get its name?

The New World received its name from another Italian sailing under the Spanish flag. He was *Amerigo Vespucci*. Vespucci wrote books about his experiences in the New World. A German mapmaker read the books and called the New World *"Terra America"* on the maps that he made. These words are Latin, meaning "Amerigo's Land." Soon everyone in Europe was calling the new lands "America."

What land did the Spanish discover?

Spanish ships sailed into river mouths and bays along the mainland of southern North America, Central America, and South America. They asked the Indians if there were lands nearby where gold could be found. Sometimes the Indians pointed to the west. A story began to grow that there were seven golden cities somewhere in the new land.

By the year 1521, the Spaniards had discovered two important things: the Pacific Ocean and the correct size of the earth. In 1513, a Spaniard named *Balboa* led a small army of men through the jungles and mountains of the country today called *Panama*. Balboa saw the Pacific Ocean beyond this narrow strip of land. Stepping into its waters, he claimed for Spain all the lands washed by the waters of the Pacific.

Balboa claimed all the lands touched by the Pacific for the rulers of Spain.

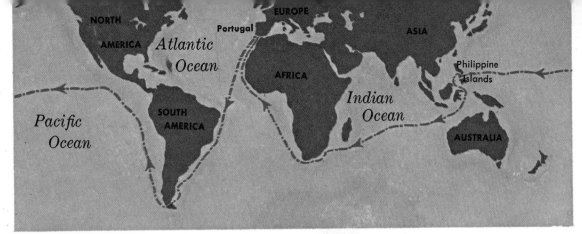

Magellan's Route Around the World

Seven years later, *Ferdinand Magellan*, a Portuguese captain sailing for the Spanish, rounded the southern tip of South America and sailed across the Pacific Ocean. Although Magellan himself was killed in the Philippine Islands, his ship was the first ever to sail around the world.

No one as yet knew how wide North America was. Maps showed it as a rather narrow band of land reaching northeastward from Mexico. Some people still hoped to find a Northwest Passage across it.

The Spanish paid little attention to the land that was to become the United States. The land to the south interested them more because it was more like the country of Spain. The gold they found among the Aztec and *Inca* Indians in Mexico and South America also held their interest.

The Spanish government kept officers in charge of the islands of the West Indies and other places they explored. One of the officers was *Ponce de Leon* on the island of *Puerto Rico*. While he was there, he heard the Indians speak of a land in which there were waters that would make an old man young again. Ponce de Leon thought that to be young again would be worth more than all the gold in the world, so he himself paid for ships and men to go to that land which we now call Florida.

That was the year 1513, the same year that Balboa found the Pacific Ocean. Ponce de Leon found no "fountain of youth" nor any gold.

Biography Outline

Vasco Nunez de Balboa

1475-1519

Spanish

Discoverer and explorer

Discovered the Pacific Ocean and claimed it for Spain—explored the coasts of Venezuela, Colombia, and the Isthmus of Panama.

Biography Outline

Juan Ponce de Leon

1460?-1521

Spanish

Explorer

Conquered Puerto Rico—discovered and claimed Florida for Spain—searched for the legendary Fountain of Youth.

Ponce de Leon returned to Florida for a second search in 1521. This time his ships were caught in a storm off the Florida coast and could not make a landing at once. When the storm was over, unfriendly Indians were lying in wait. Ponce de Leon was killed before he reached shore.

About five years later, another group of Spaniards went to Florida. In this group were five ships, hundreds of men, and horses. Part of the group traveled by land along the western coast of Florida, robbing Indian villages and seeking gold. The rest of the men started out in ships, and the two groups planned to meet. They never found each other. The men on land finally decided to build ships and sail along the coast of the Gulf of Mexico until they reached Mexico.

They melted down their swords and other bits of metal they had and made nails, saws, and axes. They cut down trees in the southern pine woods. They used the pine *resin* to seal cracks between planks, and made rope from strips of palm leaves and the manes and tails of their horses. They killed a horse every third day for food. They made sails of their shirts and set sail in September, 1528.

They sailed along the coast. They saw the mouth of the Mississippi River, but did not know what it was.

Farther on, storms wrecked their ships and many men died at sea. A few reached land and were kept alive by some Indians there. These Indians had not yet heard of the cruel treatment that the Spaniards usually gave to the Indians.

One of the Spaniards fed by the Indians was named *Cabeza de Vaca*. In order to keep from becoming a slave to the Indians, Cabeza de Vaca became a trader among them. He took shells, sea beans, and other goods of the seashore Indians and traveled inland to the west and north. He traded these items for buffalo skins, *flint*, a kind of stone used for making arrowheads, and anything else he thought the shore Indians would like to have.

Explorations of the Spanish

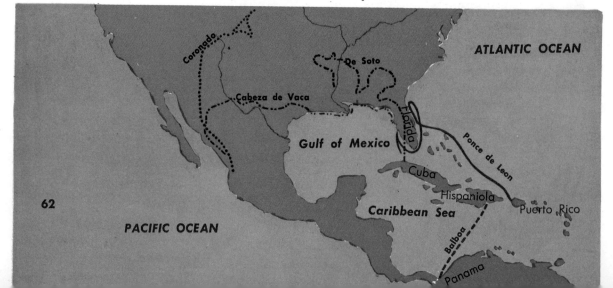

Spanish explorers journeyed through many parts of the Southwest in their search for riches and golden cities. The first Europeans ever to see the Grand Canyon of the Colorado River were a group of Spanish explorers on an expedition during the 1540's.

Cabeza de Vaca explored in Texas and perhaps in New Mexico and Arizona. He was the first European to go into these lands. He saw the great herds of buffalo that came down from the northern plains. After several years, he met two other Spaniards from the lost group and a slave they had with them. The slave was a large, strong man named *Esteban*. The four men traveled together. The Indians asked them to use the white man's power to heal sicknesses. They became known as healers among many of the tribes.

Finally, the men met a party of Spaniards out looking for Indians to take into slavery. Even the Indians who had been kind to Cabeza de Vaca and the other three men were captured, against the wishes of the men they had helped. The slave-hunters, however, helped Cabeza de Vaca find his way back to Spanish settlements.

63

The Spanish at first believed the pueblos of the Southwest Indians were made of gold.

The story of the seven golden cities was now widespread. Esteban, the slave, was sent as a guide with an exploring party led by a priest, *Friar Marcos*, to search for them.

They found one of the great pueblos of the Hopis, and from the distance, in the sunshine, it looked golden. The Spaniards guessed that the chunks of turquoise were costly jewels. But Esteban was killed by the Indians as he entered their village. The Friar hurried back to Mexico.

The Spaniards quickly planned another exploring party under the leadership of *Francisco Coronado*. This group was to go back and find the golden city where Esteban was killed, and the six other cities, too. Ships were sent up the Gulf of California under the leadership of a man named *Alarcon*. Alarcon and his men discovered the Colorado and *Gila* rivers. Coronado went overland with Friar Marcos as his guide.

Coronado and his men marched through the southwestern part of what is now the United States during the years of 1541 and 1542. Everywhere they went they fought the Indians and often won. The Spaniards took hundreds of prisoners and slaves. They found no gold.

Who was Hernando de Soto?

The same year that Esteban met his death, 1539, more ships landed in Florida, bringing another army of Spanish soldiers. The gaily dressed Spaniards brought horses, slaves to carry their belongings, and even hogs to supply food. There were six hundred men altogether, and they were led by *Hernando de Soto*.

The men marched through Florida, into Georgia, and a short distance into the Carolinas. When they reached the Appalachian Mountains, they turned southwest into Alabama. Everywhere they went, they treated the Indians badly. Word of their cruelty went ahead of them. In the part of the country now in the state of Alabama, they were attacked by Indians and lost much of their goods.

Biography Outline

Francisco Vasquez de Coronado

1510-1554

Spanish

Explorer

Led an expedition through the southwestern United States—discovered the Grand Canyon and the Continental Divide.

De Soto and his men set out toward the northwest and crossed what is now the state of Mississippi, still looking for golden cities. It was the spring of 1541 when, one day, they saw ahead of them a great river. They were not far from where *Memphis*, Tennessee, is now, and the river they saw was the Mississippi. By making rafts, they were able to cross it. They followed it northward along the bank on the opposite shore.

The Indians there had not yet learned about the men who rode on great animals and had "sticks" that could kill. They were amazed at the things the men had from the other world across the ocean. De Soto did all he could to make the Indians believe that he was more god than man, calling himself "Child of the Sun" and saying that he could not die.

De Soto and his men journeyed on and on, traveling westward and then circling back to the Mississippi River. All felt discouraged, and many were sick, including De Soto himself. De Soto died near an Indian village in present-day Arkansas, not far from the Mississippi River.

De Soto's men wrapped his body in skins, weighted it, and dropped it into the Mississippi River in the dark of night. They hoped to keep the Indians from finding out that the "Child of the Sun" had died and so was not a god after all. But the Indians did learn of De Soto's death and attacked the men who were left.

As the men with Cabeza de Vaca had done, they built ships in which to make their escape. They floated down the Mississippi, hurrying away from this disappointing land that had held such promise of riches but had turned out to be only a rough wilderness.

How did the Spaniards help change the lives of the Indians?

The Sioux and Muskogean tribes almost forgot about the Spaniards after De Soto's travels through their lands. But the Spanish left their mark on the world of the Indian. The Sioux tribes of the plains especially had their lives changed. They soon learned to use the white man's horses. On horseback, they could roam over the plains much more freely, and swiftly chase the buffalo that meant their living. De Soto and Coronado both lost many horses during their explorations. These lost horses became the parents of the herds of wild horses that roamed the Southwest in later years. The Indians of the Plains soon learned to capture these wild horses and to use them in their lives.

Biography Outline
Hernando de Soto
c. 1500-1542
Spanish
Explorer
Discovered the Mississippi while searching for treasure.

Words to Know

Alarcon (ä′lär kôn′) 64

Amerigo Vespucci (ä må rē′gŏ vĕs pōō′chĕ) 60

Balboa (bǎl bō′å) 60

Cabeza de Vaca (kä vä′thǎ dĕ vä′kä) 62

Esteban (ĕs tä′bŏn) 63

Ferdinand Magellan (fûr′dĭ nǎnd må jĕl′ǎn) 61

flint (flĭnt) 62

Francisco Coronado (frän sēs′kŏ kŏr ŏ nä′dō) 64

Friar Marcos (frī′ĕr mär′kōs) 64

Gila (hē′lå) 64

Hernando de Soto (ĕr nän′dō dē sō′ tō) 64

Inca (ĭng′kå) 61

Memphis (mĕm fĭs) 65

Panama (pǎn′å mô) 60

Ponce de Leon (pŏns′dĕ lē′ŭn) 61

Puerto Rico (pwĕr′tŭ rē′kō) 61

resin (rĕz′ĭn) 62

Terra America (tĕr′å å mĕr′ĭ kå) 60

Questions

1. Why did Spain rather than Portugal lead the way in the exploration of the New World?

2. Why was Ponce de Leon interested in exploring Florida?

3. Why were the Spanish more interested in the lands of Mexico and South America than in the lands to the north? How did the Spanish become interested in the lands to the north? Were they happy with what they found?

4. How did Cabeza de Vaca stay alive after he was shipwrecked in the Gulf of Mexico? Whom did he meet after several years? Why were these men welcomed in the Indian villages they visited?

5. Why did De Soto's men not wish the Indians to learn of De Soto's death? How did the men that were left get back to Mexico?

You See for Yourself

Make a chart entitled "Spanish Explorers." Mark off three columns on your paper. For each explorer give the name, dates, and lands explored. The explorers you should include are Ponce de Leon, De Soto, Balboa, Coronado, and Cabeza de Vaca.

Cartier explored the mouth of the St. Lawrence River.

France Looks into the New World

When Magellan's ship returned from the first round-the-world voyage in 1522, the king of France decided that his country, too, should take part in the explorations. He hired an Italian seaman named *Verrazano*. In 1524, Verrazano sailed along the coast of North America. He did not find the Northwest Passage.

In 1534, the king of France sent *Jacques Cartier*, who had been a seaman for twenty years, to North America. He sailed to Newfoundland, as Cabot had done for the English. But Cartier went farther inland, into the mouth of the St. Lawrence River, thinking that he had found the Northwest Passage. He and his men traveled upriver for a month, but found only Indian villages and wilderness.

Cartier talked with Indians in sign language. The Indians spoke of a "Great sea at end of rivers." The Indians meant one of the Great Lakes, but Cartier was sure they meant the Pacific Ocean. He had to go back to France because winter was coming, but he decided to return the next spring. He reported to the king that he had claimed much land for France and also that he now knew the way to the Pacific Ocean through North America. All he needed was time to follow the rivers far enough.

Biography Outline

Jacques Cartier

1491-1557

French

Sailor and explorer

Sailed up the St. Lawrence River as far as Montreal, claiming the land he saw for France.

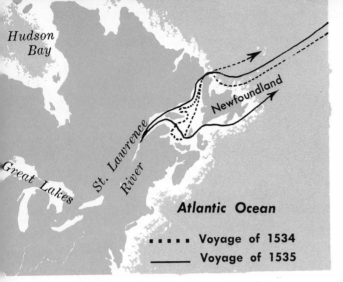

Voyage of 1534
Voyage of 1535

Cartier in the New World

Cartier was back in the New World the next year. He went to the place where the *Ottawa* River empties into the St. Lawrence. The Indians said that this was the river that led to the sea but that to follow it was a dangerous journey. There was a volcanic mountain on the right bank as the men approached the meeting of the two rivers. Cartier named the mountain *Mount Royal*, and the city of *Montreal* later was built there. It took its name from Cartier's name for the mountain.

Hope burned in Cartier's heart. He felt he would soon find the Northwest Passage. But again, winter was approaching and he had to take his ship back to France.

Unfortunately, France was not ready to go on with the explorations. War had broken out between France and Spain, and Cartier had brought back no gold to pay for more voyages. Cartier paid for another journey himself, and he may have returned for even another. But he did not get much farther than he had before. Sixty years were to pass before France sent more men back to the St. Lawrence Valley.

Words to Know

Jacques Cartier (zhăk kȧr′tyā′) 67

Montreal (mŏn′trė̇ ôl′) 68

Mount Royal (mount roi′ăl) 68

Ottawa (ŏt′ȧ wȧ) 68

Verrazano (vȧr′rä tsä′nȯ) 67

Questions

1. What was the name of the first seaman to explore for France? What did he especially hope to find?

2. What did Cartier believe the "Great sea at end of rivers" to be?

3. Tell how the present-day city of Montreal, Canada, got its name.

4. What river did Cartier explore on his trips to the New World?

You See for Yourself

In an encyclopedia or perhaps a book about Indians, read about talking by sign language. Can you learn enough signs to say something to your classmates?

Now You Know

The first Americans came to this land probably from Asia. These people became known to Europeans thousands of years later as Indians. The Indians lived as separate tribes, working out their lives according to where they lived.

During the 1400's, the Europeans began to build better ships and to study navigation in order to send trading ships to Asia. Their search for a sea route to Asia first brought them in touch with America in 1492. America was at first believed to be very near Asia. Later, Europeans realized it was a new continent.

The work of exploring the New World fell largely to Spain during the early years. The Spanish found gold in Mexico and in South America within thirty-five years after Columbus. They spent most of their time and interest in these lands. They looked into the lands to the north, but made few large or lasting settlements there.

France and England, too, sent sea captains to the New World. They hoped these men would find a way around or through America, as it stood in their way for a westward route to Asia. The French and English explored in the north, in Canada, and along the Atlantic Coast.

In the years to come, many more Europeans would take an interest in the New World. Just as events in Europe had led to the discovery of America, so events in Europe would lead to the settlement and growth of the land that would become the United States of America.

You Talk It Over

People today are living in an age of space explorations. How were the journeys of the early sea captains like the trips of space explorers today? How were they different? In which do you think there would be the greater risk to the explorer?

Do you think the Spanish felt that their treatment of the Indians was wrong? How do you think the Spanish felt about the Indians as people? Could the Spaniards have gotten what they wanted if they had been more friendly to the Indians?

Unit Questions

1. What was the land of North America like several million years ago?

2. The Indians in Mexico, Central America, and South America were more advanced than those to the north. Name three ways in which they were more advanced.

3. What were the four large language groups of Eastern Woodland Indians?

4. Tell how most of the Eastern Woodland Indians built their homes.

5. In what way did nature provide clothing for the Eastern Woodland Indians?

6. Where did the tribes of the Sioux language-family live?

7. What was the name of the home the Plains Indians built? How did these homes suit the kind of life the Plains Indians lived?

8. What did the Southwest Indians of the desert use to build their homes?

9. What is a potlatch? Where did the potlatch Indians live?

10. Who was Prince Henry? When did he live?

11. How had Europeans been getting Far Eastern goods before the time of Prince Henry?

12. How much education did Columbus have as a boy? Did Columbus need education for his work as a sea captain? How did he learn what he needed to know?

13. Was Columbus the only person of his time who believed the earth was round?

14. When did Europeans learn the correct size of the earth?

15. Who discovered the Pacific Ocean? For what country did he claim the lands washed by its waters?

16. Who explored the St. Lawrence River for France?

Puzzlers

Listed below are statements that could have been made by people who really lived or could have lived during the years covered in this unit. Read each statement carefully. Then match the letter of the statement with the number for the name of the person you think could have made it.

A
I went to Lisbon, Portugal, in 1476. I worked in the mapmaking business there. My older brother became a very famous man.

B
I led a group of men who were searching for the seven cities of gold. We traveled by ship and discovered the Gila and Colorado Rivers.

C
Both my king and I were disappointed not to have found the Northwest Passage. In later years, however, my explorations were important to my country, England.

D
I was the first Spaniard to explore the southwest. Because of my reports, other Spaniards made journeys into this part of North America.

E
I made a famous sea voyage in 1488. On this voyage, I reached the southern tip of Africa, the Cape of Good Hope.

F
I visited North America even before Columbus. Yet people do not say that I discovered America.

G
I would have used my jewels to have helped Columbus make his first voyage. I found, however, that I could help him without the jewels.

H
I shall be a man soon and must show my bravery before all my people. I am eager to go on my first buffalo hunt when I am a man. I practice running so that I can run swiftly when I am on buffalo hunts.

1. Francisco Coronado   2. Bartholomeu Diaz   3. A young Indian boy of the Dakota   4. John Cabot   5. Ferdinand Magellan 6. Leif Ericson   7. Bartholomew Columbus   8. Queen Isabella 9. Alarcon   10. Cabeza de Vaca   11. Ponce de Leon   12. Christopher Columbus

Unit Activities

You present a television program

If your school has a television viewer, make a scroll for it showing the voyage of Magellan. If your school does not have a viewer, make one from a pasteboard box. Write a story to go with the pictures to tell about Magellan's voyage. You will want to include several maps among your pictures.

Perhaps you will want to divide your class into committees, each making a scroll for other explorers.

You make an Indian display

Choose one of the large Indian groups, Woodland, Plains, or Southwest, that you learned about in this unit. Plan a display of as many items as you can that would be found among the group you have chosen. Most of the items you will be able to make or draw: tools, clay pottery, lodges, and even clothing made from material the same color as skins. If you wish, the class may be divided into three groups.

You dress a doll

Find pictures of the kind of clothes that Europeans wore during the time of Columbus. Sew a costume for a doll that is like one someone in Spain, France, or England may have worn.

You write a newspaper

Although there were no newspapers in Europe in the 1400's, it would be fun to pretend that there were, and to write news items for it. Pretend that you are a newspaper editor in Portugal during the years that Columbus was in Lisbon. Make up a front page that would suit the times. Your headline story will be about the Portuguese sea captains and their latest discoveries. You may want to make up some news items about imaginary people and put them in your paper just for fun.

You build a ship

Choose one of the sea captains you read about in this unit. In encyclopedias or history books, find some good pictures of this captain's ship. Build a small ship as much like the one in the picture as you can. Use whatever materials you feel are best and easiest for you to get.

You draw a story map

On a large piece of wrapping paper or on the chalkboard, make a picture map that tells the story of the people in this unit. You will need to show Asia, Africa, Europe, North America, and South America. Draw in the routes of the explorers and the dates of their explorations. Show where the Indian groups lived. Write important facts on the map, too, if you have room to do so.

Colonization and Settlement of America

On an April day in 1562, two little ships rolled and tossed in the waves of the Atlantic Ocean not far from the northeastern coast of Florida. On board the ships was a group of Frenchmen who were looking for more than gold or a Northwest Passage. These people, known as French *Huguenots*, were looking for a new place to live, one in which they could worship in the way they chose. Their leader was *Jean Ribaut*.

Although seventy years had passed since Columbus's discovery, there was not yet a single European community in all the section of North America that would become the United States. The French Huguenots planned to start the first one.

England's colonies became firmly established during the 1700's. The city of Philadelphia was an important business center.

The French Gain a Foothold

What was the first colony on United States soil?

Ribaut and the Huguenots first dropped anchor near the place where Jacksonville, Florida, is today. They stayed at this point long enough to set up a stone marker bearing the French coat-of-arms and to make friends with the Indians there. They even gave the chief a blue silk cape with the French lily embroidered in gold thread.

The French sailed farther north to choose a place for their new colony. A *colony* is a settlement in which the land itself belongs to another country. That country also has control over the people who live in the colony. The colony of the French Huguenots would belong to France.

Ribaut sailed into Port Royal Sound in present-day South Carolina. On the shore, he helped the men to build a fort and then sailed back to France for supplies. Ribaut was unable to return as quickly as he hoped, so the discouraged colonists built a ship and returned to France.

Three years later, a second group of French Huguenots tried to set up another colony at the place where Ribaut had left the stone marker. They called their new colony Fort Caroline. The Spanish, however, claimed all rights to Florida and started making plans to drive out the French as soon as they heard of Fort Caroline.

The Spanish took over an Indian village near the present city of St. Augustine, Florida, and used it as a base for their attack on Fort Caroline. The Frenchmen were sure that they would be attacked, so most of them left Fort Caroline in ships to make a surprise attack on the Spanish at St. Augustine.

The Huguenots at Fort Caroline were greeted by the same Indian chief whom Ribaut had met three years earlier. The chief still wore the silk cape Ribaut had given him.

The Spanish Stop the French

The French ships were destroyed in a hurricane before they reached St. Augustine. In the meantime, the Spanish had set out overland. They found Fort Caroline nearly empty and destroyed it.

Although the French were the first to try setting up a colony in land that would later become the United States, they were not the first to succeed. Instead it was the Spanish who set up the first colony in 1565, at St. Augustine.

When did the French begin setting up fur-trading posts?

The next group of French explorers set sail in 1603, thirty-eight years after the fall of Fort Caroline. On board one of the ships was a young mapmaker named *Samuel Champlain*. The ships headed into the St. Lawrence River, following up on Cartier's findings. But like Cartier, these men were forced to return to France because they did not have the supplies to last through the cold northern winter.

Young Champlain became the leader of another group that set sail from France in 1608. His ships carried tools and supplies to build shelters in order that winter would not again drive the men away before they had the chance to explore the Ottawa River. They hoped that this river would lead them to the Northwest Passage. There was also the hope that they might find rich Indian settlements like those the Spanish had found in South America. But Champlain had yet another idea for business in the New World. He planned to build trading posts for trading with the Indians. The Indians could easily get many furs which they would trade for European goods. The French hat makers had learned to use beaver fur in making gentlemen's hats, and the style was popular all over Europe. Cartier had reported thousands of beaver to be found in the many streams of inland North America. Furs of other American animals were also in demand for trimming the capes and robes of well-dressed ladies of Europe.

The Algonkian Indians were eager to trade the furs that they could get so easily for European trinkets. They brought their furs to Champlain's trading post.

Champlain built his trading post on the high bank of the St. Lawrence River. It stood two stories high and had balconies at the second-story level. The Indians watched eagerly as the Frenchmen put up fine buildings, so unlike their simple lodges. They were especially amazed when Champlain fired a shot from the cannon the Frenchmen placed on the balcony. This post was the beginning of the Canadian city of Quebec.

Biography Outline

Samuel de Champlain

1567?-1635

French

Explorer

Founded the city of Quebec in Canada—explored the St. Lawrence River, Georgian Bay and Lake Ontario—helped establish the French in North America.

The neighboring Algonkians looked upon the French as their friends. They enjoyed the iron cooking pots, metal knives, bright-colored cloth and beads, animal traps, mirrors, bells, and dozens of other items from the world of the European. They got these things through trading their furs to the French. The Algonkian chief even asked Champlain to take his guns and men and join the Algonkians in a fight against their enemies to the south, the Iroquois tribes. Champlain agreed, and the fierce Iroquois met the guns of the Europeans for the first time at a lake named for Champlain in what is now New York State. The Iroquois, from that day forward, looked upon the French as their enemies.

After a year or two, Champlain was ready to seek the Northwest Passage. He went out with small groups of men, using birchbark canoes in which the Indians could travel so easily. He finally found the headwaters of the Ottawa River. He soon learned that it was not a route to the Pacific and that the "great seas" the Indians spoke of were the Great Lakes. The first lake he discovered was Lake Huron. He and other French explorers soon found Lake Superior, Lake Michigan, Lake Ontario, and Lake Erie.

Who were some other great French explorers?

By the time Champlain died in 1653, New France, as the French called their holdings in America, was well started. In addition to the fur trade, which had grown rapidly, the French had brought the Christian religion to North America. French priests built missionary posts near the trading centers. The priests, or *missionaries*, helped the Indians in every way they could, aiding them when they were sick and teaching many of them about God.

It was a French missionary and a French explorer who found the way from Lake Michigan to the Mississippi River. Father *Jacques Marquette* and *Louis Joliet* journeyed in a canoe just about as far south as the place where De Soto had first seen the Mississippi, one hundred years earlier.

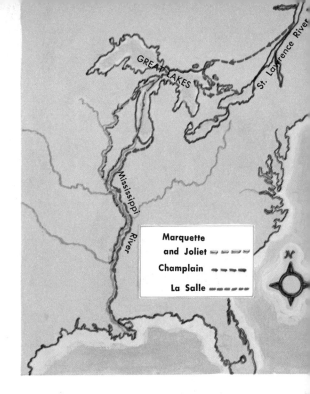

Explorations of the French

During those years, no white man is known to have visited the Mississippi Valley. The Spanish had not found it to be a place of good fortune. They built their trading posts farther west, founding Santa Fe, in New Mexico, in 1609.

Marquette and Joliet returned to the northern lands, but a few years later, another Frenchman, *Robert la Salle*, journeyed all the way to the mouth of the Mississippi.

La Salle set the flag of France into the ground at the mouth of the Mississippi in 1682, and declared that all the land whose waters drained into the Mississippi River now belonged to France. He did this in the name of King Louis XIV of France, and the land was named Louisiana.

79

Words to Know

colony (kŏl′ồ nĭ) 76

Huguenots (hū′gẽ nŏts) 75

Jacques Marquette (zhȧk mȧr′kĕt′) 79

Jean Ribaut (zhän rē′bō′) 75

Louis Joliet (lōō′ĭs jŏl′ĭ ĕt) 79

missionaries (mĭsh′ŭn ĕr′ĭz) 79

Robert la Salle (rŏ′bĕrt lȧ sȧl′) 79

Samuel Champlain (săm′ủ ĕl shăm plān′) 77

Questions

1. What business was Champlain planning to start in America?

2. What was the name of the settlement the French made in Florida? What became of this settlement?

3. Why did the French Huguenots leave France?

4. Name three French explorers of the Mississippi River. Which one claimed the mouth of the river for France?

5. How did Champlain make the Iroquois Indians enemies of the French in the New World?

6. What Canadian city grew up at Champlain's trading post?

You See for Yourself

Find "Huguenots" in an encyclopedia. Read about the trouble they had in France before they decided to come to America.

Early English Colonies in America

What was the lost colony?

While the French were busy setting up trading posts and exploring during the late 1500's and early 1600's, England, too, was busy in North America. England's ruler, Elizabeth I, sent many brave sea captains out onto the seas to try to break Spain's claims to rule almost all of the New World. Among her sea captains were Sir Francis Drake and *Sir Walter Raleigh*.

Drake attacked Spanish ships and burned down Spanish settlements in America, including St. Augustine, whenever he could. This led to serious wars between England and Spain. The Spanish rebuilt St. Augustine and kept their hold on Florida for many years.

Sir Walter Raleigh thought that England had rights in America because of the journeys of John Cabot. Raleigh felt that the best way for England to become strong in the New World would be to set up English colonies there. In 1584, he provided ships and supplies for a group of Englishmen to begin a colony on *Roanoke* Island off the coast of North Carolina. A year later seven more ships of colonists arrived at the colony.

The colonists began running low on food and were finding that the Indians were not very friendly. When Sir Francis Drake visited the colony on one of his voyages, the colonists returned to England with him.

An English supply ship, with food and more colonists, arrived a few days later to find the colony empty. Only fifteen of the new colonists were willing to stay.

A year later, John White, who was to be the English governor of the colony, arrived with over one hundred more settlers to join the fifteen. Among them were his daughter and her husband, *Ananias Dare*. White again found an empty colony, and the Indians would tell him nothing. After a couple of months, John White returned to England for supplies. But before he left, a baby girl was born to his daughter. The child was named Virginia Dare, in honor of this land called Virginia by the English. Virginia Dare was the first English child born in America.

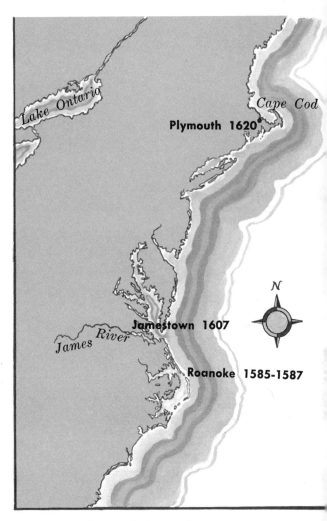

Early English Settlements

It was two years before White could return to Roanoke Island. When he arrived, he was shocked to find only empty cabins. The only sign of any message left for him was the word *CROATOAN* carved on a tree. It was the name of an Indian tribe a few miles to the south. John White searched, but he found neither the Indians nor the lost colonists. The mystery of the Lost Colony of Roanoke was never solved.

Indians looked on as John Smith directed the building of the Jamestown Colony.

What English colony was successful?

Twenty years later, in 1607, the English tried again to start a colony in the New World. A group of English merchants, known as the London Company, paid for the colony. The company would have been much pleased if the colonists had found gold in the new colony. Yet they were almost sure of getting their money back through lumber and crops the colonists would send from the New World.

Among the men the London Company chose to be leaders of the colony was Captain John Smith. Captain Smith and one hundred forty-two colonists chose a place at the south end of Chesapeake Bay, between Virginia and Maryland, for their colony. They named it Jamestown.

Illness attacked the colonists during the very first months. John Smith was among those who burned with fever. Yet if it had not been for the planning, work, and strong will of John Smith, this colony, too, would have failed.

Much work, such as cutting trees for lumber, planting crops, and building shelters, was needed in the colony. Many of the colonists had been "gentlemen" in England and felt they should do no work. John Smith saw to it that all the men worked.

Biography Outline

John Smith

1580-1631

English

Soldier and adventurer

Helped in the founding of Virginia and New England—helped establish Jamestown, Virginia, the first permanent English settlement in America.

Smith also learned how to deal with the Indians for corn and other food, without which the Jamestown colonists would have starved to death. Many of the men disliked Captain Smith for the way he gave orders and controlled the colony. They did not realize that he was undoubtedly the main reason for their staying alive.

The neighboring Indians, however, could see how valuable Smith was to the colony. They felt they had taken a real prize when they took him prisoner one day as he was out exploring. *Powhatan*, the chief, was not sure what to do with Smith. He feared the white men, yet he wanted to learn more about their secrets.

Powhatan allowed Smith the freedom of the Indian village for some time while he decided what to do with his prisoner. Smith made friends with the children, including *Pocahontas*, the chief's daughter.

Powhatan finally decided that Smith should be put to death. Pocahontas, however, is believed to have convinced her father to allow Smith to return to Jamestown.

The Jamestown colonists were very angry with Smith when he returned. Part of their anger was because some of the other men who had gone exploring with him had been killed by the Indians. Yet as they were about to hang him, a supply ship arrived and Smith was set free.

Pocahontas came often to Jamestown. She and one of the young men who came on the later ship were married. It is thought that she showed her husband, *John Rolfe*, the way the Indians grew tobacco. He soon learned to improve the crop and was sending some to be sold in England. It was through the growing of tobacco that the Virginia colony finally began to pay its own way.

In 1619, a shipload of ninety women came to Jamestown from England so that the men without families could have wives. The colony took on a more settled look, and many of the families moved to land farther from Jamestown in order to grow tobacco.

That same year, a shipload of Negroes was brought to Virginia. The Virginia planters bought them for slaves to help with the work. At the time, the work of the slaves helped the colony to grow stronger because more tobacco could be grown. But it was the beginning of later trouble.

One other important thing happened in 1619. Until that year, the colony had been ruled by a governor picked by the king, and sent over from England. In 1619, the colonists were allowed to choose people from their own group to meet with the governor and help decide how to meet the problems of the colony. These men were called burgesses and their meeting house was called the House of Burgesses.

When was the first New England colony begun?

John Smith left Jamestown after it was firmly settled. He mapped the Virginia area well and then sailed northward. He went around Cape Cod and into the bay it shelters. He made a fairly accurate map of the New England shoreline. The land north of the Hudson River was already being called "New England."

One of John Smith's maps was in the chartroom of the ship that neared the New England shore in the fall of 1620. The ship was the *Mayflower*. One hundred and two men, women, and children were on board with as much of their family belongings as the ship could hold.

The *Pilgrims*, as these people are often called, had left England because the government there would not allow them to worship as they chose. For a while, the Pilgrims had lived in Holland, but after a few years there, they decided they would be happier in the New World.

The Pilgrims received money and supplies from the London Company to make their trip to the New World. In return, the Pilgrims were to send furs and lumber back to England to repay the London Company.

The *Mayflower* dropped anchor just inside Cape Cod Bay. Before the Pilgrims went ashore, however, their leader, *William Bradford*, called the men together to draw up an agreement as to how they would govern themselves. The agreement was called the *Mayflower Compact*. In the plan was the idea of the New England *town meeting*, under which all the men of the colony could meet to give their ideas and decide what should be done in the colony.

The ship's carpenters, among whom was a young man named John Alden, built a small sailboat in which the men could explore Cape Cod Bay.

Using John Smith's map as a guide the Pilgrims spent a month exploring the bay. At last they chose the place marked *Plymouth* on John Smith's map.

The Pilgrims laid out a street and divided it into lots. The first building they put up was a "common house," twenty feet on each side, to be used as a storehouse and shelter until others could be built. The first homes of the Pilgrims were much like the first shelters at Jamestown, huts of poles and bark. These were replaced as quickly as possible by homes of lumber with thatched roofs.

The Pilgrims suffered much during the first winter from lack of good food and from illness. The *Mayflower* stayed through the winter, and Pilgrims rowed back and forth from the ship to the shore as they went about building homes and shelters. Many of the Pilgrims and sailors, too, died before spring came. One family, the Mullins, was entirely wiped out except for a daughter, Priscilla. Her later marriage to John Alden became famous because of a poem that was written about it. Another person in that poem was Captain Miles Standish. An ex-soldier, Captain Standish was one of the most helpful men in Plymouth.

The Pilgrims saw Indians in the woods from time to time during that first winter, but none of them ever came into the village. One day in spring, however, the Pilgrims were very much surprised by an Indian who came boldly walking into their village. Fearless Captain Standish was the only one willing to approach the stranger. Yet even he was shocked when the Indian put forth his hand to shake hands and said, "Welcome, Englishmen! Me *Samoset*. Me friend to Englishmen!"

Later, the Pilgrims learned that the place they had chosen for their settlement had been visited by another English ship just ahead of theirs. The captain of that ship was Thomas Dermer. Captain Dermer had an Indian slave named *Squanto*. Captain Dermer was a kind man. He gave Squanto his freedom. He made friends with the Indians in the region and even taught some of them, including Samoset, to speak a little English.

Samoset startled the Plymouth colonists when he greeted them in their own language.

Soon afterward, Samoset brought Squanto to Plymouth. In turn, Squanto helped the Pilgrims win the friendship of *Massasoit*, chief of the Algonkian tribes that lived nearby. Massasoit soon signed a peace treaty with the Pilgrims, which he kept for the rest of his life.

Squanto stayed with the Pilgrims the rest of that spring and summer. He taught them how to plant corn, or *maize* as the Indians called it. He showed them how to enrich the earth by burying certain rotting fish with the seeds. He taught the Pilgrims the uses of wild roots and herbs for food and medicine, how to hunt deer and other wild game, and how to use deerskin in everyday living the way the Indians had done for so many years.

That fall, the Pilgrims wanted to show their thanks both to God and to their Indian friends. Their corn had grown well and they had much fish, turkey, duck, and deer meat stored for the winter. They invited Massasoit to join them in a Thanksgiving Feast. Massasoit arrived with ninety braves, and the feasting lasted for three days. The story of this feast has been told in many different ways. Probably no one knows exactly what took place, but it has become known to Americans as the first Thanksgiving Day.

The neighboring Indians joined the Pilgrims in a Feast of Thanksgiving after the Pilgrims' first harvest.

Words to Know

Ananias Dare (ăn′a nī′ăs dâr) 81

CROATOAN (krō′tăn) 81

John Rolfe (jŏn rŏlf) 83

maize (māz) 86

Massasoit (măs′a soit′) 86

Mayflower Compact (mā′flou′ĕr cŏm′pakt) 84

Pilgrims (pĭl′grĭmz) 84

Plymouth (plĭm′ŭth) 85

Pocahontas (pō′ka hŏn′tăs) 83

Powhatan (pou′a tăn′) 83

Roanoke (rō′a nōk) 81

Samoset (săm′ȯ sĕt) 85

Sir Walter Raleigh (sûr wôl′tĕr rô′lĭ) 80

Squanto (skwŏn′tō) 85

town meeting (town mēt′ĭng) 84

William Bradford (wĭl′yăm brăd′fĕrd) 84

Questions

1. What are the names of the first three colonies that Englishmen tried to set up in America?

2. Who paid the way for the colony at Roanoke?

3. Why was John Smith so important to the success of Jamestown?

4. Who were Pocahontas and Powhatan?

You See for Yourself

Find the word "perseverance" in your dictionary and study its meaning. Why is it correct to say that the New England Pilgrims had much perseverance? Would you say the early settlers of Roanoke and Jamestown had perseverance? Why or why not?

The Dutch Come to America

Who explored for the Dutch?

During the same years that the French and English were settling Quebec and Jamestown, the Dutch, too, became interested in America. Holland had a great navy at that time, so it is not surprising that her ruler was interested in looking for the Northwest Passage.

The Dutch hired an English sea captain named Henry Hudson to look for the Northwest Passage. In the summer of 1609, his ship, the *Half Moon*, followed the North American coast southward from Newfoundland as far as Jamestown. At Jamestown he turned around and started back up the coast. He explored the mouths of numerous rivers as he sailed along the coast.

Early in September, the *Half Moon* reached the mouth of the Hudson River, in present-day New York State. Other explorers had passed this place, but none had taken their ships northward into the fine harbor that was to mean so much in the later growth of New York City.

Hudson was carrying trading goods in the *Half Moon*. When he saw Indians on Manhattan Island, he exchanged these gifts for furs to take back to Holland. Leaving the island, he sailed on up the Hudson River to the point at which the city of Albany, New York, later grew.

Dutch Settlements in the New World

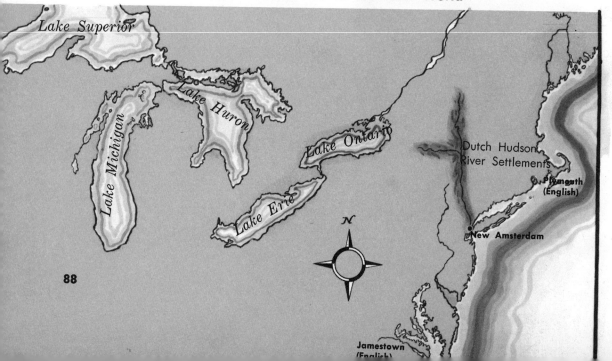

88

"This would be an excellent place for a trading post," Hudson decided when he saw the joining of the Mohawk River with the Hudson.

Hudson knew that he had not found the Northwest Passage, but he charted the rivers and claimed the land for Holland.

Where did the Dutch settle?

The Dutch were quick to start making the most of Hudson's claims. They set up a fur-trading post about where the city of Albany is today. The town grew quickly because of its location. It was a good place for Indians to bring furs by canoe from the upper Hudson or from the Mohawk Valley. A shipping port on the ocean became necessary, so a second settlement began to grow at the mouth of the Hudson.

This shipping port later became New York City, but it was called New Amsterdam at first in honor of the large and important city of Holland. The Dutch bought Manhattan Island from the *Manhattas* Indians for about twenty-four dollars' worth of trinkets.

The Dutch were the best bankers and businessmen of Europe during those years. New Amsterdam soon became an important business center. Many people from countries besides Holland came to New Amsterdam.

The Dutch bought Manhattan Island from the Indians. Here they built the city of New Amsterdam as a shipping port for the furs from their inland trading posts.

England's Thirteen Colonies

Once Plymouth and Jamestown were firmly set up, one English colony after another sprang up along the Atlantic Coast of North America until there were thirteen in all. All belonged to England, but people from many European countries besides England came to live in them. All during the 1600's and the first part of the 1700's, shipload after shipload of people left Europe to live in America. Many of the people left their European homes for religious freedom. Others hoped to find jobs and a chance to better their way of living in the New World. Still others were unhappy with their governments in European countries.

How were the New England Colonies settled?

The city of Boston was begun in 1630 by a group of English colonists who wanted to worship in a way different from that followed by the Church of England. These people were known as *Puritans*. The Puritans found the religious freedom they were seeking in the New World, yet they did not give freedom of worship to others in their colony. They wanted only those who believed as they did to live in their colony, called the Massachusetts Bay Colony. They were often very cruel to people of other beliefs, and even drove some of them from their homes in the colony.

The Puritans of the Massachusetts Bay Colony held to simple living and strict beliefs.

Several groups of people who could not accept the Puritans' way of life left or were driven from the Massachusetts Bay Colony to set up new colonies more to their own liking. Two such groups were those led by Roger Williams and Mrs. Anne Hutchison. Together, these groups began the colony of Rhode Island, in which everyone was allowed more religious freedom. The colony of New Hampshire was begun in much the same way.

Massachusetts, Plymouth, Connecticut, and New Hampshire became known as the Northern Colonies, or New England. When Indian troubles came, the people of the four colonies worked together as the New England Confederation.

Who settled the Southern Colonies?

The king of England looked upon the Atlantic Coast of North America as his property. Because of this, he claimed the right to give it away if he chose. He sometimes gave sections of land in America to people to whom he owed money or favors. The Indians living on the land were seldom asked if they wished to sell the land until the people from Europe had already moved in.

Lord Baltimore was a man to whom the English king owed money. The king gave Lord Baltimore a large section of land northeast of Virginia, around Chesapeake Bay. After Lord Baltimore's death, his son decided to move to this land and go into the tobacco-growing business.

Young Lord Baltimore belonged to the Roman Catholic Church, which was unpopular in England at the time. Baltimore saw America as a place to practice his beliefs in peace. He allowed other people to come to his colony, no matter what their church as long as they were Christians. Baltimore's colony was named Maryland. It was started in 1634.

South Carolina and North Carolina were settled in a little different way. Settlers of the Virginia colony had always grown much tobacco.

The tobacco growers soon learned, however, that tobacco draws great amounts of plant food from the soil. After a few years, a tobacco field becomes too worn out to grow a good crop. The Virginia planters answered this problem by taking great amounts of land, much more than they could plant in one year. When one tobacco field wore out, they just began a new one. In time, there was not enough land to go around.

North Carolina and South Carolina were settled by Virginia tobacco growers in search of new land. The longer growing season in the Carolinas made it possible for the colonists to grow rice; *indigo*, a plant used in making dye; and a little cotton. Yet, tobacco, the gift of the Indian, was the crop that brought wealth to the colonists, just as corn, another gift of the Indian, had brought life to settlers in earlier years.

The Thirteen English Colonies

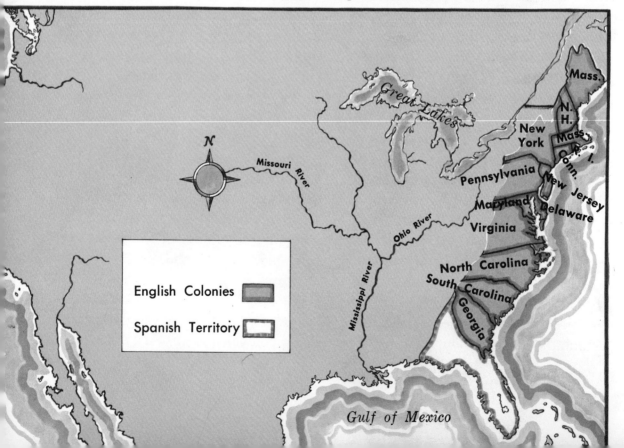

English Colonies

Spanish Territory

Facts About the Colonies

Name	Year of Settlement	Founder(s)	Purpose for Settlement	Nationalities Besides English
Virginia	1607	London Company	Tobacco growing	Scots, Germans, French Huguenots
Massachusetts	1620	Pilgrims	Religious freedom	Irish, French Huguenots
New Hampshire	1623	David Thompson	Need for new land, Religious freedom	Irish, French Huguenots
New York	1624	Dutch West India Company	Fur trade, Farming	Dutch, German, Irish, French Huguenots
Maryland	1634	Lord Baltimore	Religious freedom	Germans
Connecticut	1635	Thomas Hooker	Establish separation of church and state	French Huguenots
Rhode Island	1636	Roger Williams	Religious freedom	French Huguenots
Delaware	1638	Peter Minuit	Fur trade, Farming	Swedish, Finnish
North Carolina	1653	Eight English Noblemen	Need for new land, Individual freedom	Scots, Welsh, Germans, Swiss, French Huguenots
New Jersey	1664	Lord Berkeley, Sir George Carteret	Fur trade, Farming	Swedish, Finnish
South Carolina	1670	Eight English Noblemen	Plantation farming	Scots, Germans, Swiss, French Huguenots
Pennsylvania	1682	William Penn	Religious freedom	Scots, Welsh, Dutch, Germans, French Huguenots
Georgia	1733	James Oglethorpe	Religious freedom, Freedom for debtors, Hold back Spanish	Swiss, Italians, Germans, Scots

James Oglethorpe made careful plans when he founded the city of Savannah, Georgia.

No one paid much attention to religious beliefs in the Carolinas. People of many different religions came to live there. Among them were some French Huguenots, whose forefathers had tried so hard to begin a colony in the same area years before.

The Spanish, still holding on to Florida, fought back people who tried to take up land in the area that is now the state of Georgia. Not until 1733, over one hundred years after the settlement of Jamestown, was England able to start a colony there.

In that year, a man named *James Oglethorpe* brought a group of colonists to Georgia. Among the colonists were people who had been in jail because they could not pay money that they owed. Oglethorpe thought this was unfair, so he asked the king for permission to bring them to America. The king was willing to release these prisoners to help fight the Spanish and to work the land.

Oglethorpe tried to raise silkworms in Georgia at first, but they did not do well. The colonists later began to raise the crops of the other Southern Colonies. With this mistake in choice of crops, and fighting back the Spanish and Indians, too, Georgia's start was not only late, but slow.

Maryland, Virginia, North Carolina, South Carolina, and Georgia made up the Southern Colonies.

Where were the Middle Colonies?

The land between New England and the Southern Colonies was also rapidly settled.

In 1664, both New York and New Jersey became English colonies. The king gave the New Jersey land to two of his officers, one in the navy and the other in the army. The two owners offered religious freedom to all in their colony. Many people, both from European countries and other colonies, came to live in New Jersey.

New York, which was first settled by the Dutch and called New Netherland, became an English colony in 1664. The people living there did not care whether they were living in a Dutch colony or an English colony. They gave up easily when English ships appeared in the harbor. The English renamed the colony New York. Most of the people stayed on in the colony under English control. The colony continued to grow.

In 1681, the king gave William Penn the land for the Pennsylvania colony. The king had owed Penn's father money, and William Penn asked for land to settle the matter after his father died. William Penn belonged to a religious group in England known as the *Quakers*. Quakers were not allowed to live at peace in England. Penn invited the English Quakers to settle in his colony. Many Quakers did come to Pennsylvania, but Penn also sold land to people from other European countries.

Some of the Swedish people who first lived in Pennsylvania later separated from it and formed a new colony. The new colony was Delaware.

New York, New Jersey, Pennsylvania, and Delaware belonged to neither the New England nor to the Southern Colonies. They became known as the Middle Colonies.

By 1733, all thirteen English colonies were formed. They would, within just sixty years, become the first thirteen states of the United States of America.

Although Pennsylvania was begun by Quakers, people of all Churches were welcome.

Words to Know

indigo (ĭn′dĭ gō) 92

James Oglethorpe (jāmz ō′g′l thôrp) 94

Puritans (pū′rĭ tănz) 90

Quakers (kwāk′ērz) 95

Questions

1. Name the four colonies in the New England group.

2. How was the Massachusetts Bay colony formed? How were the other New England colonies begun?

3. Who claimed the right to give away land along the Atlantic Coast of North America? Why did he often do so?

4. How did Virginia tobacco growers solve the problem of worn-out land?

5. Why did the English at first have trouble starting the Georgia colony?

6. Name the five Southern Colonies.

7. Who were the Quakers? What colony did they settle? Who was their famous leader?

You See for Yourself

In an encyclopedia or history book, read about William Penn and how he planned the Pennsylvania colony. How did he deal with the Indians who were living in that land?

Find Florida on the map on page 92. To whom did Florida belong during the 1600's and the 1700's? Why would the owners of Florida not wish another country to start a colony in Georgia?

Do you believe in witchcraft? Some of the people of the colonies did. Find the word "witchcraft" in an encyclopedia. Read what is said about it. What happened in Salem, Massachusetts, in the year 1692?

Life in the Colonies

How did New England change?

For many years, the Puritans and their strong beliefs set the rules for life in New England. The little group of Pilgrims at Plymouth soon became part of the Massachusetts Bay Colony and followed the Puritan way of life. The Puritans held tightly to their belief that hard work and simple living were the proper way to live. Their beliefs were shown even in their clothing, which was plain in style and dull in color.

It was well that these were the kind of people who settled in the wilds of New England. The long, cold, and snowy winters left only a few short months during the year in which crops could be grown. The soil itself was often covered with stones. The early New England farmer had to clear away so many stones that he usually had enough to build a stone fence around his land.

The blade of the farmer's plow would hit the roots of the many trees and these also had to be removed. Most farmers could clear only small fields in which to grow corn, a few vegetables, and a little grain. There was fine pasture for cattle, but the man who chose to plow the soil and plant crops picked a hard life.

The Puritan Church, especially during the early years, was the center of both religion and government. The Puritans were as strict in their church-going as they were about the work of their daily lives. The whole village went to church almost all day on Sunday. No work, not even cooking, was done on this day of worship. There were no holidays, religious or otherwise. There was room for almost no gaiety of any kind in the lives of the Puritans.

New England farms became known for their many stone fences.

The Puritans carried on the town meetings begun by the Pilgrims. All the men of the church met to decide on community matters and to select community leaders.

How did business grow in New England?

With farming giving such a hard life, it is not surprising that the New England settlers began to look for other ways to make a living. They did not have to look far, for they were surrounded by forests from which came fine lumber and by seas swimming with fish.

Since Pilgrim days, New Englanders had built ships with lumber from the forests and used them as they fished along the coast. As the colonies grew, so did fishing and lumbering. Along with fishing and lumbering came shipbuilding. New England shipbuilders made such fine ships that trading companies all over Europe were eager to buy them. It was not long until New England people themselves became shipowners with trading businesses of their own. Many New England businessmen made fortunes in this way.

New England Shipping Business

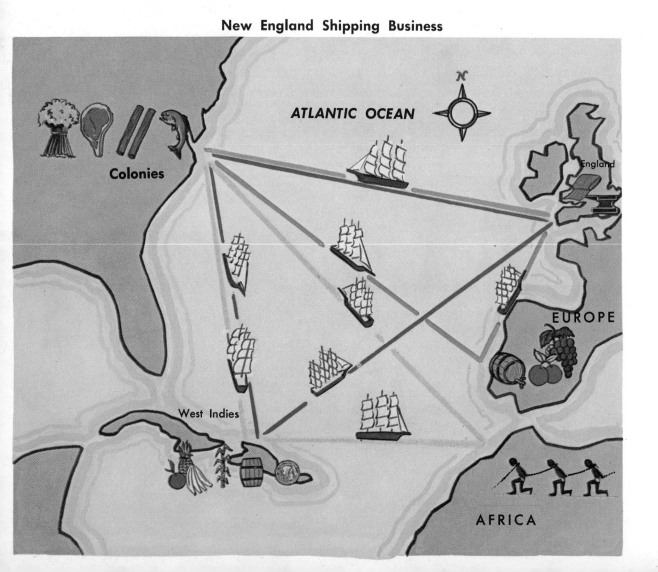

Boston was a leading city among the colonies.

Iron found in New England also brought business to the colonies. Within twenty-five years after the Pilgrims landed, there were furnaces for melting iron in New England.

New England grew in other ways as well. More and more Europeans came to live in the colonies, so many that the Puritans were not able to spread their teachings and beliefs throughout every community as they had done in the beginning.

People from all over Europe were attracted to the growing towns and cities of New England. They crossed the ocean looking for a new and better life in a new land. The newcomers brought their skills and talents from Europe. There were carpenters, brickmakers, cabinetmakers, and people with many other skills that were useful in the building of a new community.

Merchants and other businessmen became wealthy. These people wore clothing of the latest styles in Europe and built fine, beautiful homes. Even some of the Puritans themselves drifted away from the strictness and simple living of earlier days in the colonies.

The New England Primer was one of the first books printed in the colonies.

What were New England schools like?

Schools and education were important in New England from the very beginning. One of the first things the people did at their town meetings was to arrange for a school. Massachusetts passed a law in 1642 that all parents must see that their children were taught to read and that some were taught a trade by which to make a living. Five years later, a law was passed that every *township*, or community served by one meeting house, of fifty families or more must provide a school in which children would be taught to read and write. Townships of one hundred or more families were also to provide a school in which boys could be taught the things they would need to go to college. In those days, this meant that they must learn Latin and Greek. In 1636, the first New England college was opened. It was named Harvard College, and it is still open today.

Children were taught to read with a *hornbook*, which was really not a book at all. It was a small thin board with a handle. Onto the board was pasted a paper printed with the small and capital letters, syllables to sound, and the Lord's Prayer. The paper was protected with a thin sheet of *horn*, which was something like clear plastic made from the horns of animals. This is how the hornbook received its name. After the hornbook lessons, the children read the Bible.

When printing became more widespread, readers called the *"New England Primer"* were used. The Primer had a picture for each letter of the alphabet and a rhyme, usually intended to teach a lesson in behavior or an idea from the Bible.

Small children, in colonial days, often went to a *dame school*. Housewives were called "Dames" in those days just as they would be called "Mrs." today. A dame school was held in a home, where the housewife would often go on with her spinning or knitting as she listened to the children say their lessons.

Beginners learned the alphabet from a hornbook.

A school for older children might be held at the meeting house, which served as the church on Sundays. The teacher was usually a man, called the "master." The schoolmaster allowed no mischief and kept a stick handy or a *cat-o'-nine-tails* for punishments. This was a stick with stinging leather straps at one end.

A girl was seldom taught more in school than reading, writing, and some arithmetic. After that, she spent her time learning to sew, spin, weave, embroider, cook, and to do all the other tasks that women did.

A boy who was to become a minister or a lawyer usually stayed in school until he was a young man and had gone through a university. Many of the other boys left school between eleven and thirteen years of age to become apprentices.

An *apprentice* was a boy, or sometimes a man, who worked for a number of years without pay for a shopowner or other tradesman. During these years, the apprentice was expected to learn the trade of his master, as the tradesman was called. When the apprentice knew the work well enough, he could begin to earn a little money for his work.

An apprentice could learn one of many different trades in the New England colonies. He might learn to be a glassmaker, spending long hours turning the blow pipe with its mass of melted glass on the end until he was ready to learn the more difficult

A boy could choose from a number of different trades in which to work as an apprentice.

parts of the trade. He might work the great bellows to keep a blacksmith's fire burning white hot until the smith at last taught him to twist and hammer the iron into tools and other useful items. He might learn to shoe horses, to make saddles and harness, to make fine furniture, beautiful silver vases and teapots, or to print a newspaper.

Sometimes an apprentice grew tired of his long hours of work, often work which did not interest him. Some of these boys ran off to become sailors. If a boy was large for his age, or strong, he could probably become a "ship's hand." He soon learned, however, that the life of a sailor or a fisherman was not any easier than that of an apprentice.

Although the strictness of the early Puritan life was beginning to fade out during the early 1700's, it left its mark on New England. New Englanders were strong people, willing to work hard and long to bring about something they believed was good or right. They were the kind of people who had much to give to a new country and homeland.

How did colonists live in the South?

Life in the Southern Colonies was very much different from that found in New England. The wealthy colonists lived on plantations. A *plantation* was something like a very large farm. It included many fields, the *mansion*, or large house of the plantation owner and his family, and homes for all the people who worked on the plantation.

Tobacco was the main crop of the South during colonial days. It was hard work to grow tobacco and get it ready for shipment to markets in Europe. The easiest way for the landowner to get the help he needed was to "buy" Negro people from the slave traders who brought them to America in slave ships. The Negro slaves received no wages, for a slave was the property of the man who paid for him, as much as were the man's horses or his house. The landowner gave his slaves housing, food, and clothing. The slave was expected to do whatever his master ordered.

Another way to get help was to pay the passage across the ocean of someone who wanted to come to America but did not have the money to pay his way on a ship. Such a person was *indentured* to the landowner who paid his passage. This meant that he had to work for a certain number of years, usually from five to ten, just as if he were a slave. At the end of that time, he was free.

Many of the indentured servants had some special skill or had learned a trade in Europe. Some were even well-educated. Since the plantations were large and far from towns, each one had to provide most of the things the village community in New England provided for its people. The skills of an indentured servant could be used in doing the work of blacksmith, carpenter, weaver, shoemaker, cook, or even a teacher for the children. With so many people living on a plantation, each with its center many miles from the next, the plantation was a community in itself.

Southern tobacco growers often used slaves.

The southern planters had little need for a town. Until all the land along the rivers was gone, each plantation owner built his home facing a stream. When the tobacco was ready to be shipped, it was loaded onto boats at the plantation landing and taken to a point in deeper water. Here it was loaded onto an ocean-going ship that could not come all the way to the plantation because of the shallow water near it. That same ship might be bringing European goods that the plantation owner had ordered for himself and his family. There might be fine clothing, furniture, or toys for his children.

There was little need for wagon roads until the land bordered by streams and rivers was all taken. To ride around his plantation or to join his neighbors for a party or a hunt, a planter rode horseback. Narrow trails through the South were all that were needed for many years.

The planter's children were usually taught at home. After the boys had learned all that the *tutor*, their private teacher at home, could teach them, they often were sent back to England for college. In 1694, William and Mary College opened at the capital of Virginia, Williamsburg, making it possible for a young man to be educated in America.

Southern planters chose lands along the rivers and streams whenever possible.

Who besides plantation owners lived in the Southern Colonies?

Not all southerners were plantation owners or plantation workers. There were some people who came to the South with little money and with no way to get enough land to start a plantation. There were also the indentured servants who had finished their time as workers for a plantation owner. These people either worked in the few towns of the South or moved farther west than the plantation owners went. Many lived in the foothills of the Appalachian Mountains, which in colonial days stood as a wall between the coastal colonies and the unexplored lands west of the mountains.

These people lived a life completely different from that of the planters. They cleared small patches of land on which to grow just what they needed to feed themselves.

Settlers in the southern hills lived the lives of pioneers.

They built log cabins or simple houses of board. Often the man of the family spent much of his time hunting, not only to get meat for the family, but also to get furs. These he traded for sugar, salt, gunpowder, and the other things he could not grow or make for himself.

Some people came into these foothill lands of Virginia and the Carolinas from other colonies, especially from Pennsylvania. Many of them were a restless kind of people. Many were Scotch-Irish. They were not usually satisfied with staying on their clearings when their neighborhood began to fill up with new people moving in. They seemed to be ever pushing westward.

How were the Middle Colonies different from the South and from New England?

The Middle Colonies, New York, New Jersey, Pennsylvania, and Delaware, were like the North in some ways and like the South in others. In general, the soil was better and the fields larger than in New England. The climate was not as mild as in the South so the crops could not be the same. Grain crops grew well.

In almost every way, the Middle Colonies seemed to take a middle path. Farms were medium size. Government was neither as close to the people as the New England town meeting, nor so far removed from the common people as it was in the South.

Manufacturing and trades were carried on, but not as much as in New England. Religious beliefs were generally not so strict as in New England, but took on more importance for everyday life than they seemed to do in the South.

For many years, the most important city of the Middle Colonies was Philadelphia. Grain from Pennsylvania farms was shipped from Philadelphia. The fur trade was still important there as well as in New York City, which in those days was smaller than Philadelphia.

The people living in the Middle Colonies seemed to differ from each other more than did the people of either New England or the South. The people of the Middle Colonies were more relaxed than the strict New Englanders. Yet they did not try to copy the upper class ladies and gentlemen as the southern planters often seemed to do. There was a mixture of all classes, with people coming from many different countries.

Philadelphia was a shipping point for the Middle Colonies.

What famous people lived in the colonies?

Among the boys and girls growing up in the colonies between the years 1725 and 1750 were many who were to play important parts in the future of America. They were the ones who would help to change the Thirteen Colonies into the first Thirteen States of the United States of America.

In 1741, for example, a six-year-old boy named John Adams was learning to read at Dame Belcher's school in the village of Braintree, between Plymouth and Boston. He was to become the second President of the new United States. He would bring to this office much of his strict New England background.

Little John Adams had never met his cousin Samuel Adams, who was already a young man of nineteen. The Puritan touch was much lighter on Sam, for he lived in the greatest city of the colonies, Boston. In Boston, many ideas besides those of the Puritans were present. Sam was a Harvard graduate, and he spent much time talking with other educated young men of the city. During their talks, they often questioned the way people in far-away England handled the problems of the American colonies. Samuel Adams would help to spread this kind of questioning among the other colonies until finally the colonies would break away from all English control.

Boston was also the home of a six-year-old boy who would one day be-

Biography Outline

Benjamin Franklin

1706-1790

American

Statesman, scientist, and printer

One of the men who helped build the United States—helped win the War for Independence as minister to France—signer of the Declaration of Independence—proved that lightning was electricity—invented an efficient heating stove—was a civic leader and a publisher—founded the first public library—backed the first city hospital—invented bifocal eye glasses—was one of the first to favor daylight-saving time during the summer.

come famous for carrying messages back and forth among those men who wanted to see a new nation born. The boy's name was Paul Revere. Paul Revere's father came to America from Italy and was the owner of a Boston silversmith shop. Paul became an apprentice to his father and afterwards became the best of the colonial silversmiths.

Another boy who was to become famous had already grown to manhood by the year 1741. The young man, Benjamin Franklin, grew up in Boston and became an apprentice to a printer there. He ran away to live in Philadelphia and became important in Philadelphia through a printing business he owned. Before many years passed, Ben Franklin would take part in the first meetings in which men of all the colonies talked over the shaping of a new nation.

Samuel Adams and his friends often talked about the way England ruled the colonies.

People in Philadelphia knew Franklin well in 1741. He was known as a printer and inventor, but people were also interested in the things he had to say. They watched for the wise and clever things he wrote for his newspaper and for "Poor Richard's Almanac," a kind of yearly magazine. Ben Franklin played many roles in the shaping of the new country, but it is probably his wit and wisdom for which he is best remembered.

Not many miles from Philadelphia, but a world apart in way of living, was a seven-year-old boy named Daniel Boone. Daniel's father was one of Penn's Quakers, but he did not like living in a city. He opened a blacksmith shop in an outlying village and had cattle pastured in the open country beyond. The boy, Daniel, often helped tend the cattle. In a few years, Daniel would be heading down the valley trail to begin his role of helping the colonies to become a nation that reached beyond the Appalachian Mountains.

Down in Virginia, a nine-year-old boy was learning to ride horses and getting an education, as befitted a southern planter's son. The boy was unable to continue his education, however, beyond fourteen or fifteen years of age. His father died when the boy was eleven years old. Going to school beyond this would have meant going to England, and his mother disliked having him that far away from home. The young boy dreamed of becoming a sailor, longing for a life of adventure. He nor anyone else probably ever dreamed that this boy was to become one of the most important and probably the most famous of all the boys growing up in the colonies. One day he would be called the "Father of His Country." His name was, of course, George Washington.

George Washington grew up in Virginia.

107

Words to Know

apprentice (ă prĕn′tĭs) 101

cat-o′-nine-tails (kăt′ŏ nīn′tālz′) 101

dame school (dām skōōl) 100

horn (hôrn) 100

hornbook (hôrn′bŏŏk) 100

indentured (ĭn dĕn′tụ̆rd) 102

mansion (măn′shŭn) 102

"New England Primer" (nū ĭng′ glănd prĭm′ẽr) 100

plantation (plăn tā′shŭn) 102

township (toun′shĭp) 100

tutor (tū′tẽr) 103

Questions

1. What was an apprentice? Name four things an apprentice might learn to do?

2. In which group of colonies would you have found the greatest number of apprentices? Why?

3. What was the name of the New England school to which small children were sent? Who was the teacher?

4. What is a tutor? In which group of colonies would children most likely have had a tutor?

5. What kind of people were the Puritans? Why were they the kind of people needed to settle New England?

6. Why did the southern planters have little need for towns or villages?

7. What was the name of the first New England college? In what year was it opened?

8. What was the name of the first southern college? What year was it opened?

9. What was an indentured servant? What did many indentured servants in the South do after they were free?

10. How did the farms of the Middle Colonies differ from those in the South and those in New England?

11. In what trade was Paul Revere an apprentice as a young boy? In what city did he live?

12. What did Samuel Adams and other young men often talk about when they were together?

13. In what city did Benjamin Franklin have a printing business?

You See for Yourself

Learn more about the production of iron in the New England colonies from encyclopedias and other sources. Where were the first ironworks? How was the ore refined? How was the iron used?

Now You Know

During the last half of the 1500's, both the French and the English tried to set up colonies in America. The first Frenchmen came to Florida and South Carolina, but the Spanish quickly drove them out.

In the early 1600's, the French began setting up trading posts in the St. Lawrence region. Later, Frenchmen explored the Great Lakes and the Mississippi River.

The English first tried to start a colony in Roanoke, North Carolina, but the colony failed. The first lasting English colony was begun at Jamestown, Virginia, at about the same time the French opened their fur trading posts in the St. Lawrence region. All during the 1600's, one English colony after another grew up along the Atlantic Coast.

The Thirteen Colonies are often divided into three groups: the northern New England Colonies, the Middle Colonies, and the Southern Colonies. Farms were small and poor in New England, so most of the colonists looked to business and trade to make a living. The Middle Colonies had medium-sized farms on which grain crops could be grown successfully. There were also large and important cities where business and trade grew. The southern colonists were largely farmers, and tobacco was the main crop. The growth of towns was slow in the South.

The English colonies were firmly settled by the first half of the 1700's, yet before the end of the 1700's, they would become American states rather English colonies.

You Talk It Over

What do you think America might be like today if the English and French had not been interested in colonizing North America?

Do you think the colonists believed that "all men are equal"?

In what colonies, Northern or Southern, do you think the people were better educated? Why? Would it be easier for England to control educated or uneducated people? Explain your answer. Why were boys given more education than girls?

Unit Questions

1. What was the name of the first lasting colony on United States soil? Where was it and to whom did it belong?

2. What Frenchman set up the first French fur-trading post in America? Where was the trading post?

3. How did the Europeans use the furs from the American fur-trading business?

4. Who claimed for France the lands drained by the Mississippi River? What did he name this land?

5. What was the name of the first successful English colony in America? Where was the colony and in what year was it started?

6. Who was John Smith and why was he important to American history?

7. What crop helped to bring about the success of Virginia and later Southern Colonies?

8. What important idea about government did the Pilgrims write into the Mayflower Compact of 1620?

9. What important step in government was taken by the Virginia colonists in 1619?

10. Tell three ways in which the Indians helped the Pilgrims to learn to live in the New World. How do we know the Pilgrims were grateful for the Indians' help?

11. What country first sent settlers to the New York region?

12. What particular reason did the Puritans have for coming to America?

13. Why did some groups of people leave Massachusetts, the colony settled by Puritans?

14. Who started the Maryland colony? The Georgia colony?

15. What businesses did the forests help the New England colonists start?

16. What was the name of the first New England college? In what year was it begun?

17. Tell two ways in which southern planters got the help they needed to run their plantations.

Puzzlers

Look carefully at each picture shown below. Be able to describe what is happening in each picture. Then tell in which of the three colonial areas, Northern, Middle, or Southern, you would most likely have seen what each picture shows.

A.

F.

B.

G.

C.

H.

D.

I.

E.

J.

Unit Activities

You give a style show

Dress up in a costume that shows one of the different kinds of dress that would have been found in colonial days. Be prepared to tell the rest of the class in which colonial region your costume would have been seen and a little about the life of a person who would have worn it.

You draw a picture

On a large sheet of manila paper, draw a picture that shows life in one of the colonies. You may show a street of Boston, a New England home, a dock scene in Philadelphia, or a southern tobacco field, for example. Divide all the pictures drawn by your class into three groups and display them under one of these headings:

Life in the New England Colonies

Life in the Middle Colonies

Life in the Southern Colonies

Look in an encyclopedia and in history books for ideas and to make certain your drawings are correct.

You may also make a display of pictures you draw of the homes of famous people of the colonies.

You make cutout models

Draw and cut out pictures of different items made by colonial New England shop owners. Mount your pictures on cardboard or stiff paper, and put a brace on the back of each model so that it will stand up. Some of the things you will want to make models of are glassware, silverware, furniture, leather goods, and iron cook ware. You will be able to find pictures of these items in library resource books.

Display the finished cutouts on a large table and make a large label that reads:

"From the Shops of New England"

You build a log cabin

Study the article about log cabins in an encyclopedia. Make a model log cabin from a pasteboard box or collect sticks and build your cabin from them. Use the encyclopedia article to help you make your cabin look like those built in colonial days.

You read a poem

Below is a list of several poems about early days in America. Practice reading one of them until you can read it aloud to your classmates.

"The Courtship of Miles Standish"

"The Village Blacksmith"

"The Song of Hiawatha"

The Colonies Become a Nation

"Hats for sale!"

"American beaver hats for sale!"

This is the way signs in many store and shop windows of Paris, France, read during the 1600's and early 1700's. Signs like them could be found in store windows throughout Europe. The shopkeepers did a good business, for every gentleman in Europe felt that it was important to have a stylish fur hat.

The hatmakers' business grew bigger with Champlain's success in the New World. Many young Frenchmen interested in a life of adventure came to the wilds of America to take part in the fur-trading business. Some of them set their own traps. Others bought furs from the Indians.

Dressed as Indians, angry Boston colonists destroyed many crates of English tea by throwing them into the harbor.

115

France and England Clash in America

During the same years that the English were working to set up the Thirteen Colonies along the Atlantic Coast, the French were building up their fur trade to the north and west. Many fur-trading posts appeared in the St. Lawrence River Valley and around the Great Lakes soon after Champlain came to America. In addition to the trading posts, the French built many armed forts.

The French built forts and trading posts along the Mississippi River, too. By the time the Thirteen Colonies were set up, the French holdings formed a curved chain north and west of the English colonies. Spain still held Florida.

French missionaries continued to come to North America. They built log churches near the trading posts. They invited the Indians to come to them not only to learn about Christ, but also to learn how the Europeans cured sickness, and sometimes how to read and write.

Few Frenchmen came to America to build homes and settle the land. Since the traders and missionaries did not seem to be taking land away from the Indians, the Indians were usually friendly to the French. Only the Iroquois, who had first met the Frenchmen when Champlain fought against them with the Algonkians, did not welcome the French.

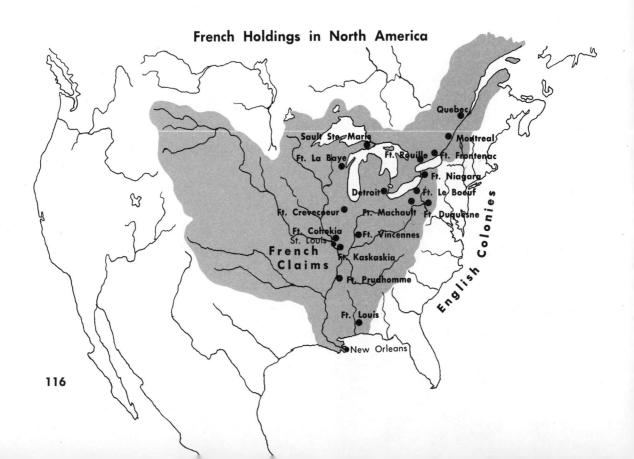

French Holdings in North America

Quebec

Sault Ste. Marie

Montreal

Ft. La Baye

Ft. Rouille · Ft. Frontenac

Ft. Niagara

Detroit

Ft. Le Boeuf

Ft. Crevecoeur

Ft. Machault · Ft. Duquesne

Ft. Cahokia
St. Louis

Ft. Vincennes

French
Claims

Ft. Kaskaskia

English Colonies

Ft. Prudhomme

Ft. Louis

New Orleans

Some of the French trading posts, forts, and missionary stations were to grow into great cities. In the north, Detroit was the greatest of these. It was begun in 1701.

The city of New Orleans was begun in 1718. It was not only a trading post, but also a shipping point. Ocean-sailing ships could come to its harbor, bringing supplies and trading goods from Europe. Furs could be sent back on the ships. A few years later, the French found silver and a great deal of lead in the land that is today southern Missouri. Soon the ships were taking both lead and furs from New Orleans to France.

In their search for furs, the French also followed the rivers that led into the Mississippi River. They built up an especially good trade along the Missouri River. In 1763, a fur-company post was built just below the place where the Missouri flows into the Mississippi. This was the beginning of the city of St. Louis.

How did the English meet the French?

While the French were learning about the great river valleys of central North America, most of the English knew very little of the land that lay west of the Appalachian Mountains. For many years, there seemed to be plenty of space for their settlements along the coast.

Now and then an English adventurer would journey westward across

The French built many forts in America.

the mountains to search for a passageway to the Pacific Ocean. By the year 1700, however, the English were sure there was no quick way from their colonies to the Pacific.

The English had carried on fur trading with the Indians in their colonies for years. Some of the more adventurous made a few trips into the land west of the mountains.

English traders found two ways to go through the mountains. One way was to follow old Indian trails through Cumberland Gap. *Cumberland Gap* is an opening in the mountain wall at the point where the states of Virginia, Kentucky, and Tennessee meet today.

A second way the English traders crossed the mountains was by following the *Shenandoah* River northeast.

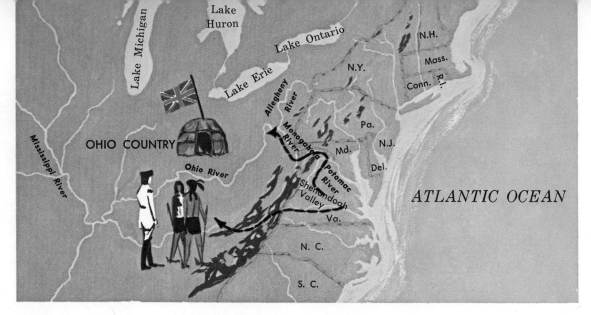

The English in the Ohio Country

The Shenandoah Valley had been settled by southern tobacco growers in search of more land. The Shenandoah River took the fur traders to the Potomac River. By following the Potomac upstream, they could go northwest for some distance. Journeying even farther, they went over a dividing ridge that separates the rivers that flow into the Ohio River. They found the *Monongahela* River and followed it northward to the point where it joins the *Allegheny* River from the northeast. This point was very important, for it was the beginning of the Ohio River, which led to the Mississippi.

The French explorer La Salle had journeyed down the Ohio River as early as 1669. Because of this, the French claimed the lands near the river. Yet, they were so busy with their trading posts along the St. Lawrence River, the Great Lakes, and the Mississippi River, that they did little about building up trade along the Ohio.

It was the English traders who took a real interest in the *Ohio country*, as the land between Lake Erie and the Ohio River was called. Around the year 1740, traders from the English colonies began making regular trips into this land.

The greatest of the English traders was a man named *George Croghan*, who came from Ireland to eastern Pennsylvania in 1741. He knew how to get along with the Indians as well as with the men he hired to work for him. He soon had a pack-train route across Pennsylvania and down into the Ohio Valley. In each *pack train* were usually twenty horses roped together in a line. Each horse carried about one hundred fifty pounds of trading goods, and each could bring back the same weight in furs.

In a few years, Croghan had traveled as far as the Wabash River to the west, Lake Erie to the north, and the Ohio River to the south. He built trading posts at some of the Indian villages, and he and his men made friends with many of the Indians. They did not try to take anything but furs from the Indians. They paid the Indians what seemed a fair price.

What did the French think of having the English in the Ohio country?

The French soon learned that English traders were visiting the Ohio country, and they were not pleased. "The English are trespassing on our land," said the French. "It is our land by right of La Salle's journeys."

From their forts on the south shore of Lake Erie, the French sent out a party of men to tell the Indians not to trade with the English. They also planned to place markers here and there to show that the Ohio country was French territory. The leader of the group was a man named *Celoron*.

Celoron, dressed in his finest clothes, and with silken French flags flying, called the Indians to watch as he and his men buried lead plates near the mouth of each river that flowed to the Ohio River. The lead plates, he told the Indians, had the mark of France on them and were put into the soil to show that it belonged to France. Celoron nailed markers on trees, too.

"Trade only with French traders," he ordered the Indians. "Fly French flags over the lodges of your chiefs." He made them take down the English flags that Croghan had left.

Croghan, of course, returned later to the villages in which Celoron had stopped. He saw the French flags waving over the lodges. "Take down the French flag," Croghan told the Indians. "I will give you more for your furs than the French traders do. Save your furs for the English."

The Indians knew that what Croghan said was true. The English did give them more for their furs than the French did. The flags were changed; English flags flew again.

English traders led their pack trains across the mountains and into the Ohio country.

What did Washington tell the French?

The Colony of Virginia claimed to own land as far west as the Mississippi River and north almost to Lake Erie. The claim was based on the official papers signed by the king of England when Jamestown was started. When an English land company wanted to begin settlement in the Ohio country, the Virginia Colony sold some of the Ohio land to it. In 1751, the land company sent a man named *Christopher Gist* to explore the territory and study the land. Gist reported to the company that there was fine land for settlements.

Soon after Gist returned from his Ohio journey, Governor Robert Dinwiddie of Virginia learned that the French were becoming active in the Ohio country. Governor Dinwiddie sent George Washington, who was by then a young officer in the Virginia army, to deliver a message to the French in Ohio. Gist was to go with young Washington as his guide.

Washington and Gist traveled to the French forts near Lake Erie. Washington talked with the French officers, explaining that the Ohio country was English territory belonging to the colony of Virginia. The French were polite, but just as sure that the land belonged to France, not England.

Washington could see that trouble with the French would come very soon. He planned to take a shortcut across the Allegheny River in order to get back to Virginia as quickly as possible. He almost lost his life crossing the Allegheny. Gist had to pull him from the icy river waters.

Back in Virginia, Washington reported to the governor. "The French are strong, and they want the Ohio country as badly as we do. But I believe that we could control the Ohio country if we had a fort at the point where the Monongahela and Allegheny rivers meet."

Washington suggested the building of a fort to protect the Ohio country.

Governor Dinwiddie lost no time. He sent men to build a fort at the meeting of these rivers, where the city of Pittsburgh, Pennsylvania, now stands. He also ordered Washington to train one hundred soldiers to hold the fort against the French.

The Virginia governor tried but failed to get help from other colonies. The colonies had not yet learned to work together for the good of all.

The Virginians began to build the needed fort, but before it was finished, the French soldiers attacked. The French took this important piece of land and built there a large fort for themselves. They named it *Fort Duquesne*. This was the beginning of the French and Indian War, fought by France and England in battlefields on both American and European land.

Words to Know

Allegheny (ăl′ĕ gā′nĭ) 118

Celoron (sā′lô rōn′) 119

Christopher Gist (krĭs′tŏ fĕr gĭst) 120

Cumberland Gap (kŭm′bĕr lănd găp) 117

Fort Duquesne (fōrt dōō kān′) 121

George Croghan (jôrj krō′g′n) 118

Monongahela (mŏ nŏn′gȧ hē′lȧ) 118

Ohio country (ȯ hī′ō kŭn′trĭ) 118

pack train (păk′trān) 118

Shenandoah (shĕn′ȧn dō′ȧ) 117

Questions

1. What reason did the Virginia colonists have for thinking the Ohio country belonged to Virginia?

2. What reason did the French have for thinking that the Ohio country belonged to France?

3. What are three United States cities that were first begun as French fur-trading posts? On what waterways are they located?

4. Locate Cumberland Gap on a map. Why was it important?

You See for Yourself

Find New Orleans and the Mississippi River on a map. With your finger, trace the route that French fur traders used to send their furs all the way from Indian villages along the Missouri to ships headed for France. By what route would they have had to send their furs if they had not had the port of New Orleans?

The French and Indian War

France and England had quarreled and fought over their claims in America for more than one hundred years. The fighting that began when the French took Fort Duquesne, however, would finally settle their quarrels once and for all.

The French received the help of the Algonkian Indians in their fight against the English. The French had long been friendly with the Indians, but the Indians were especially eager to keep the English out of the Ohio country. They had seen how the English took over the land of the Indians along the Atlantic Coast, and did not want the same thing to happen in Ohio. The Indians taught the French soldiers how to fight in the woods. They showed them how a rather small number of men could attack a larger force that fought in the ways used by an army in Europe.

George Washington, now a lieutenant colonel in the English colonial army, was having a hard time getting enough men to fight back the French. He hoped to get supplies from English settlers who had pushed westward from the coastal colonies and were living on the frontier. A *frontier* is the outer edge or border of an area that faces foreign territory or territory that has not been settled or explored. Washington found the frontier settlers unwilling to give much help.

Who won the first battles?

Washington and his men lost a battle soon after he met the French soldiers for the first time. He had to retreat. He built Fort Necessity on the trail between the Potomac and Monongahela Rivers. There he worked to train his little army.

General Braddock directed his army in the building of a road to Fort Duquesne.

The king of England saw that Virginia must have help to keep the French from taking the Ohio country. He sent a good military leader, General *Edward Braddock*, and some soldiers from England to help.

Braddock made plans to take Fort Duquesne almost at once. The first thing he did was to begin widening the trail from Fort Necessity to Fort Duquesne into a road. His men were able to move forward at about two miles a day, with workmen chopping down trees ahead of the march. Braddock hired wagons and drivers from Pennsylvania, Maryland, and Virginia, to move supplies.

Braddock's army was almost up to Fort Duquesne in July, 1755, when the French and Indians made a surprise attack upon them. Braddock knew nothing of fighting in a frontier wilderness. He had not sent scouts ahead to see if there were French and Indians in the woods.

From behind trees, the French soldiers and Indians found the red-coated Englishmen easy targets as they moved in regular lines down the open road. The attack was so great a surprise that the men of Braddock's army fell by the hundreds. Braddock himself was killed. Washington was luckier; he was only wounded.

Three out of four of the English were shot down. The rest turned back quickly. Wagoners, frontier soldiers, and Virginia soldiers all hurried back down Braddock's Road. Among the wagon drivers was Daniel Boone, whose family had just moved from western Pennsylvania to the *Yadkin* River Valley of western North Carolina.

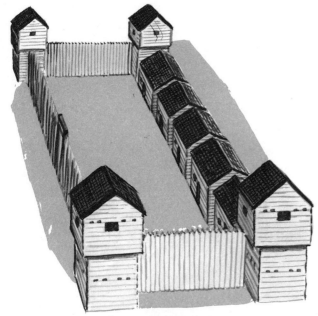

Some forts were a single blockhouse.

Some forts had several blockhouses, plus cabins for several families.

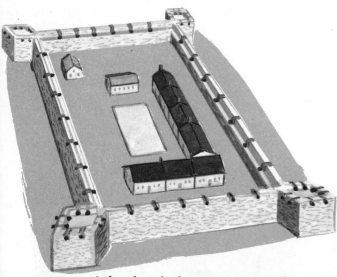

A few forts had stone or brick walls.

What was the frontier fighting like?

The war went on. It was especially bad for the colonists who had made their homes on the frontier, as the Boones had done. Particularly open to attack were the settlers in western Pennsylvania. A man never knew when there would be a sudden yell from the edge of his clearing and a small band of Indians would be upon him and his family.

It became necessary for the frontiersmen to build a number of forts. When word reached a frontier area that a family had been attacked, settlers hurried to the nearest fort. There they all lived until they felt it was safe to return to their homes.

Some of the forts were only one building—a square blockhouse, two stories high, with the second story overhanging the first. Other forts had several log cabins in them and were able to hold several families. There were a few large forts with strong thick walls built up of earth and logs, sometimes with outer walls of stone or brick.

The soldiers helped build the forts when a company of them was to stay for a while or when the fort was at an especially important location. Even though they built many forts, it was five years after Braddock's fall before the English were able to win back what they had lost to the French. Part of the trouble was that the colonists still had not learned to work together.

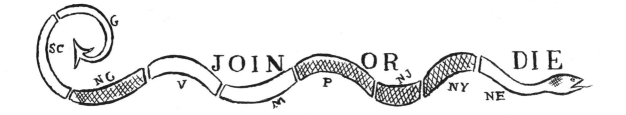

JOIN OR DIE

Benjamin Franklin was one of the first to see that unless the colonies could learn to work together, they would never become strong. He printed a cartoon in his Philadelphia newspaper that brought out this idea. The cartoon was printed right after the English government had called a meeting of the Thirteen Colonies and men from only seven had gone to it.

How did the war end?

During the fighting, the English learned much about fighting in the frontier way. They also received the help of the Iroquois Indians, old enemies of both the French and their Algonkian helpers. In 1760, Fort Duquesne fell to the English. The English changed the name to Fort Pitt, in honor of an English leader, William Pitt.

A peace treaty was signed in Paris, France, in 1763. Under this treaty, France lost all her holdings in America. England's territory now included all the land between the Atlantic Coast and the Mississippi River except the city of New Orleans and the mouth of the Mississippi River. England also took all the French lands in Canada.

The war that began in America had become a war in Europe also. Spain had helped France fight against the English in Europe and expected to be paid for this help at the end of the war. France paid by giving Spain New Orleans and the land the French had claimed between the Mississippi River and the Rocky Mountains. Spain gave up her claim to Florida to the English. England now held much of North America.

English Holdings in 1763

Unexplored

Spanish Territory

English Territory

Mississippi River

Great Lakes

ATLANTIC OCEAN

Gulf of Mexico

Edward Braddock (ĕd'wẽrd brăd ŭk) 123

frontier (frŭn tēr') 122

Yadkin (yăd'kĭn) 123

Questions

1. Why were the Algonkian Indians willing to help the French fight the English?

2. Which Indians helped the English during the war? What reason did these Indians have for siding with the English rather than with the French?

3. What kind of help did Washington hope to get from the frontier settlers? Did he get this help?

4. Why did the English build forts along the frontier?

5. Who won the French and Indian War? Where was the peace treaty signed and in what year?

You See for Yourself

Read more about George Washington's early life in other books. What did he do as a boy at Ferry Farm? What work did he do along the frontier as a young man?

Find the article about Daniel Boone in an encyclopedia or read more about him in other books. How did young Daniel learn so much about the ways of the Indians? How old was he when he got his first rifle? Whom did Daniel Boone marry? Why was she a good match for someone like Daniel Boone?

The Frontier in Last Colonial Days

As the French and Indian War drew to a close, a young Indian chief, living where the state of Michigan is now, called upon other Algonkian chiefs to work together. This young chief was *Pontiac*, and he was chief of an Ottawa tribe.

"It is clear that the white man plans to take our hunting grounds," Pontiac told the chiefs at a great council of chiefs. "Are we to sit back like women while these strangers take what is not theirs, but ours? Are we to die by the hundreds as our hunting grounds are turned to the plow of the white man? Are we to be left without the game of the forests that is ours by right of our birth?"

Then he said, "Gather your war-riors while there is still time! We can yet drive back the trespassers and keep what rightly belongs to us!"

What was Pontiac's plan?

It was Pontiac's idea to attack all the English forts on the same day. The tribes prepared for war. On May 7, 1763, all the forts were attacked. All along the line of the frontier, they fell—all except three.

The three forts that the English held were very important forts. They were Niagara, Detroit, and Pitt. At Fort Detroit, on Lake Erie, the Indians found that they could not break into the fort as they had hoped. Someone had warned the English of the secret plans of the Indians, so the attack was no surprise. The Indians decided to starve out the soldiers by not allowing any food or supplies to be taken into the fort. They surrounded the fort.

The Indians were unable to take Fort Detroit because ships brought supplies to the fort.

This did not stop the English, however. They made plans to move supplies into Fort Detroit by water instead of by the usual land route. They built two warships on Lake Erie, beginning an inland navy. The two ships, with cannons holding off Indians who tried to stop the ships, moved in the needed supplies. The Indians gave up at Detroit, and then at Niagara and Fort Pitt, too.

Pontiac kept on trying to gather new Indian forces from all over the Mississippi Valley. But before he could bring them together in a new attack, he was killed.

Daniel Boone often stayed in the woods for weeks at a time.

What did Daniel Boone do after the war?

Daniel Boone, living with his wife and children on his Yadkin Valley farm, grew restless with each new year. Hunting rather than farming was the life he loved. He often left the corn patch and the garden for his wife and children to tend while he went into the woods for weeks at a time to hunt.

One day, a peddler named John Finley came to the Boone cabin. Finley had known Boone when they were both driving supply wagons for Braddock's army.

"Best hunting grounds you ever saw are over the mountains, Dan'l," Finley told him. "We ought to go on a long hunt in Kentucky."

Soon it was arranged. Finley, Boone, and four other frontiersmen packed up for a hunting trip that would last a full season. They set out over the old trails through the mountains to Cumberland Gap. They turned northwest through the foothills on the western side of the Appalachians. Then they were in the Indians' favorite hunting grounds—Kentucky.

On that trip, in 1769, a dream was born in Daniel Boone's heart. He saw a place in the bluegrass lands of north central Kentucky that looked to him like a perfect homeland.

For six years afterwards, Boone tried to take family and friends into Kentucky to settle. This was done at great risk and hardship for him and his family. The Indians tried to stop his every move. They tortured and killed his eldest son.

In 1775, a man named Richard Henderson called together the chiefs of the Cherokee Indian tribes. He felt that these were the Indians who had the strongest claim to Kentucky. He paid the Cherokees a great pile of trading goods for a section of their land, which he named *Transylvania*. He planned to start a colony of that name in Kentucky.

Daniel Boone was to lead a group of men into Transylvania and to cut a pack-horse trail through the woods. They were to build a fort in the wilderness, at a spot Daniel had chosen six years earlier.

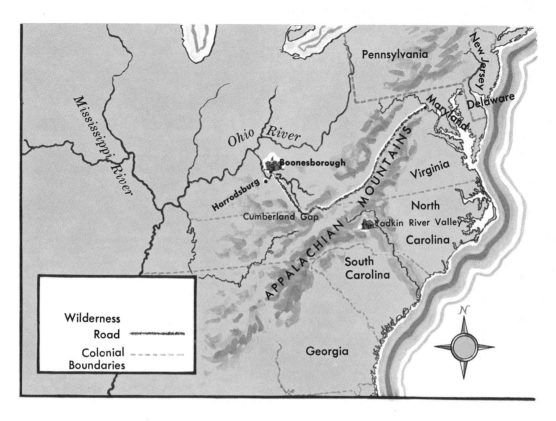

Boonesborough and the Wilderness Road

Boone and his men marked the trail from Cumberland Gap to the place where the fort was to be built. The route was called the *Wilderness Road,* but it was really no more than a pack-horse trail. They built a fort and named it *Boonesborough.*

In the fall, a group of brave pioneers traveled the Wilderness Road to Boonesborough. In the group were Boone's wife, his children, his brother Squire, and other relatives and friends from North Carolina.

One month before Boonesborough was started, another group of pioneers led by a man named James Harrod, had come to Kentucky. They built a fort and cabins a few miles southwest of Boonesborough. Their settlement was named *Harrodsburg.* Harrodsburg and Boonesborough were the first English settlements in the lands west of the Appalachians.

Settlement soon began on the upper Ohio River, too. Pittsburgh was growing around Fort Pitt. A group of pioneers built a fort where Wheeling, West Virginia, is now. Hunters and traders were beginning to use the Ohio River as a route to the west, although the Indians were fighting harder than ever to hold them back.

Words to Know

Boonesborough (boōnz′bûr ỏ) 129

Harrodsburg (hăr′ŭdz bûrg) 129

Pontiac (pŏn′tĭ ăk) 126

Transylvania (trăn′sĭl vān′ya̍) 128

Wilderness Road (wĭl′dēr nĕs rōd) 129

Questions

1. How did Pontiac feel about the white men's moving west?

2. Why were the Indians unable to take Fort Detroit?

3. Why did Boone make his first trip to Kentucky? Who went along?

4. Where did the Wilderness Road begin and end?

5. What were the names of the first two English settlements in the land west of the Appalachian Mountains?

You See for Yourself

Daniel Boone had many adventures during his years at Boonesborough. Read about these days in an encyclopedia or a book written about Boone. What was the name of the Indian chief who adopted him as his son? How was Boonesborough saved from an Indian attack?

The Colonies Break Away from England

How did misunderstandings begin?

England had been in many wars. Her government needed money badly at the close of the French and Indian War.

"The colonies should help pay the cost of the war," said the men of the English Parliament. *Parliament* is the group of officials who govern England. Right after the close of the French and Indian War, Parliament began passing a number of laws that called on the colonies to pay taxes to England.

The government of England was led by a king, but the king did not rule alone. Parliament was in charge of making new laws. The members of Parliament were divided into two parts, or houses. The *House of Lords* was made up of nobles, and the *House of Commons* was made up of Englishmen elected by the people who could vote.

Each of the Thirteen Colonies had a government similar to that of England. A governor, chosen by the king of England, was at its head.

Many speeches against English taxes were made at meetings of colonial representatives.

The colonial governor was helped in governing the colony by a kind of little parliament, again with two houses. The upper house members were selected by the governor. The lower house members were elected by the people of the colony.

No colony, however, elected members to *represent*, or speak for it, in the English Parliament. For this reason, the colonists felt that they had no part in the making of laws that came to them from England. They were very unhappy with the new taxes, not because they were so high, but because the colonists had not had a chance to vote on them.

"Taxation without representation is unfair!" said leaders in the colonies. Samuel Adams, in Boston, was one who talked a great deal about how unfair it was for the colonists to have to pay taxes for which they had not had the chance to vote.

Samuel Adams and his friends in Boston formed a group called "The Sons of Liberty." The Sons of Liberty were especially unhappy with the

Stamp Act, by which Parliament ordered that certain goods sent from England to America could not be bought by the colonists unless they paid a tax. A stamp was placed on each item sold to show that the tax had been paid.

The Sons of Liberty called meetings at which they talked against paying the tax. They put up signs that read, "Liberty, Property, and No Stamps!" If they heard of a store owner who had paid this tax, they sometimes found ways to punish him.

"We'll get along with the things we make and the food we grow right here in the colonies," said many people in the colonies. "If we don't buy the goods sent from England, we won't have to pay the tax on them."

Biography Outline

Samuel Adams

1722-1803

American

Patriot and politician

Organized the Boston Tea Party—was a leading spokesman for American independence—stirred discontent among the colonists before the war with his speeches and writings.

Many Boston colonists hated the sight of English soldiers in their city streets.

The colonies had been protected during the French and Indian War by the many English soldiers sent to America. The colonists were helping to pay for this help through their trade with England. It was important to the businessmen of England as well as to the government that the colonists buy English goods.

The English king again sent soldiers to America. This time they were to keep order and to try to make the colonists pay the taxes. The "redcoats" marched each day in the city streets, especially in Boston. The colonists began to hate the sight of the soldiers. The soldiers themselves were unhappy living so far from their homes in England. Sooner or later, trouble was sure to come.

Trouble came on March 5, 1770, in the streets of Boston.

"Lobster backs!" the Sons of Liberty shouted at the soldiers. Someone threw a stick and hit one of the ten soldiers who were drilling in the street. Another soldier was suddenly knocked down by someone who pushed at him as he passed by. Suddenly, the soldiers turned on the crowd and fired their guns. Eleven colonists were killed or wounded.

This event became known as the *Boston Massacre*. It was the first shooting that took place between the Americans and the English.

What did England think of the trouble in the colonies?

In England, King George III and the Parliament were very angry with the colonists. In order to please the colonists, England had already removed the Stamp Act and taxed only a few things. To quiet matters, the English now removed all the taxes except the one on tea. They kept this one just to prove to the colonists that England had the right to tax the colonies if she chose to do so.

The colonists were not satisfied. Samuel Adams was keeping the flame of anger alive. He wrote pamphlets and made speeches, telling the colonists it would be better to get along without tea than to pay the tax.

In December of 1773, three English ships were anchored in the harbor of Boston, each loaded with wooden crates of tea. The Sons of Liberty asked that the ships return to England and the tea be taken back to the company that had shipped it to America. Orders came from England that the ships were to be unloaded in the colonies by no later than December 17.

On the night of December 16, colonists with painted faces, pretending to be Indians, rowed out to the ships. They climbed aboard, overcame the English crewmen guarding the ships, and broke open the crates of tea. They dumped the tea into the water of the harbor. Among the "Indians" was a silversmith named Paul Revere. This event has become known in American history as the *Boston Tea Party.*

The next day, as tea leaves made a brown edge around the Boston harbor, Paul Revere left Boston on horseback. He was going to warn the other Sons of Liberty in New York and Philadelphia of what had happened in Boston. He was also to urge the Sons of Liberty in those two cities to stand strong against the taxes as Boston had done.

How did the colonies begin to work together?

Members of the English Parliament became very angry after the Boston Tea Party. They passed more laws for the colonists, some aimed at punishing them. One of these laws said that no ships could go in or out of the Boston harbor until the colonists paid for all the destroyed tea.

In September of 1774, the leaders of the colonies called a meeting to which twelve of the thirteen sent representatives. The purpose of the meeting was to talk over the problems that all of the colonies were facing. During the months and years ahead, a number of these meetings would be held. This group was the *First Continental Congress.*

The fifty-five members of the First Continental Congress met in Philadelphia. Here Samuel Adams, John Adams, and George Washington came together for the first time, along with other important men. John Hancock, from Boston, was elected president of the group.

Biography Outline
Paul Revere
1735-1818
American
Patriot
Warned patriots in Lexington and Concord of the approach of British soldiers—discovered the process of rolling sheet copper—built the first copper rolling mill.

Biography Outline
John Adams
1735-1826
American
Politician
President of the United States—played a leading role in the adoption of the Declaration of Independence—maintained peace with France as President.

The Continental Congress was trying to find a way in which the colonists would have a right to help decide the laws made by Parliament. "If we don't buy the goods from England, Parliament will be forced to give us that right," the men said.

Again, King George and Parliament were angered. Their answer was to send more soldiers to the colonies. Neither side would give in. The Sons of Liberty kept chicken feathers and kettles of hot tar ready to "tar and feather" any colonists who bought goods from England.

A group of colonists was trained to be ready for action in case fighting came. These men were called the *minutemen*. They had guns and gunpowder stored at Concord, a town about twenty miles from Boston.

One of the most famous speeches of this time was made by Patrick Henry before the House of Burgesses in Virginia. "Give me liberty or give me death!" he shouted in one of his speeches. His words became a saying that helped draw people together.

How did open battle begin?

English soldiers were sent to Boston with orders to capture the two men the English felt had the biggest part in causing the trouble in the colonies. One of these men was Samuel Adams, and the other was John Hancock. The soldiers also had orders to find and take the guns and gunpowder stored at Concord.

The Sons of Liberty went on duty to watch the movement of the English soldiers as they arrived at the Boston Harbor. Paul Revere was again ready to act as one of the messengers. He had his horse saddled and was ready to carry the word of the soldiers' attack as soon as the Sons of Liberty learned which way the redcoats would come. Paul Revere, and others, too, rode all through the night of April 18, 1775, to spread the alarm.

Gunfire at Lexington and Concord

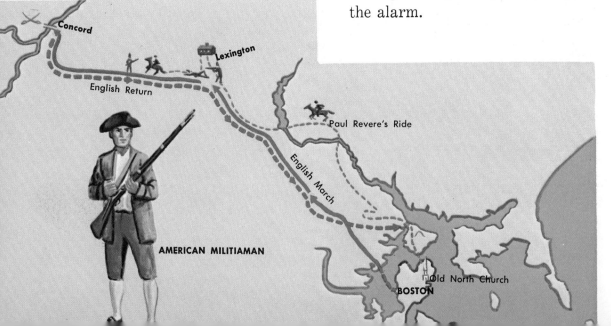

AMERICAN MILITIAMAN

The English soldiers, in their bright red uniforms, were fired upon all the way back to Boston. It seemed that a fighting colonist was behind every barn and each stone wall fence. The English soldiers could not understand how the colonists could dare to stand against "His Majesty's Men," making war on the greatest nation in the world.

At dawn the next morning, the minutemen and the *militia*, private citizens who fought with the army in case of emergency, were on hand at Concord to defend their war supplies.

The first shots were fired as the English soldiers marched into Lexington, a town on the road between Boston and Concord. Eight colonists were killed and more wounded. Adams and Hancock, who had been hiding at Lexington, had left during the night.

The redcoats met the minutemen and militiamen at the bridge just outside Concord. Some of the redcoats were able to get across the bridge. They searched the town for the supplies, which the colonists had hidden during the night. By noon, the redcoats turned back.

Colonists fired upon the English soldiers all the way from Concord to Boston.

Many colonists, too, wondered how their fellow colonists dared to start a fight with England. Thousands of English soldiers arrived in America during the weeks that followed. There were some people in the colonies who really believed that it was wrong for the colonies to turn against England, the "mother country." But there were many more whose anger could not be put down and who were ready to fight for their rights. Their hatred for the British soldiers had grown even stronger than before.

Some of the men who helped bring forth a new nation. . .

Thomas Paine—
who urged the people on to freedom

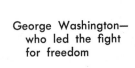

George Washington—
who led the fight for freedom

The redcoats made matters worse by killing cattle and taking other food from the colonists. It was their wasteful ways that angered the colonists most of all.

What did the Second Continental Congress do?

The Second Continental Congress met about three weeks after the battle at Concord. They selected George Washington to be Commander-in-chief of the Continental Army. They voted to give him money to pay the soldiers and to buy supplies for them. Yet the Continental Congress had no money to give him and no power to raise money by taxing the colonists.

The fighting was going on full force. The colonists, taking the English by surprise, captured two forts in upper New York. Then came the Battle of Bunker Hill, just outside Boston. Again the straight-shooting militia and the angry Sons of Liberty held back the English.

King George hired some German soldiers called *Hessians*, to help put down the colonists. When the colonists saw that the soldiers were hired, they became even angrier and more eager to win. But things went badly for them for a while.

Benjamin Franklin—
who pointed out that working together was very necessary

The English set fire to the Virginia town of Norfolk in the South, and forced the Americans out of Boston.

When did the colonists decide to fight for complete independence?

Until 1776, the idea of breaking away from England completely had not been taken seriously. The Americans were fighting only for rights as colonists. But in January of 1776, a booklet called *"Common Sense"* was printed. In this booklet, Thomas Paine, the author, pointed out that the colonies might just as well fight for their complete freedom. His words influenced the thinking of many of the colonists. Paine had come from England a year earlier, but he was already as strong a patriot as Samuel Adams. A *patriot* is a person who loves his country strongly and fights hard for it.

When the Continental Congress met again, in June of 1776, the members voted that "These United Colonies are, and of right ought to be, free and independent states. . ."

A young Virginia lawyer named Thomas Jefferson was asked to head a committee to write an official paper telling what the Congress had decided. The paper written by Jef-

Biography Outline
Thomas Paine
1731-1809
English
Patriot
Wrote pamphlets defending the colonists' cause before the War for Independence.

Biography Outline
Thomas Jefferson
1743-1826
American
Statesman
President of the United States—author of the Declaration of Independence—founder of the University of Virginia.

ferson is known as the *Declaration of Independence*.

The Continental Congress voted on it on July 4, 1776, and John Hancock signed it. That day became the birthday of the United States.

The big bell in the Pennsylvania State House, where the meeting was held, was rung. The words carved into the bell read, "Proclaim liberty throughout all the land unto all the inhabitants thereof." The bell became known as the Liberty Bell.

Benjamin Franklin, now an old man, was one of the men at the signing of the Declaration of Independence. He said, "We must indeed all hang together now, or assuredly we shall all hang separately."

Thomas Jefferson—who put into words the call for freedom, The Declaration of Independence

Words to Know

Boston Massacre (bŏs'tŭn măs'á kēr) 132

Boston Tea Party (bŏs'tŭn tē pär'tĭ) 133

Declaration of Independence (dĕk'lá rā'shŭn ŏv ĭn'dĕ pĕn'dĕns) 137

First Continental Congress (fûrst kŏn'tĭ nĕn'tăl kŏng'grĕs) 133

Hessians (hesh'ănz) 136

House of Commons (hous ŏv kŏm' ŭnz) 130

House of Lords (hous ŏv lôrdz) 130

militia (mĭ lĭsh'á) 135

minutemen (mĭn'ĭt mĕn) 134

Parliament (pär'lĭ mĕnt) 130

patriot (pā'trĭ ŭt) 137

represent (rĕp'rĕ zĕnt') 131

Stamp Act (stămp ăct) 131

Questions

1. How was the government of each of the English colonies like the government of England?

2. Why did the colonists dislike having to pay the taxes set down for them by the English Parliament?

3. How did the Sons of Liberty and other colonists plan to keep from paying the Stamp Tax?

4. Why did the English government decide that the colonies should pay taxes to England?

5. Tell the story of the Boston Massacre.

6. What happened in Boston Harbor on December 16, 1773?

7. Why were the English soldiers sent to the town of Concord?

8. What job did George Washington receive at the first meeting of the Second Continental Congress?

9. In June of 1776, the Continental Congress made an important decision. What was this decision?

You See for Yourself

Look up "Philadelphia" in an encyclopedia. What buildings are still standing there today that were important in the birth of the new nation? What happened in each of them? What else would you like to see if you visited Philadelphia?

Find a copy of the Declaration of Independence in an encyclopedia or history book. Read the first ten or fifteen lines. Memorize the statement that begins: "We hold these truths. . ." Talk about the meaning of this statement in class.

The War for Independence

Washington's army suffered at Valley Forge.

In the days that followed, it sometimes seemed that the flame of liberty would go out. In many battles, the well-trained English soldiers easily pushed back the American farmers, shopkeepers, and others who had taken arms against the English. Boston, New York, and Philadelphia were all in the hands of the English.

It was part of the English plan to cut off the Northern Colonies from the Southern Colonies by marching right down the Hudson River Valley. The southern end of the valley had already fallen to the English. But New England soldiers stopped the English troops led by *General Burgoyne*. The English general was forced to surrender 6,000 men to the American leader in the north, General Gates. This victory helped to give the Americans the courage they needed.

Washington's army, farther south, became a tired and worn group of men. Their clothing and their shoes wore out, and Washington had no way to get new ones for them. The winter of 1777 was the coldest any of the people then alive could remember. Washington and his army spent that winter in the little village of Valley Forge, near Philadelphia. The men did not have proper food, clothing, or shelter that winter. It was one of the worst times during the war for Washington.

How did the French help the Americans?

While the patriots fought shooting battles at home, Benjamin Franklin was fighting for America in another important way. He was in France, using his wisdom and wit to get the help of France for the struggling Americans. In February of 1778, Franklin's work was rewarded. France signed an agreement to send America men, ships, and supplies.

Burgoyne Is Stopped

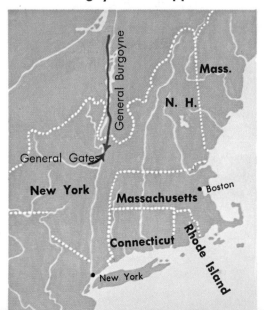

General Burgoyne

General Gates

Mass.

N. H.

New York

Boston

Massachusetts

Connecticut

Rhode Island

New York

139

John Paul Jones commanded the Bonhomme Richard against the English Serapis.

Five of the ships received from France were commanded by Captain John Paul Jones. The ship on which Captain Jones himself sailed was the *Bonhomme Richard*. The meeting of the *Bonhomme Richard* and the English ship *Serapis* has become a famous sea battle in American history. When it seemed that the *Bonhomme Richard* was lost, Captain Jones moved his ship so close to the heavily armed English ship that its guns were useless. The English thought Captain Jones was surrendering his ship, but he cried, "We have not yet begun to fight!" With these words, he and his men began hand-to-hand fighting on the decks of the ships, although the *Bonhomme Richard* was sinking. The battle ended when the *Serapis* surrendered.

Even before the French government agreed to help the colonists, many interested soldiers from France and other European countries had come to America to fight on the side of the colonists. One of the French soldiers was *Marquis de Lafayette*, a young man of the French noble class. After France openly entered the war on the side of America, French troops were sent to Virginia to fight under the command of Lafayette. They were of great help in the final battles of the war. In October of 1781, Washington and Lafayette together brought about the surrender of 7,000 English soldiers under General Cornwallis at Yorktown, Virginia.

The surrender of Cornwallis marked the end of most of the fighting. Some fighting broke out once in a while, mainly in the South, for almost a year. Yet it was clear that both sides were ready for peace.

Who won the western frontier?

Not all the fighting in the War for Independence took place within the Thirteen Colonies themselves. The frontier settlers had to fight both the Indians and the English for their homes and their freedom.

General Hamilton, with headquarters in Detroit, led the English forces in the fight for the western frontier. George Rogers Clark, a settler in Kentucky, headed the Americans.

When Clark saw that General Hamilton was urging the Indians to attack the American settlers and to drive them from the frontier, he decided that the war should be carried west of the Appalachians. He went to the capital city of Virginia, where he spoke with Thomas Jefferson and Patrick Henry. They helped him to get some supplies he needed.

Back in Kentucky, Clark set about training a small army of frontiersmen. Each man used his own long rifle. His own hunting clothes, usually a buckskin outfit, became his uniform. Among Clark's captains were Daniel Boone, James Harrod, and Clark's brother, Benjamin. His chief scout was the famous pioneer, Simon Kenton.

Clark sent spies to learn how many English soldiers were in the old French forts at *Kaskaskia* and *Vincennes*, in the Illinois region. He learned that there were not many, and planned to attack. But even he could see that it would be foolish to attack with no more soldiers than he had. Some of his best men, including Daniel Boone, had been captured by the Indians and turned over to the English.

Patrick Henry, who had become governor of Virginia, wanted to help Clark, but most of the Virginia men were needed for the fighting in the East. All Clark could get were 150 men and only part of the supplies for which he asked. He set up training quarters for his men at Corn Island, near present-day Louisville.

With his tiny army, George Rogers Clark crept up on Fort Kaskaskia, after a journey partly by boat and partly on foot. They took the fort by surprise, as they had hoped. Fort *Cahokia* fell to Clark, too.

Clark planned to turn back eastward to Vincennes, hoping to take that fort before Hamilton had a chance to send more men to defend it.

Biography Outline
George Rogers Clark
1752-1818
American
Soldier
His victories in the Northwest Territory during the War for Independence gave the United States claim to boundaries west to the Mississippi and north to the Great Lakes.

Clark in the West

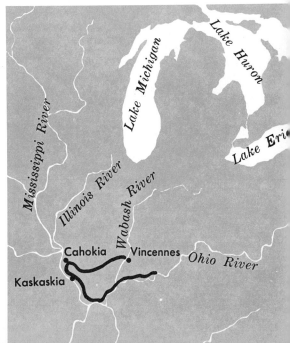

A surprised English general surrendered to Clark and his men at Fort Vincennes.

The rivers were flooding because of a February thaw after a heavy snowstorm. Marching through miles of mud and flooded land, the men often had to carry their rifles and powder above their heads to keep them dry. Some asked Clark if it wouldn't be wise to wait for a better time to travel.

"No," Clark told them. "Hamilton would not expect us to attack through these waters. We must take the fort by surprise, or we surely will not win it. We'll keep going."

How a New Nation Came Forth

1763
English Parliament begins to pass laws that check the westward movement of the colonists, cut down on their trading business, and ask them to pay more taxes to the English government.

1765
England continues to keep soldiers in the colonies even though danger from French or Indians is mostly past.

1767
More and more colonists show their displeasure at England's attitude toward the colonists. Some grow angry enough to speak openly against the "mother country."

1770
English soldiers fire upon American colonists in Boston, where a crowd has gathered to watch them march through the city streets.

Clark was right. Hamilton himself had come to Vincennes, but he did not think it possible for an army to cross the Wabash River when it was flooding so badly. Clark placed his men so that it seemed to Hamilton that the firing was coming from a great attacking force. The sharp-shooting frontiersmen picked off the English soldiers as quickly as their heads appeared above the walls of the fort. Hamilton surrendered the fort, and with it, all the western holdings of the English. The English general was greatly embarrassed when he saw the handful of ragged frontiersmen who had defeated him.

What did peace mean to the Americans?

When the fighting ended, Benjamin Franklin went back to Paris. With him went John Adams and a young leader from New York, John Jay. The three Americans met with French, British, and Spanish officials. When the meeting was over, they had drawn up the Treaty of Paris of 1783. According to this treaty, the United States of America was now an independent country.

The treaty gave to the United States all the land that England had held south of the Great Lakes except for the land around the mouth of the Mississippi. Spain had taken Florida back from England so America's southern limit was a little north of the Gulf of Mexico. Because of George Rogers Clark's fight in the west, the Mississippi River was the western limit of the United States.

The Americans were pleased with the terms of the treaty. But they soon saw that they had many, many problems to face. The young nation needed wise and strong leaders.

1776
The colonists decide to claim their full independence from England. They draw up a statement known as the Declaration of Independence.

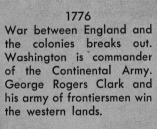

1776
War between England and the colonies breaks out. Washington is commander of the Continental Army. George Rogers Clark and his army of frontiersmen win the western lands.

1781
General Cornwallis, head of the English forces, surrenders his army to George Washington. Except for a few battles farther south, the war ends.

1783
England and America sign a peace treaty. The United States becomes an independent nation. Western lands between the Appalachians and the Mississippi River are American territory.

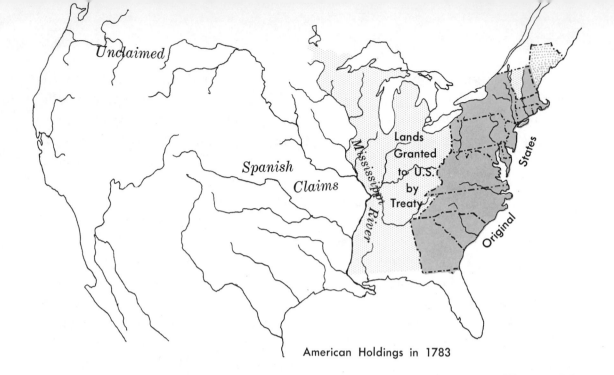

American Holdings in 1783

Words to Know

Bonhomme Richard (bŏn'nôm' rē' shàr') 140

Cahokia (kà hō'kĭ à) 141

General Burgoyne (jĕn'ẽr ăl bûr goin') 139

Kaskaskia (kăs kăs'kĭ à) 141

Marquis de Lafayette (màr kē' dẽ lä'fĭ ĕt') 140

Serapis (sẻ rā'pĭs) 140

Vincennes (vĭn sĕnz') 141

Questions

1. Why did the English want to take the Hudson River Valley?

2. Who was General Burgoyne? Who defeated him?

3. Where did Washington's army spend the winter of 1777? Why was this a bad time for him and his soldiers?

4. Why was Benjamin Franklin in France during the War for Independence?

5. Who was John Paul Jones? What now-famous words did he say?

6. What land did George Rogers Clark win for America?

You See for Yourself

Learn more about Benjamin Franklin from books in your library. List all the ways in which he made himself famous. What was "Poor Richard's Almanac"?

Now You Know

Between the years of 1754 and 1783, many events that were to have a lasting influence upon America took place. The French and English had had disagreements that sometimes led to war since the beginning of their interests in the New World.

In 1754, the last war over French and English claims in the New World broke out. At the end of this war, France had lost out entirely in the New World. England held Canada and almost all the land between the Atlantic Coast and the Mississippi River.

This war, as well as others, left the English government badly in need of money. Parliament, feeling that the colonies should help pay the war bill, decided to tax the colonies.

The colonists were bitter about the laws, namely because they had not been represented when the laws were passed. "Taxation without representation!" was their angry cry.

This angry cry turned into open war between the colonists and the English. The colonists were willing to fight for their rights as colonists, their right to be represented in the making of laws that they had to obey. Before the war ended, however, the colonists drew up and signed the Declaration of Independence, which meant that they had decided to fight for complete separation from England.

After more than six years of fighting, the war finally dragged to an end. The peace treaty of 1783 gave the Americans all of the land along the Atlantic Coast plus the land between the Mississippi River and the Appalachian Mountains.

You Talk It Over

Do you think the colonists were right to cause so much trouble over the taxes they were asked to pay? Why or why not? Did it seem to you that England cared how the colonists felt about the matter? Explain your answer.

Do you think the colonies were right or wrong to go to war against England? Why or why not? Can you think of ways the colonists could have got what they wanted without going to war? Do you think that war was bound to come sooner or later?

Unit Questions

1. On a map, compare the location of the French and English colonies. (page 116) Which colonies were strung out along many miles of river valleys? How was this important in the colonists' chief business? Which country's colonies were "fenced in" by mountains? Why would it be easier for the people of the English colonies to work together than for the people of the French colonies to do so?

2. Why had the French not built up their fur trade in the Ohio country?

3. Why was the city of New Orleans important to the French in America?

4. Who was Celoron and why did he make a trip through the Ohio country?

5. Why did George Washington visit the French along Lake Erie? What did he suggest the English do after he returned from his trip?

6. How did the frontier settlers protect themselves from the Indians during the French and Indian War?

7. What new American lands could the English claim after the French and Indian War?

8. How did the Indians plan to stop the English after the French and Indian War? Who was the Indian leader of this plan?

9. How did the English at Fort Detroit hold out against the Indians?

10. What was the Wilderness Road? Who first marked this road?

11. Why did the colonists object to paying taxes Parliament placed upon goods sent to the colonies?

12. Who were the "Sons of Liberty"? Tell three things they did to show how they felt about the Stamp Act.

13. Why did Parliament close the port of Boston?

Puzzlers

The American colonists and the English argued over many things before the United States was finally separated from England. The two men shown here are an American and an Englishman. The statements at the bottom of the page could have been made by either an Englishman or a colonist. Read the statements, and decide which of the two men would have said each one.

American Colonist

Englishman

A. "The purpose of the colonies is to bring wealth to the mother country."

B. "The colonists are better off to do without tea or any other English goods than to pay Parliament's tax on them."

C. "English soldiers are unnecessary in the colonies. The colonies are able to defend themselves without English help."

D. "England must send more troops and continue to tax the colonies. The colonies must be taught that England has the right to control them."

E. "The colonies send no representatives to the English Parliament. Because of this, Parliament has no right to tax people in the colonies."

F. "The tax on tea is so small that the colonists could not possibly mind having to pay it."

G. "Colonists have the rights of Englishmen. Only their own colonial governments have the right to tax them."

H. "Fighting off the French and Indians cost England much money. The least the colonies can do is to help pay the cost of that war."

147

Unit Activities

You Give a Play

Study one of the important events you read about in this unit, and with the help of your classmates, plan to give a play that tells the story of this event. For example, you might act out the story of Washington's visit to the French, beginning with a scene in which Governor Dinwiddie gives him his instructions, then his trip through dangerous Indian country, his meeting with French officers, his return trip, and his suggestions to Governor Dinwiddie.

The whole story of the War for Independence would make a very good play. Everyone in your class could have a part.

You Learn about Famous People

You read about a number of people in this unit, yet there are many other interesting and important people who lived during the War for Independence. Choose a name from the list below and read about that person in books from your library. Be prepared to report to the class.

Simon Girty
Molly Pitcher
Betsy Ross
Baron von Steuben
Ethan Allen
Benedict Arnold
Nathan Hale
Anthony Wayne

You Make a Map

Make a large table map showing the United States between the Atlantic Ocean and the Mississippi River. On your map, show the mountains, rivers, lakes, etc., which were important in the way the country grew. Mark with "flags" such important places as Cumberland Gap, locations of forts and cities, etc. If you make your map large enough, you may even be able to show such things as Independence Hall at Philadelphia and the famous bridge at Concord.

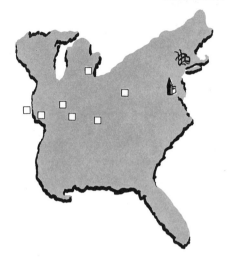

You Interview People of the Times

Choose another class member to be your partner. One of you will play the part of someone who either really lived or someone who could have lived during the years you read about in this unit. The other person should pretend to be a newspaper reporter who is interviewing this person. For example, you might interview a man who led a wagon train of settlers over the Wilderness Road to settle in Kentucky. You could interview George Croghan, Benjamin Franklin, or another famous person. Use encyclopedias and other books to help you plan a good interview.

You Sing a Song

"Yankee Doodle" was frequently sung by American armies during the War for Independence. Learn to sing all the verses to this tune as they were sung then. Most of the words are just for fun, but tell what you think the words mean.

You Read a Poem

Several poems have been written about the Americans' fight for freedom. Read one of the poems listed here and be able to explain what it is about.

The Concord Hymn—Ralph Waldo Emerson

The Midnight Ride of Paul Revere—Henry Wadsworth Longfellow

Building the New Nation

The United States was at peace. The English troops were gone. The American soldiers were back working on their farms, in their shops, and tending their plantations.

Not all the Americans' problems left with the English. One of the first things the Americans had to do was to decide upon a government that would satisfy all the people. This was not an easy thing to do. Each state wanted to keep many rights for itself. All the states wanted to be sure that the *federal government*, the one that would have powers over all the states, would not take over almost all the work. Different groups of states often did not agree on what they wanted.

The nation did much growing and changing during its first years of independence. Travel methods grew and improved.

Government Under a Constitution

The Continental Congress worked during the War for Independence to set up a government under which all the Thirteen States could work together. The members drew up a plan known as the *Articles of Confederation*. According to the Articles, a group of representatives from the states would govern the nation. This group was called the *Congress of the Confederation*. By the end of the war, all the states had joined.

What work was done by the Congress of the Confederation?

One of the first jobs of the federal government at the end of the war was to make plans for the ownership of the new lands west of the Appalachian Mountains. The land between the Ohio River and the Great Lakes became known as the *Northwest Territory* instead of the Ohio country, as it was called during earlier, colonial days.

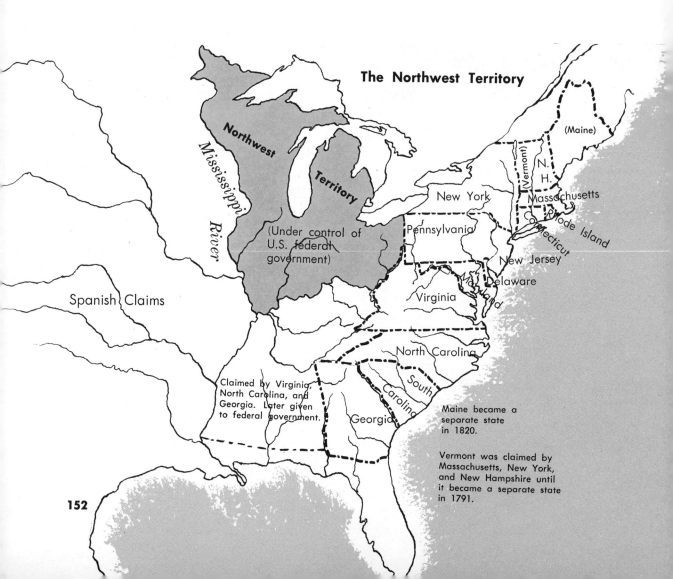

The Northwest Territory

Northwest Territory

(Under control of U.S. federal government)

Mississippi River

Spanish Claims

Claimed by Virginia, North Carolina, and Georgia. Later given to federal government.

New York

Pennsylvania

New Jersey

Delaware

Md.

Virginia

North Carolina

South Carolina

Georgia

(Maine)

(Vermont)

N. H.

Massachusetts

Rhode Island

Connecticut

Maine became a separate state in 1820.

Vermont was claimed by Massachusetts, New York, and New Hampshire until it became a separate state in 1791.

The Congress of the Confederation divided the Northwest Territory into squares called townships. Each township was six miles long and six miles wide. The townships were divided into thirty-six equal squares called *sections*. The sections were numbered, and section sixteen was set aside for schools. The government could sell the rest of the land to private persons or companies.

The idea of townships and sections written into the plans for the Northwest Territory became a model for the planning of territories added to the United States in later years. It was an early step toward free public education in this country.

6	5	4	3	2	1
7	8	9	10	11	12
18	17	16	15	14	13
19	20	21	22	23	24
30	29	28	27	26	25
31	32	33	34	35	36

Two years later, the Congress passed the *Northwest Ordinance*, which gave further plans for the Northwest Territory. Land that belonged to the United States would first be known as a territory, with a governor chosen by the Congress. When there were at least 60,000 people living in a territory, they could ask that the territory be made a state. Not more than five states were to be made from the land of the Northwest Territory.

One part of the Northwest Ordinance had special importance. Many Americans believed strongly that all the people under the government should have equal rights. The Declaration of Independence stated this belief clearly. "If we really believe this," said some of the leaders in the Congress, "then slavery should not be allowed in the United States."

Many of the leaders of the Congress had slaves themselves. George Washington and Thomas Jefferson were slaveowners. The plantation owners needed their slaves to do the work. A planter paid a high price for a good slave, and he could not afford to give away his worker. But Jefferson and others agreed that the idea of slavery was wrong. They voted that slavery be against the law in the Northwest Territory.

The plans made for the Northwest Territory became a model for the planning of all new lands that were later added to the United States.

Representatives at the Philadelphia meeting decided to give up the Articles of Confederation and to write an entirely new Constitution.

How was the government changed?

The Congress of the Confederation did a good job of providing for new lands. But there were many other serious problems that this congress did not have the power to do anything about. Washington, Jefferson, and others could see that the government would have to be changed if the nation was ever to act as one.

In 1787, the government leaders agreed to meet in Philadelphia for the purpose of rewriting the Articles of Confederation.

Biography Outline

James Madison

1751-1836

American

Politician

President of the United States during the War of 1812—did much toward building a strong federal government.

Among the fifty-five men at the meeting were George Washington; Benjamin Franklin; Alexander Hamilton, a brilliant young lawyer from New York; and James Madison, a Virginia representative who helped to solve many disagreements.

The men chose George Washington to act as chairman of the meeting. They met in the Pennsylvania State House, where the Declaration of Independence was signed. They locked the doors and agreed to keep their work secret until they were finished.

The idea of rewriting the Articles of Confederation was soon forgotten. Instead, the men began making plans for an entirely new government. They wrote their plans into a document that has proved to be one of the greatest accomplishments in the history of man—the Constitution of the United States of America.

All during the hot summer of 1787, the men worked. They often argued, and at times it seemed they would never reach agreement. Sixteen of the representatives became so angry that they left and went home before the end of the meeting.

Benjamin Franklin and James Madison were two men whose ideas often ended arguments. James Madison's ideas and speeches were so helpful that he has become known as the "Father of the Constitution."

Finally, in September, the Constitution was finished, and the meeting came to an end. Although the men still had doubts about some things, they felt they had drawn up a plan that would provide for a federal government strong enough to do what was needed. At the same time, the states were allowed certain rights.

According to the Constitution, the federal government was divided into three parts. Each part had its own duties and powers. The writers of the Constitution used this plan to keep any one person or one group of persons from becoming too powerful.

When did the Constitution become the law of the land?

The Constitution was ready to be presented to the states. Before it could become law, the states had to *ratify* it, which meant to vote to follow it. The Constitution was the subject of much talk throughout the states during the months after it was first presented.

The writers of the Constitution planned the federal government to have three branches, each with its particular powers and duties. The writers also hoped that the three branches would act as a check on each other so that no one person or group of persons could ever have complete control of the government.

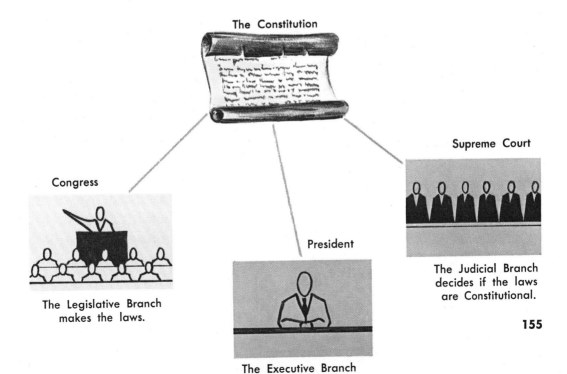

The Constitution

Congress

The Legislative Branch
makes the laws.

President

The Executive Branch
carries out the laws.

Supreme Court

The Judicial Branch
decides if the laws
are Constitutional.

155

George Washington took office in 1789.

Some people thought the Constitution took too many powers away from the states and gave them to the federal government. People who favored a strong federal government were ready to ratify it right away.

The District of Columbia

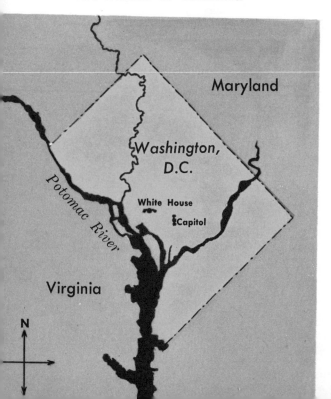

Delaware was the first to ratify the Constitution, and so became the first state in the Union. A promise of greater protection for the personal rights of citizens was needed to get some states to ratify it.

After eleven states had ratified the Constitution, the new government began its work. George Washington was elected as the first President of the United States. John Adams was the Vice-President. Both men took office on April 30, 1789.

What was the work of the first Congress?

The first thing Congress had to do was to keep the promise made to some of the states to include protection of personal rights in the Constitution. Congress did this by adding ten laws, called *amendments*, to the Constitution. Other amendments have been added through the years. The first ten are often called the *Bill of Rights*. The Bill of Rights gives certain freedoms to all Americans. Among them are freedom of speech and freedom of religion.

Another thing the first Congress did was to choose a place for the capital. The District of Columbia was to be part of no state at all. It was formed of land that belonged to Virginia and Maryland, which was a central location in those days. Government buildings were to be built there as soon as possible. In the meantime, Philadelphia served as the capital.

A new nation had fought for and won its freedom. It had set up a kind of government in which the people themselves had the right to make and change their laws. The people also had the right to choose their own leaders. Their new government was called a *democracy*.

Questions

1. What group was governing the United States at the end of the War for Independence?

2. What is a federal government?

3. How did the federal government divide the Northwest Territory?

4. According to the Northwest Ordinance, how many people did a territory need before it could ask to become a state in the Union?

5. Why did the leaders of government meet in Philadelphia in 1787? How did the purpose of their meeting change?

You See for Yourself

Find a copy of the United States Constitution. Study the short paragraph, sometimes called the Preamble, that is at the beginning of the Constitution. Discuss this paragraph in class, making sure that you understand its meaning. You will need to use your dictionary to understand some of the words. Your teacher will help you, too.

On the map, study the section that was once the Northwest Territory. What states were formed from this large section of land? Find out in what year each of these states joined the Union.

People of the New Nation

In its first years as a nation, the United States of America was divided into three parts and three groups of people. In some ways each group seemed to be living in a world of its own.

The people along the eastern coast lived in communities which already seemed old. Their life was much different from that of the second group, the frontier settlers west of the Appalachian Mountains. The third world was that of the Indian, pushed out of his old homelands and away from his hunting grounds into whatever lands the white man had not yet chosen to settle.

How was the eastern world changing?

The southern states had been farming states since the beginning of colonial days. The northern states had turned to *manufacturing*, or the making of goods to sell. After the War for Independence, both the North and the South saw their business interests grow bigger and richer. The main reason for this growth was the invention of machines that could do certain jobs faster, cheaper, and more easily than they could be done by hand.

Southern plantation owners had started growing much cotton in addition to tobacco a few years before the War for Independence began. England had begun to use two machines that made the manufacture of cotton cloth easier than it had been before. English businessmen paid a good price for American cotton.

During and after the war, this trade with England stopped. The South had no place to sell its cotton crops. But machines came to America, too. In 1793, Samuel Slater built the first American factory at Pawtucket, Rhode Island. At Slater's Mill, cotton was spun into yarn, for weaving.

Trade Among the States

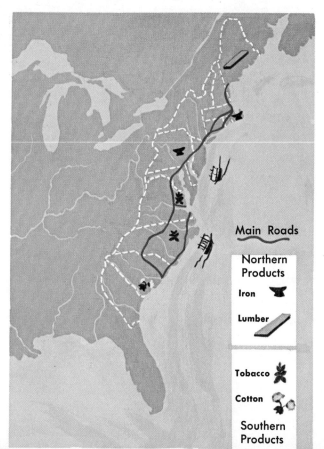

Main Roads

Northern Products

Iron

Lumber

Tobacco

Cotton

Southern Products

One of the problems of using cotton had always been picking out the seeds that stuck to the fibers. In 1793, Eli Whitney, a great American inventor, solved this problem with a machine called the *cotton gin*, short for cotton engine.

In 1813, Francis Cabot Lowell built a factory at Waltham, Massachusetts. In his factory, were machines for weaving cotton yarn into cloth.

All of these machines and factories in the North gave the South a place to sell the cotton crops. New England was growing into an important manufacturing center, and the South was becoming more and more important as a farming center.

In the eastern world, other changes were taking place, too. Northern cities were growing larger. A great many people from the different countries of Europe were coming to live in America, bringing customs and ways that were different from those the older, English colonists had brought. The American "melting pot" was already beginning, especially in New York, New Jersey, and Pennsylvania.

In the North, more and better roads were being built because of the growing trade. Postal service improved. River travel grew to new importance after 1807, when Robert Fulton's steamboat made its first successful trip up the Hudson River.

Most of the cotton crop was shipped to the northern states or to Europe. Southern port cities were less busy than the northern cities, and road-building in the South took place much more slowly.

Slater's Mill, built in 1793, was the first factory in America.

The first factory for weaving cotton yarn into cloth was at Lowell, Massachusetts.

The invention of the cotton gin in 1793 made the cotton crop even more important.

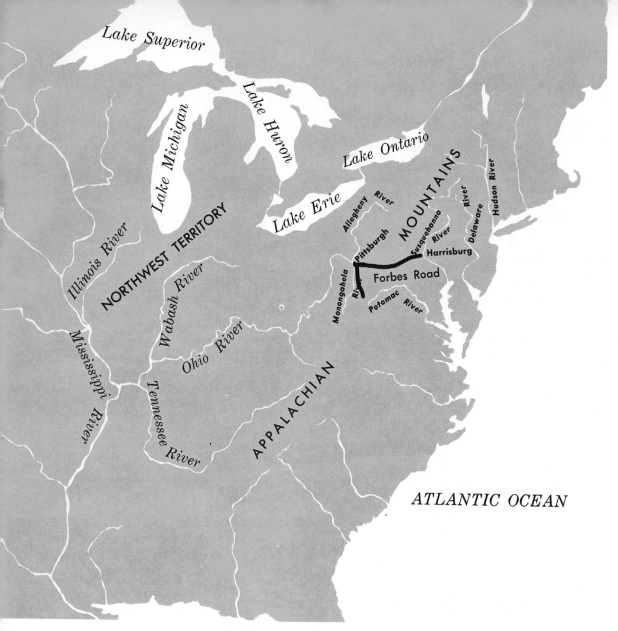

Lake Superior

Lake Michigan

Lake Huron

Lake Ontario

Lake Erie

Illinois River

NORTHWEST TERRITORY

Wabash River

Ohio River

Mississippi River

Tennessee River

APPALACHIAN

Allegheny River

Pittsburgh

MOUNTAINS

Susquehanna River

Harrisburg

Forbes Road

Monongahela

Potomac River

Delaware River

Hudson River

ATLANTIC OCEAN

The Western Frontier Around 1800

How did people live on the frontier?

The settlers west of the Appalachians, with the wilderness still in sight all around them, lived a life much different from that of the easterners. Here, most of these families lived for days or even weeks at a time without seeing an outsider.

As soon as a region was free from the danger of Indian attacks, the frontiersmen and their families settled farther and farther away from the protection of the forts. They first chose land near water. The first trees they cleared were used for log houses, furniture, and fuel.

The number of trees seemed to be endless, and the pioneers wasted many of them. They often burned the wood just to get the land cleared. The early settlers, however, needed only a small patch of cleared land for the corn and few garden vegetables they grew. They took most of their living from the woods around them.

Deer, brought down by the frontier hunter, gave his family deerskin clothing and fresh meat or dried meat, called *jerky*. Bears provided fur robes, fine meat, and good cooking fat. Wild turkey, quail, and squirrel or rabbit helped fill out the meat supply. Beaver meat was not good except for the tail, but the fur was very valuable. It could be traded at the nearest post for iron tools, lead for bullets, or perhaps coffee.

The first settlers found even sugar in their wooded surroundings. There were sugar maple trees, and wild bees often left honey in hollow trees. Fish from the streams added another food. The children learned to watch for greens in the spring and wild grapes and berries in the summer.

As time passed, and more and more settlers moved into the frontier lands, much of what the woods provided was used up. The settlers had to look to farming for a living, and more and more land had to be cleared.

Some plants were brought along from the East. Many mothers brought cuttings of lilacs and some flower seeds to their new homes.

Some brought fruit-tree cuttings, too. Many orchards were begun from the young fruit trees grown along the frontier by a New Englander named John Chapman. Chapman spent his life taking apple trees and religious teachings to the frontier. He was known as *Johnny Appleseed.*

Amusements had to be homemade, at first. Work was sometimes turned into fun as neighbors gathered to help a newcomer put up a cabin, husk corn, work on a quilt, or prepare apples for drying. When the work was done, the fun began. Someone might bring a fiddle and play music for dancing far into the night.

Before churches and schools were built, the traveling preacher made his rounds, and the people saved up weddings and christenings for his arrival. Sometimes a young man who wanted to be a teacher would hold a *subscription school* in any empty cabin he could find. Children whose parents had something with which to help pay the schoolmaster, might attend his school.

How did improved transportation help in the settling of the frontier?

After the War for Independence, the Appalachian wall no longer held people back from the western frontier. One reason was that most of the good land along the coast was taken, and settlers were looking farther and farther for good land. Another reason was that travel became easier.

161

Flatboats carried goods and people down the Ohio River to frontier settlements.

Both wars led to the building of roads, for armies cannot easily move along a trail wide enough only for a man on horseback. Braddock's Road had almost reached Fort Pitt at the time of the French attack. After the French and Indian War, the English finished the work. Soon wagon drivers were using it to go from northern Virginia to Pittsburgh.

A man named Harris was running a ferry boat across the *Susquehanna* River at the place now called Harrisburg. Traders such as Croghan had crossed the river there and followed a trail westward to Pittsburgh. Near the end of the French and Indian War, this trail had been widened into a road called Forbes Road. Trading settlements and inns began to appear.

Traders and travelers could find rest and food at inns along the early trails.

Wagon travel, especially between the eastern cities and Pittsburgh, had grown a good deal by the time of the War for Independence. A new type of wagon was being made in the valley of Conestoga Creek in Pennsylvania. These wagons were made especially for the carrying of supplies to the frontier settlements.

Conestoga freight wagons carried goods over the rugged mountain trails.

The frontiersman of the woodlands needed only a small garden patch.

The forest provided the pioneer family with material for building their home.

Several pioneer families might gather for an evening of fun and dancing.

Children of frontier families might attend a subscription school in a log cabin.

Many fruit orchards were begun by an unusual man called Johnny Appleseed.

The ends of the Conestoga wagon bed were slightly higher than the center.

The Pennsylvania drivers and their wagons traveled in groups, with each driver handling a team of four to six horses. At night, they stopped at inns along the road. The horses were cared for in the yard, and the men slept on the floor in front of the fire in the "great room."

Now and then, a stagecoach with mail and passengers journeyed over the freight roads. Smaller wagons, carrying the household goods of people leaving their eastern homes to take up new land in the west, were also seen on these roads.

How did people travel west from Pittsburgh?

At Pittsburgh, the roads ended. Those people headed farther west changed to water transportation. They could go all the way down the Ohio to the Mississippi and then down the Mississippi all the way to New Orleans if they chose.

Near the beginning of the Ohio River, many people went into the business of building boats. *Flatboats* were the most common kind. Each of them began with a flat platform, perhaps twelve or fifteen feet wide and twenty-five or thirty feet long. This became the bottom of the boat. Low sides were added. Some of the flatboats were roofed over, and some were left open to the weather. Most of them had a roof over at least part of the boat to protect some of the cargo from bad weather during the trip.

Conestoga wagons continued to carry freight across America for many years. They were used until railroads crossed the country. The wagon bed was made with both ends higher than the center so that as a wagon went up or down the steep hills, the goods inside would not all slide to one end. Wooden hoops were arched over the wagon bed to hold a canvas cover over the goods. Great red wheels, the front ones smaller than the back, and a sturdy tongue, were attached to the bed, which was often painted blue.

All flatboats were too clumsy to be moved upriver against the current. They were used for downriver travel only, and were steered by means of a big oar at the back of the boat. They usually had a few poles on board to be used for pushing in shallow water. At the end of the journey, the boat was broken apart, and the boards used for lumber.

The boatmen who took flatboats of freight from the upper Ohio down to New Orleans had to walk back home. They usually followed the shore of the Mississippi River as far as Natchez, Mississippi. There they turned to take a shortcut trail through the wilderness, called the *Natchez Trace*. It led to Nashville, Tennessee. Often, robbers were waiting behind trees to take from the boatmen the money they had been paid for their work or for the freight they had sold.

The only freight boat that could be taken back up the river was the *keelboat*. Its building began with the laying of a keel, to which curved braces were attached so that it would have a rounded shape. The finished boat was shaped like a fat cigar. It had a mast above its cargo box with a square sail attached. Once in a while, the sail was of some help in moving the boat along. Mostly, however, its upstream travel depended upon the muscle power of its crewmen. The boatmen either poled it or pulled it with a rope as they walked along the bank of the river.

It took strong men to pull a keelboat upstream. The keelboatmen were proud of how tough they were. They were the "half-horse, half-alligator" men, of whom Mike Fink was the most famous. Sometimes the boats were attacked by river pirates, but the keelboatmen were as tough as any of the pirates who tried to rob the boats.

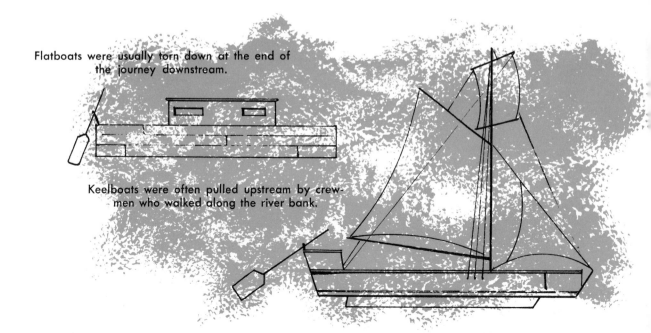

Flatboats were usually torn down at the end of the journey downstream.

Keelboats were often pulled upstream by crewmen who walked along the river bank.

The keelboatmen were the "kings of the river." Since the frontier settlers greatly needed the things carried by the riverboats, it was a good thing for the new nation that it had men equal to the work.

What new states were added to the Union?

Many flatboats were used to take families and all their goods to the frontier settlements along the Ohio River. New towns began to appear, even before the peace treaty with England was signed. When George Rogers Clark finished his work in the winning of the Northwest Territory, he began a settlement on the south bank of the Ohio, near his old training camp. It became the town of Louisville, Kentucky.

Farther up the Ohio, the town of Marietta, Ohio, was begun in 1788. Soon Cincinnati and other towns along the Ohio River were started.

Next, settlers followed the rivers that emptied into the Ohio to take up the land along the smaller rivers, too.

People continued to follow other trails over the mountains, too. The circle of thirteen stars on the field of the first United States flag had to be changed as new states joined the Union. The fourteenth state was Vermont, settled by New Englanders shortly before the War for Independence. Ethan Allen and his "Green Mountain Boys," who helped fight the war, were from the region that became the state of Vermont. Kentucky became the fifteenth state, in 1792. Four years later, Tennessee joined the Union.

For a long time, Ohio had been the home of several Algonkian tribes especially the Shawnee, the Miami, and the Delaware. They were deeply angered when settlers began to take their lands from them.

River transportation helped Americans to settle more and more new states. Keelboats and flatboats were both widely used.

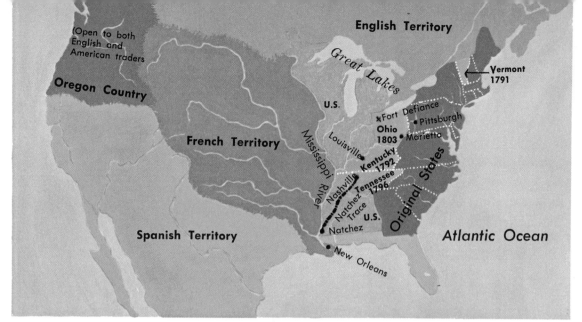

The United States in 1803

Many Indians did not feel that they had to follow treaties signed by the chiefs. American settlers had a way of pushing over treaty lines, too, in spite of being told by the government to stay back. There were many Indian attacks on frontier settlers.

The United States government sent men to forts along the Ohio River to try to keep peace. Finally an army was sent north from Cincinnati to force the Indians back. Twice the army failed to do so. Then in 1793 and 1794, General Anthony Wayne trained an army to try again, taking much more care than had been taken before. They began to move northward up the Miami River, building a fort after each advance. The Indians backed off until they finally met Wayne's men near *Defiance*, in northwestern Ohio. The Indians were badly beaten. They signed a treaty that left all but a small corner of Ohio open to white settlers. Ohio became a state in the year 1803.

How was the Indian's world changing?

The third world in the United States after the War for Independence was that of the Indian. Some tribes lived outwardly much as they had before the coming of people from Europe. The only difference was that now they had a few of the things that the white men had brought.

They had iron pots in which to cook, guns to bring down game or enemies, steel traps for catching beaver, and a place to sell furs. Another thing the Indians now had was the horse. Sometimes the measure of how great an Indian brave was depended upon how well he could steal horses from the white man. The Indians saw no wrong in that, although they had strict rules about property rights within their own tribes.

The great change in the life of the Indian was in his loss of freedom to go wherever he chose. This was the most dangerous change of all, for it caused some of the Indians to think of how things once had been and of how each year the white man pushed farther and farther into Indian land.

Into the hearts of some crept a deep hatred of the people they had once welcomed into the wilderness. Some were deeply unhappy over what was happening to their people. An attack upon the cabin of a white settler was the only way of striking back. It was payment for wrongs done to the Indian, and a warning of more trouble to come.

Words to Know

Conestoga wagons (kŏn′ĕs tō′gȧ wăg′ŭnz) 164

cotton gin (kŏt″n jĭn) 159

Defiance (dė̇ fī ăns) 167

flatboats (flăt′bōts) 164

jerky (jûr′kĭ) 160

keelboat (kēl′bōt′) 165

manufacturing (măn′ů̇ făk′tůr ĭng) 158

Natchez Trace (năch′ĕz trās) 165

subscription school (sŭb skrĭp′shŭn skōōl) 161

Susquehanna (sŭs′kwė̇ hăn ȧ) 161

Questions

1. Where did southern planters sell their cotton crops before the War for Independence? Where did they sell them after the war?

2. Who was Samuel Slater? Eli Whitney? Francis Lowell? How did these men help the business interests of the country?

3. How did the early frontier settlers make a living? Why did their way of making a living change?

4. What kinds of schools were there on the frontier?

5. What was a Conestoga wagon? How was it important to the settlement of the frontier?

6. How were flatboats and keelboats used by the people of the new United States?

You See for Yourself

Be a detective. Find out how the Englishman, Samuel Slater, got to the United States even though it was against the English law for a man who could build machines to leave England.

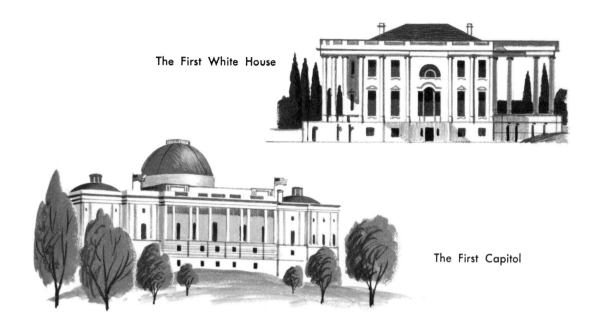

The First White House

The First Capitol

New Lands and New States

As the 1700's ended, and the 1800's began, the young nation entered a period of rapid growth. It grew greatly in size, but it also grew in wealth and trade. The new growth brought the world of the pioneers west of the Appalachians closer to the world of the people along the Atlantic Coast.

Who was President in 1800?

When the year 1800 came, the United States had just lost one of its great leaders, George Washington. Washington had finished his work as President in 1797 and gone home to Mount Vernon, where he died in 1799. John Adams was President after Washington. The White House was not yet finished. It is said that Mrs. John Adams dried the laundry in what is now the beautiful East Room. It was still unplastered in those days.

The *Capitol*, the building in which Congress meets, was ready for use. It was not the same building, however, that is used today.

How did frontier farmers get their products to market?

As it became harder to make a living by hunting on the frontier, more and more frontiersmen became farmers. The result was that the farmers were soon producing more farm products than they could use themselves. They needed a place to sell their extra products, or a *market*. They also needed a way to get their products to the markets where they could sell them.

Many farm products were shipped out of the port of Cincinnati during the early 1800's.

Corn grew especially well in the new land. Some of it was used for food for the farmer's family. Some was fed to hogs. The rest the farmer could sell for *profit*, money left after he had paid all his bills.

Some corn was shipped out as grain, but it did not bring a very good price. The farmers found they could make more money by using their extra corn crops in other ways. Eastern cities and even European cities bought much pork for food. The frontier farmers fed much of their corn to hogs, which they butchered. They then either smoked the meat or salted it in barrels to keep it from spoiling. The meat was then shipped by wagon or flatboat to the markets in the East. So much pork was shipped from Cincinnati that it was sometimes called "Porkopolis."

Another way corn was used was in the making of whiskey. Many, many gallons of whiskey were made on the frontier and used in place of money. A great deal of whiskey was used as trading goods for furs from the Indians, too. This made new problems among the Indians.

Many flatboats loaded with frontier products were sent down the Ohio to the Mississippi and then on to New Orleans. At New Orleans they were loaded onto ocean-going ships. New Orleans and the rest of the old French claims west of the Mississippi belonged to Spain, but they were open to Americans.

How did the United States get the port of New Orleans?

Thomas Jefferson became the third President of the United States in 1801. At that time, the French government was in the hands of *Napoleon Bonaparte,* who wanted to conquer as many countries in Europe as he could. The Spanish government gave Spain's land in America to Napoleon. Jefferson could see that this change of power might cause trouble for American shipping through the port of New Orleans. Jefferson made plans to get control of the mouth of the Mississippi and the New Orleans port.

Jefferson sent a message to Robert Livingston, the American representative in France, to offer to buy New Orleans from Napoleon. Congress had voted to spend two million dollars for this city and the land around it.

Napoleon was not interested in selling the mouth of the Mississippi. He offered, instead, to sell the United States the whole Louisiana Territory for a price of fifteen million dollars. The *Louisiana Territory* included the huge amount of land west of the Mississippi River as well as the mouth of the Mississippi.

The United States was not yet thirty years old and still had more land than its people could use. The huge Louisiana Territory would make it twice as big as it was. No one even knew what that part of the country was like.

Buying the Louisiana Territory would also mean that about 50,000 more people would be added to the United States' population, including many Indians.

Exploration of the Louisiana Territory

Columbia River
Missouri River
Mississippi River
Louisiana Territory
N

Pike Expedition ....
Lewis and Clark – – – –
Lewis's Return – – – –
Clark's Return – – – –

Spanish Territory

A few Americans had gone to live in the Louisiana Territory under the Spanish government, which was giving large sections of land to settlers. These were known as Spanish land grants. Most of the people lived in the area that is the state of Missouri today. Daniel Boone and his family had moved there to live.

President Jefferson could find nothing in the Constitution giving him the power to buy all that land. But his advisers told him he should not let this chance slip through his fingers. They said he should sign the papers before Napoleon sent further word that he had changed his mind. President Jefferson signed, and in 1803, the Louisiana Territory became part of the United States.

Who explored the Louisiana Territory for the United States?

President Jefferson sent two young men, Meriweather Lewis and William Clark, to lead an exploring party to find the starting point of the Missouri River. William Clark was the younger brother of George Rogers Clark.

Lewis and Clark were to make maps; keep notes of what the land was like, the animal and plant life found there; and look for minerals. If possible, they were to go even farther than the starting point, or source, of the Missouri to find a certain river that led to the Pacific. Americans had learned of such a river through the reports of fur traders in that part of the country. It was the Columbia River, that flows through the Pacific northwest region of the United States and the southwestern corner of Canada.

Lewis and Clark started their trip up the Missouri River from St. Louis in May of 1804. In their party were twenty-one soldiers, nine young Kentuckians, eleven boatmen, a man who could speak many of the Indian languages, and Clark's servant. For much of the journey, the boatmen had to walk along the shore, pulling the big keelboat against the strong currents of the Missouri River.

By the start of winter, the explorers reached the Mandan Indian villages in the present state of North Dakota. They spent the winter there. When spring came, Lewis and Clark sent seven soldiers and nine boatmen back down the Missouri with the keelboat. They took with them Lewis and Clark's report, for President Jefferson, of their journey so far.

Lewis and Clark set out again in April. They continued up the Missouri River in smaller boats and Indian canoes. With them were a man named Charbonneau and his Indian wife, whom they had met and hired at the Mandan villages. The Indian woman's name was Sacajawea, which means "Bird Woman." She had been captured and taken from her own tribe, the Shoshones of the northwest, when she was just a girl.

Lewis and Clark started up the Missouri River from St. Louis in a large keelboat.

Since Lewis and Clark planned to go into the land of the Shoshones, they knew Sacajawea's knowledge of the language and country would be useful to them.

By the end of June, they had reached the source of the Missouri, one of the points they had set out to find. The explorers left their boats and canoes at the source of the Missouri, and set out on foot to look for the Columbia River. They needed horses, and hoped to buy some from the Shoshone Indians, whose country they had now reached. It was here, that Sacajawea, who had already proved to be the most useful person in the party, was of greatest service.

When the men sighted a group of Shoshones, it seemed they were planning an attack rather than a friend-ly meeting. But Sacajawea ran forward to meet the chief. He was her own brother, whom she had not seen since the day she was captured. She explained that the men came in peace and helped Lewis and Clark to get the horses they needed so badly.

Lewis and Clark found guides at a Mandan Indian village.

With the help of Sacajawea, Lewis and Clark found the Columbia River.

Soon afterward, with the help of the Indians, Lewis and Clark found the Columbia River. They followed its course and reached the Pacific Ocean in November of 1805.

In September of 1806, Lewis and Clark were back in St. Louis with much to tell about their adventures and the lands they had seen.

Where did Pike explore?

A young army officer named *Zebulon Pike* also helped to explore the new western lands about the same time as Lewis and Clark made their journey. Pike followed the Arkansas River to the Rocky Mountains. He and his men reached the mountain which was named for him, but they did not climb it. Winter was coming on, so the men had to head southward. Pike found the source of the Rio Grande. This river flowed into the Gulf of Mexico, so its shores could not be claimed as part of the Louisiana Territory. Pike's homeward journey was through Spanish land.

These explorers made known the general size and shape of the great Louisiana Territory. Yet, there were many parts of the plains and the Rocky Mountains that would not be explored or mapped for many years to come. Much of the later exploring was done by the hunters and trappers who soon swarmed into the new west to find game and adventure.

Who followed the trails westward?

Stories about the new western lands excited many of the American people. Many a young man headed toward St. Louis to outfit himself as a hunter or trapper and then set out for the Rocky Mountains.

The American frontier was moving farther and farther west. As with the earlier frontiers, first came the traders, hunters and trappers, and then the settlers.

Two of Daniel Boone's sons opened a road from St. Charles, Missouri, that reached westward for 150 miles. It was known as *Boone's Lick Road.* Settlers soon followed this road. A town named Franklin was begun on the banks of the Missouri River.

One of the families that settled in the area was named Carson. One son, named Christopher, but better known as Kit, became a very famous fur trapper, scout, and explorer. Kit's first trip to the west was along the *Santa Fe Trail*, which began in Franklin, Missouri, and reached all the way to Santa Fe, a Mexican city during those years.

Travelers across the grasslands of the Great Plains called this area "The Great American Desert." For years, people believed it to be useless land.

Fur companies built trading posts on the Missouri River and bought furs from Indians.

Beginning in 1821, the Santa Fe Trail was traveled by many traders with pack trains and wagons. They took American goods, brought to Franklin by steamboat, farther west. They traded for Mexican-Spanish silver dollars or for the sure-footed and strong mules needed for hauling more goods.

Travelers on the Santa Fe Trail saw the grasslands of the Great Plains, but for many years no one thought of them as possible farming land. People called the land the "Great American Desert" for many years. This "desert" covered the eastern parts of the present states of Colorado, Wyoming, and New Mexico; and the western parts of North Dakota, South Dakota, Nebraska, Kansas, Oklahoma, and Texas.

Keelboats began journeying far up the Missouri River as soon as the Lewis and Clark journey ended. The boats belonged to St. Louis fur-trading companies. Small fort-like trading posts were built along the Missouri River and its larger branch rivers. Traders on duty at these posts bought furs from hunters.

Rivers and Trails Leading West

Great Plains

Santa Fe Trail

Boone's Lick Road

State Lines

Missouri River

Mississippi River

Platte River

Illinois

Independence

Franklin

St. Louis

Missouri

Ky.

Tenn.

Arkansas River

Mississippi

Louisiana

Santa Fe

When did Missouri and Louisiana join the Union?

With the port of New Orleans in American hands, shipping out of the city grew to even greater importance. The main products that passed through it were the grain and pork from the Ohio valley and the furs, lead, and salt from the land farther west. Soon, enough people had moved to the area to form the state of Louisiana. It joined the Union in 1812.

St. Louis and many new settlements along the rivers of Missouri were growing, too. The state of Missouri joined the Union in 1820. It was the first state that lay entirely west of the Mississippi River.

Words to Know

Boone's Lick Road (bōōnz lĭk rōd) 175

Capitol (kăp'ĭ tŏl) 169

Charbonneau (shär'bŏn nō') 172

Columbia (kȯ lŭm'bĭ a̍) 172

Louisiana Territory (lŏo'ĭ zĭ ăn'a̍ tĕr'ĭ tō'rĭ) 171

market (mär'kĕt) 169

Napoleon Bonaparte (na̍ pō'lḛ̆n bō'na̍ pärt) 171

profit (prŏf'ĭt) 170

Sacajawea (săk'a̍ ja̍ wē'a̍) 172

Santa Fe Trail (săn'ta̍ fā trāl) 175

source (sōrs) 172

Zebulon Pike (zĕb'ṷ lŭn pīk) 174

Questions

1. Who was the second President of the United States?

2. Tell two ways the farmers of the Ohio Valley frontier used their extra corn to make money.

3. By what route were farm products from the Ohio Valley sent to market?

4. Why did President Jefferson want to buy New Orleans?

5. What two things were Lewis and Clark to look for as they explored the Louisiana Territory?

You See for Yourself

Look at a map of the United States. In which direction did the frontier move? How does nature seem to separate the Louisiana Territory from the Pacific Coast? Look up the "Great Divide" in an encyclopedia. Point to where you think the Great Divide is on your map of the United States.

Troubled Times Again

One of the important needs of the new United States was to build up trade with other nations. This meant that American sailing ships had to carry goods across the oceans, mainly to Europe.

During the first years of the 1800's, England needed a strong navy to hold off the powerful Napoleon. A strong navy needs many men. When there were not enough sailors willing to work on ships, men were sometimes captured and then forced to work on a ship. This is called *impressment* of seamen. Sometimes American men were impressed into the English navy.

Sometimes English sailors escaped from their own ships and looked for work on American ships. American sea captains often hired them.

Trouble over impressment of seamen led to battles between the Americans and the English.

What was the Embargo Act?

One day in 1807, an English ship fired upon an American ship, the *Chesapeake*, because there were English sailors on board it working as members of the American ship's crew. President Jefferson felt the English should be punished. He knew that English factories greatly needed American cotton. American grain and tobacco were also wanted, in other European countries as well as England. He decided to punish England by stopping trade. He ordered all American ships to stay away from foreign ports. This was called the *Embargo Act.*

Not being able to trade with other countries caused American businessmen as well as English to lose money. Jefferson saw this, so he lifted the embargo from all countries except England. This made England very angry. English and American ships often attacked each other at sea.

Francis Scott Key wrote the words to "The Star Spangled Banner."

How did troubles start on the frontier?

The Indians were becoming more and more restless as white settlers pushed them farther and farther back, especially in the Northwest Territory. The chief known as *Tecumseh* urged the tribes to work together as Pontiac had done.

Tecumseh and his brother, *The Prophet*, began getting an army together. Their headquarters were at *Tippecanoe* Creek, in northern Indiana. But the territorial governor, William Henry Harrison, heard of the gathering army. He led an attack against it while Tecumseh was away. The Battle of Tippecanoe went badly for the Indians, and they were forced to move farther west.

How did war with England start?

The Americans learned that many of the guns and knives used by the Indians in their attacks upon white settlers were English-made. They were sure the English were urging the Indians to make many attacks.

Congress declared war on England in 1812. Tecumseh and his Indians joined the English against the Americans. Hope again rose in the heart of the Indian leader. But before the war was over, Governor Harrison's men had pushed both Indians and English into Canada.

Important battles were fought on both Lake Erie and Lake Champlain. The Americans won the victory at both places.

English ships, however, moved into Chesapeake Bay and captured Washington, D. C. They set fire to the Captitol and the White House. President James Madison, who had taken office just before the beginning of the war, had to flee the city. British ships moved into the bay to take Baltimore.

Baltimore was ready, and able to hold out against the attack. While the firing went on, an American prisoner on an English ship in the harbor, saw at dawn that the American flag was still flying over Fort McHenry at Baltimore. The prisoner was Francis Scott Key, and it was then that he wrote the words of "The Star Spangled Banner."

The third point of attack was at New Orleans, where Andrew Jackson became a hero. Jackson was from Tennessee. He had fought Indians in the South for many years, with the help of such frontiersmen as Davy Crocket. Jackson and his men fought bravely at New Orleans and many were killed. But New Orleans stayed in American hands. The men who died at the Battle of New Orleans in January of 1815, could have lived if communication had been faster. They did not know that two weeks earlier the peace treaty had been signed and the war was over.

The United States did not gain any new lands through the War of 1812. But there have never been any attacks on the border between Canada and the United States since then.

The main result of the War of 1812 was that the nations of Europe did not look down upon the United States any more. They had thought that the young country would not last long, but the war changed their ideas about America.

Words to Know

Embargo Act (ĕm bär′gō ăct) 178

impressment (ĭm prĕs′mĕnt) 178

Tecumseh (tḛ kŭm′sĕ) 179

The Prophet (thē prŏf′ĕt) 179

Tippecanoe (tĭp′ḛ kȧ nōo′) 179

Questions

1. What is meant by the "impressment" of seamen? How did this become a cause for anger in the United States during the 1800's?

2. How did Jefferson punish the English for firing on the American ship, *Chesapeake?* In what way was his plan bad for Americans? How did he change his plan later?

3. Who was Tecumseh? At what battle was his army defeated?

4. Who wrote the "Star Spangled Banner?" Where was he when he wrote it?

5. Why should the Battle of New Orleans never have been fought?

You See for Yourself

Read about Commodore Oliver Perry's battle with the English on Lake Erie. What famous words were written on the flag of Perry's ship?

Study carefully the words of the first stanza of the "Star Spangled Banner." How do the words tell about the battle that Francis Scott Key watched while he was on the English ship?

A Nation from Sea to Sea

The purchase of Louisiana from France doubled the size of the United States. Yet at the end of the War of 1812, there was still much land claimed by England and Spain west and north of the Louisiana Territory.

The northern boundary of the United States west of the Great Lakes had never been really clear. After the War of 1812, the United States and England agreed on the line that still today separates Canada from the United States.

West of the Louisiana Territory was a large territory called the "Oregon country." The *Oregon* country reached westward to the Pacific Ocean, northward to Alaska, and southward to the lands still claimed by Spain. Both the United States and England claimed to own this land. Nothing final was decided about the Oregon country after the War of 1812. For the time being, it was simply agreed that both American and English fur traders should be allowed in the Oregon country.

How did Florida become United States territory?

Florida, still claimed by Spain, was the only land east of the Mississippi River that was not owned by the United States. Spain was having so much trouble with her Mexican and South American colonies that she did not pay much attention to Florida. As a result, Florida became a hiding place for such persons as criminals, runaway slaves, and Indians. These people sometimes banded together and made attacks upon American settlers to the north.

In 1817, President James Monroe sent Andrew Jackson and troops to the Florida border to stop these attacks. Jackson was not supposed to enter Florida itself since it was Spanish land, but he did so anyway. He had a number of people including French and English citizens put to death. This angered both Spain and England. The best way to settle the problem seemed to be to buy Florida from Spain. The United States bought Florida in 1819.

What was the Lone Star Republic?

Many Americans had gone to live in Texas even though it belonged to Spain. In 1821, Mexico won its freedom from Spain, so Texas became Mexican territory.

Moses Austin, from Missouri, and his son Stephen led many Americans to Texas. By 1827, 12,000 Americans had settled in Texas, including many cotton growers with slaves.

That same year, the Mexican government passed a law that there could be no slavery in Mexico.

The Texas-Americans decided to break away from Mexico and to become an independent state. The Mexican General Santa Anna marched against Texas with an army of 7,000 men. Near San Antonio was an old mission which had been made into a fortress called the *Alamo*. One-hundred-eighty Americans met Santa Anna at the Alamo. All the American men were killed, including such famous frontiersmen as Davy Crockett and Jim Bowie.

It looked as if Texas would have to bow down to Santa Anna, for he swept through the land, meeting no army strong enough to stop him. Finally, in 1836, a Texas army surprised his men while they slept and defeated them.

The Republic of Texas was formed. Sam Houston, who had led the surprise attack, was the Texas president. Texas became the *Lone Star Republic*, with a flag like that of the United States except that only one star was in the field of blue. The Lone Star Republic lasted until 1845, the year Texas entered the Union as the twenty-eighth state.

When was the Oregon Territory added to the United States?

Even though the ownership of the Oregon country was uncertain, many Americans went there to live. The first American settlement west of the Rockies was in Oregon, at *Astoria*, near the mouth of the Columbia River. There John Jacob Astor, a fur trader, built a trading post in 1811.

Marcus Whitman and his wife made the difficult journey to Oregon in 1836, and opened a mission there. The first wagon train of settlers arrived to live near his mission in the year 1843. By 1845, 5,000 American settlers lived in Oregon.

In 1846, the question of who owned Oregon was finally settled. England suggested that the border line west of the Great Lakes be lengthened all the way to the Pacific Ocean. The United States agreed to this plan, and the Oregon country south of this line was added to the United States.

In the same year, a religious group known as the "Mormons" began a settlement south of the Oregon Territory. Led by Brigham Young, they settled near the Great Salt Lake in the present state of Utah.

How did the United States gain the Mexican lands of the southwest?

In the same year that Texas joined the Union, the United States went to war with Mexico. The Mexican government felt that the United States had no right to Texas.

At the end of the war in 1848, the United States had again grown greatly in size. All the land now in the states of California, Nevada, Utah, Arizona, and New Mexico was won for the United States, except for a section along the Gila River. This land was bought in 1853.

1846
Oregon Country

1848
Mexican Cession

1853
Gadsden
Purchase

1803
Louisiana Purchase

1845
Texas Annexation

1783
Original Lands
after
War for Independence

1819
Florida Purchase

American Land Holdings in 1853

The United States, except for Alaska and Hawaii, had reached the size and shape it is today, extending from the Atlantic to the Pacific Ocean.

How were the new western lands settled?

All during the years that the United States was adding new territories, wagon trains of settlers were streaming farther and farther west. The town of Independence, Missouri, became the main starting point for settlers going west. Here the travelers bought wagons and supplies needed for their trip.

Steamboats brought load after load of supplies as well as travelers to the landings around present-day Kansas City. Missouri was like the neck of a funnel through which people from all over eastern United States poured to spread out along the trails to lands in the west.

What was the California Gold Rush?

In January of 1848, gold was found on the land of a California settler named John Sutter. Sutter tried to keep the discovery a secret, but the news soon leaked out. That summer, Sutter found his land overrun with people from all over California. Even sailors on ships in the harbors left their ships to go gold-hunting.

The word reached the eastern section of the country, too. By the spring of 1849, wagon trains were forming so fast near Kansas City, Independence, and St. Joseph, Missouri, that the workers and store owners could not keep up with the demand for supplies.

The gold seekers formed an almost unbroken line of wagons over all the known trails to California.

Between 1849 and 1851, the hillsides and valleys of California were heavily spotted with the diggings of miners. Many people found much gold. Others found that it was hard work to find even enough gold to pay for their daily needs. The little village at the Golden Gate became the busy city of San Francisco. Other towns sprang up, too.

When the gold mining had slowed down a bit, California's other businesses, especially farming, kept many people there. Wagon trains continued to take people westward.

As the 1850's began, the Great Plains were still mainly unsettled. But the far west had become an important part of the United States. Distance separated its people from the states in the East. Communication and transportation between them were very slow.

Words to Know

Alamo (ăl′à mō) 182

Astoria (ăs tōr′ĭ à) 182

Lone Star Republic (lōn stär rĕ pŭb′ lĭk) 182

Oregon (ŏr′ĕ gŭn) 181

Questions

1. When was the northern boundary line of the land west of the Great Lakes decided?

2. Why did the United States place troops along the Florida border in 1817? How did Florida become part of the United States?

3. Why did the Texas-Americans decide to become independent?

4. Who was Marcus Whitman?

5. What was the name of the group of settlers led to the west by Brigham Young?

6. What land did the United States gain through war with Mexico?

7. Of what importance was the town of Independence in the settling of western lands?

8. During what three years did many people stream to California to look for gold?

You See for Yourself

Learn more about the frontiersmen, Davy Crockett and Jim Bowie, by reading encyclopedias or other books in your library. Which man was sent to Congress? Which man is said to have invented a useful frontier weapon?

Now You Know

In 1789, the new government went to work under the Constitution. The Thirteen States were united under a strong federal government, yet they kept many of the rights they had always had before the Constitution.

The people of the country pushed farther and farther west across the Appalachian Mountains to settle in Kentucky, Tennessee, and the Ohio River Valley. Even before the government bought the Louisiana Territory, Americans had pushed across the Mississippi River and begun settlement in Texas and Missouri.

In 1812, the new nation was back at war with England, proving its strength to the whole world.

Soon after this war, the United States bought Florida from Spain, making all the land east of the Mississippi United States territory.

Between the years of 1845 and 1853, the United States added the rest of the western lands to her territory. First came Texas, the Lone Star Republic. A year later, through an agreement with England, part of the Oregon country was added.

At the end of the war with Mexico, California and most of the land that now makes up the southwestern states were added to the country. Another small section was added some time later. The new country had grown from sea to sea.

You Talk It Over

You have learned that President Thomas Jefferson was uncertain about his right to buy land in the name of the government. How do you think the future of our country might have been changed if Jefferson had decided not to buy the Louisiana Territory? Did the government buy any other land in later years?

According to what you have learned about democracy in this unit, what part do all the people play in the government of the United States? Do you think people would be happier living under this kind of government or one in which the government was controlled by one person or one group of persons?

Unit Questions

1. What is the federal government?

2. Why did some members of the Congress of the Confederation feel that slavery should be against the law in the United States? How did this belief influence their plans for the Northwest Territory?

3. Describe the meeting at which the Constitution was written. Name four men who attended.

4. How are personal rights of citizens protected by the Constitution?

5. Why did southern plantation owners begin growing more cotton shortly before the War for Independence? Where did they sell their cotton after the war?

6. How was the growth of cities different in the northern and in the southern states along the Atlantic Coast?

7. How did people living on the frontier west of the Appalachian Mountains get supplies?

8. On what two large rivers were flatboats used for travel and transportation? Between what two cities did they often travel?

9. What was done with flatboats at the end of a journey? How were keelboats taken back up the river at the end of a journey?

10. How did General Anthony Wayne help the settlers of Ohio?

11. From what country did the United States buy the Louisiana Territory? In what year was this? Who was President at the time?

12. Name three explorers who made the land of the Louisiana Territory known to the Americans.

13. Why did an English ship fire on the American ship *Chesapeake?* What did President Jefferson do to punish the English for this act?

14. How did the United States add Florida to its territory? In what year was this?

Puzzlers

Write the letters A through J on a piece of paper. Find all these letters on the map. Then look at the pictures at the bottom of the page. Match the number of each picture with a letter on the map to show in what section of the new United States you might have seen what the picture shows.

Unit Activities

You Learn a Folk Dance

Dancing was a popular form of fun among the early Americans. One famous dance was the Virginia Reel. With the help of your teacher, learn to dance the Virginia Reel. For music, you may have someone play the piano or use a recording.

You Draw a Wall Frieze

Use a long sheet of wrapping paper and colored chalk to draw a wall frieze that shows the journey an Illinois family makes from their frontier cabin to a new home in California during the 1850's. Divide the strip of paper into eight sections. The first section should be a map that shows the route the family takes. The other seven sections will show drawings of different parts of the trip. Begin the series by showing the family packing their household goods. Next, show their journey to Independence either by flatboat or by steamboat, buying supplies and a wagon at Independence, starting out with a wagon train, camping with others from the train, and going through a mountain pass. Finally, show the family building their new home in California. If you like, you might add more excitement to the journey by showing the wagon train crossing a swift, dangerous stream or having Indian trouble.

You Make a Map

As a class project, plan and make a map of the United States from the Atlantic Coast to the Pacific Coast showing the different kinds of land and the important lakes and rivers.

Begin by drawing a map on a large sheet of stiff paper or pasteboard. On this map, mark off the different regions you are going to show. For example, draw in the coastal plains along the Atlantic Ocean and along the Gulf of Mexico. Mark off the inland plains and the mountain areas. Show the Great Lakes and the Great Salt Lake. Ask your teacher to check your work as you mark off each region.

When you have finished drawing in correctly all the regions, make a thick flour-and-water mixture. Use food coloring to add different colors of this mixture. Then cover each type of land with a different color. You will be able to use this mixture to show the mountains as higher and rougher than other regions. You will want to smooth it out to show the plains. Add small trees and little tufts of paper grass to show which of the plains regions were wooded and which were mostly grasslands in the early days of settlement. You could

use blue yarn or ribbon to make the routes of the rivers. Or, if you wish, use blue paint to show the rivers. Be sure that your paint is thick enough so that it does not cause the flour-and-water mixture to "run."

You Learn about Your Community

Find out what your community was like during the 1850's. There may be books in your library to help you. Perhaps you know an adult who has made a study of your community and its growth. Make a report on what you have learned, using pictures or interesting items to illustrate your talk.

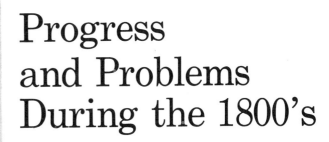

Progress
and Problems
During the 1800's

During the years the United States was growing so greatly in size, other changes, too, were taking place. One important change was in the land between the Appalachian Mountains and the Mississippi River.

The nation's problems changed, too. Serious difficulties arose when people with different interests tried to live together as a nation. Before these problems were smoothed out, the one nation almost split into two separate nations.

Improvements and inventions in transportation and communication brought many changes to the nation. Americans had much to look back on by the time the United States was one hundred years old.

American settlers pushed farther and farther into western lands. The years brought many new changes and some new problems.

Communities west of the Appalachian Mountains quickly took on a settled look.

Inventions Help Build the Country

Frontier ways disappeared rapidly in the land between the Appalachian Mountains and the Mississippi River. People who wanted to live the life of a pioneer in untamed lands had to look farther west, across the Mississippi River. The Indians, too, were pushed steadily westward. The separate worlds of the Indian and the pioneer steadily gave way to the settled American, whose world was growing more widespread.

Lone cabins in the wilderness clearings were replaced by larger houses, new barns, and acres of land cleared for farming. Tiny frontier communities grew into towns or cities. Iron and coal mines were opened. Shops and factories appeared in the towns.

In time, the farms, mines, and factories produced more goods than the people of the community could use. There were more and more products to sell to other communities and to other countries. Trade grew quickly.

What new inventions helped the farmers?

Raising grain, especially wheat, had always been hard work. A farmer first had to plow the field with a poor kind of plow, often made of wood. An iron-tipped plowshare came into use early in the 1800's. The *plowshare* is the part that cuts into the ground. Before long, manufacturers were making better and better iron plows as well as other tools that were of great help to the American farmers.

The slowest and most tiresome job of the farmer was the *harvesting*, or the gathering in of ripened grain. In the early days, grain stems had to be cut by hand, by a person swinging a *scythe* or a *sickle*. These tools are sharp-bladed knives with long handles. After the grain stalks were brought in from the field, the grain itself, which is the seed of the plant, had to be separated from the stalks. This, too, was hard work.

In 1834, there came an invention that greatly eased the work of harvesting grain. Several men had tried to invent a machine that would cut grain in the field and gather stalks into bundles. It was a Virginian named *Cyrus McCormick* who first succeeded in producing such a machine. It was called a *reaper*. The McCormick reaper made quick work of the back-breaking job of cutting grain. Farmers were able to grow much more wheat than ever before.

South of the Ohio River, cotton became almost the only crop grown. The demand for cotton became great because of the growing number of northern cotton mills, in which new machines were being used. As the Indians were forced off the lands in the South, cotton growers cleared fields in Alabama, Tennessee, Mississippi, Louisiana, Arkansas, and later Texas. These states were often called the *Cotton Kingdom*. Cotton became the most important product shipped out of New Orleans.

Early wheat farmers had to harvest their crops with hand tools.

The invention of the reaper greatly cut down the work in harvesting wheat.

Later improvements in the reaper brought even greater changes in wheat harvesting.

How did steam power improve water transportation?

New Orleans and the other seaports, river ports, and lake ports could move the products of the nation only as fast as ships and boats could carry them. On the ocean, the only ships in use during the early 1800's were ships powered by wind and sails. The clipper ship was the fastest of the sailing ships. Many of these were used to carry on trade with other countries. Yet it was a long, long journey across an ocean.

In 1838, the first ship powered by steam crossed the Atlantic Ocean. Steamships cut the trip across the Atlantic to fifteen days.

Steamships were used inland, on the lakes and rivers even earlier than 1838. The inventor, Robert Fulton, proved as early as 1807 that steam engines were powerful enough to move boats upriver against strong currents. People laughed at Fulton when he first took his steamboat, the *Clermont*, up the Hudson River. They called the boat "Fulton's Folly." But these people had to change their minds, for Fulton soon had a number of steamboats carrying goods and people on most of the deep rivers in the eastern states.

Fulton saw that businessmen needed steamboats on the rivers farther west, too. In 1811, he directed the building of a steamboat called the *New Orleans*. The *New Orleans* was built at Pittsburgh. It was to carry passengers and freight up and down the Ohio and Mississippi rivers. Late in the year, the people of the Ohio River towns were startled by the sound of the hissing and clanking engines of the *New Orleans*, making its first trip from Pittsburgh to New Orleans. The steamboat stopped at Cincinnati and at Louisville. At both towns, it made short trips upstream against the current.

The New Orleans showed the crowds that steamships could travel against the current of the river as well as with it.

Steamboats replaced keelboats on the rivers.

Deep water steamboats were on the Great Lakes.

Leaving Louisville, the *New Orleans* headed for the Mississippi River. Just as the ship neared the meeting point of the Ohio and Mississippi, a great earthquake took place. The earthquake felled trees, crumbled the banks of the river, and even moved the bed of the river in many places. The crew and passengers of the *New Orleans* were greatly frightened, but they kept on going.

The ship reached the city of New Orleans early in January of 1812. After a stay at the city, the *New Orleans* started the return trip up the Mississippi. But it went only as far as Natchez, Mississippi. Its engines were not powerful enough to pull the boat against the strong currents.

The *New Orleans* pointed the way for water transportation in the years that followed. Steamboats were rapidly improved so that they were able to go up both the Ohio and the powerful Mississippi. The Missouri River, with its muddy waters and dangerous sand bars, was more of a problem to steamboat travel at first.

A special kind of steamboat that could replace the keelboat on the Missouri was built, and the first one reached Franklin, Missouri, in 1819. Before many more years passed, steamboats were making trips up the Missouri to the fur-trading posts and bringing back loads of furs.

The big, double-decked river steamboats were making regular trips up and down both the Mississippi and the Ohio by 1819. New Orleans, St. Louis, Memphis, Louisville, and Cincinnati became busy and important shipping points. Business grew bigger and bigger. Steamboats were lined up along the docks to unload, load, and move out again.

On the Great Lakes, deep water steamboats helped in the growth of cities along the shores of the lakes. The new towns of Cleveland, Ohio; Toledo, Ohio; and Chicago, Illinois; grew rapidly. Older towns, such as Buffalo, New York, and Detroit, Michigan, grew in size and importance, also.

How did canals aid the growth of good transportation?

With the use of steamboats, water travel seemed to be the best answer to the young nation's transportation problem. The only trouble was that there were not always rivers or lakes in the places where they were needed. One way to meet this difficulty, was to dig canals where there were no rivers.

The first American canals were dug during colonial days, but none of these was more than thirty miles long. Then Governor DeWitt Clinton of New York began work on an idea that would make it possible for goods to be shipped by water all the way from New York City to Buffalo. From Buffalo, the goods could be taken on to the Ohio cities of Cleveland and Toledo on Lake Erie. Governor Clinton wanted to dig a great canal, 363 miles long, that would reach westward from the Hudson River, across New York State, to Buffalo, on Lake Erie.

Just as people had made fun of Fulton's steamboat, so again they laughed at the Governor's idea. "Clinton's Ditch" was the name they gave to the canal as work was begun. Hundreds of men worked on the canal. They used horses and mules to pull iron scoops shaped like giant shovels. They used hand shovels and wheelbarrows, too, when they were needed. The ridges and hills of New York State made it necessary to build locks in many places. *Locks* are a kind of water stairway that can lower or raise boats in the water.

One day in 1825, the first boat to travel the full length of the canal floated away from the city of Buffalo. The boat was decorated with many flowers to celebrate the event. It had no engine, for canalboats were pulled by horses or mules. The animals were driven along a path, called the *towpath*. The towpath was built along the edge of the canal. Lines led from the boat to the team of animals.

Horses and mules were used to pull the canalboats along the many canals built from rivers to towns or cities which did not have other water transportation.

Canal and Steamship Lines

The canal begun by Governor Clinton was called the *Erie Canal*. There was soon enough traffic on it to prove that it was certainly no joke. The boats that traveled it went only about five miles per hour. But it was the best form of transportation of its day to connect steamboat lines.

The next step in canal-building was to connect the cities along Lake Erie with the cities along the Ohio River. Enough canals were dug so that goods could be floated all the way from Toledo or Cleveland to any city on the Ohio or Mississippi River. It became cheaper to ship goods from New York City to Pittsburgh by way of the canals and the Ohio River than to send them overland in freight wagons. In addition to the main canals, many shorter ones were connected to them so that inland towns became canal ports and trading centers.

With the canals as connecting links, the inland cities had a complete network of water transportation. Lake steamers, in summer, could go all the way from Buffalo to Chicago. Chicago was in fine farming country. The city's leaders saw that if they could build up good transportation, the city could become an important trading center. They changed the flow of the Chicago River to make it flow out of Lake Michigan instead of into it. Then they connected the river with other rivers flowing into the Illinois River by means of a canal. The Illinois River flowed into the Mississippi River. Using this network, it was possible to travel by water from Buffalo to New Orleans.

What kinds of roads were built?

Land travel in the years between 1820 and 1840 still depended largely upon the horse. Freight wagons, small farm wagons, stage coaches, and single riders on horseback continued to carry goods, people, and mail as they had done for years. The only change that took place in land travel was in the building of roads.

At first, roadbuilding meant only the widening of a trail. Tree stumps and large rocks were left in the roadway. Carriages and wagons either straddled the stumps and rocks or rolled over them with their wheels. Ruts, formed when the road was muddy, added to the roughness of the roads. During a long period of dry weather, the roads were dusty.

Here and there, the especially busy roads were paved. A man named McAdam found a way in which crushed stone could be used to make a road that would pack into a hard surface. It drained well in wet weather, too. Roads paved in this way were called *macadam* roads.

Sometimes a road was covered with planks that were laid on logs placed lengthwise along the sides of the road. During a rainy season, the planks and logs often sank deep into the mud. After a year or two, they almost always began to rot.

A quick way to build a covered road or to lay a bridge over a small stream was to cut down young trees and lay the logs crosswise on the ground. This was called a *corduroy* road. It gave travelers in coaches and carriages a very bumpy ride. These roads were also dangerous for the horse, who could easily break a leg by stepping between the logs.

The macadam roads were the best by far, but they were very costly to build. It was a long time before macadam roads were built between even the main cities.

Plank roads would soon rot.

Corduroy roads were very rough.

Sometimes businessmen would build a good paved road and then charge travelers who wanted to use it. To keep people from using the road without paying, they put up gates at the ends of the road. The gates had sharp points or "pikes" on top. After the traveler had paid his money, the pike gates were turned aside to let him pass through. The name *turnpike* began to be used for such roads.

One of the first turnpikes in America was the Lancaster Turnpike, built in 1790. It was a macadam road that connected Philadelphia and Lancaster, Pennsylvania. It was still used in the 1800's.

When James Madison was President, the federal government entered the roadbuilding business. The old army road going westward from Cumberland, Maryland, was to be improved and lengthened to reach the Ohio River at Wheeling, West Virginia. At Wheeling, travelers would be able to cross the Ohio River on a ferryboat. They could then continue their journey across Ohio, where the road stretched almost straight west to Zanesville.

This road later became part of the *National Road*. By 1852, the National Road stretched 591 miles from Cumberland, Maryland, to Vandalia, Illinois.

Travelers stopped at a gate to pay a fee for using a turnpike road.

Horse-drawn wagons or coaches were used on the first railroads in America.

When did railroads come into use?

During the years that canals were being built and a few roads were being paved, there was a group of people working on a different transportation idea. They felt their idea would give the country far better transportation than either rivers or roads. These were the people who were trying to find a way to pull wagons over rails with a locomotive.

The first "railroads" in the United States were laid to make it easier for a horse to pull a heavy load. There was, for example, a thirteen-mile railroad between Baltimore and Ellicott's Mills in Maryland. A wagon was set on the rails, and a horse, running between the rails, could pull a wagon very fast.

Just as many people had laughed at Fulton's idea of using steam engines in ships, so many people laughed at the idea of steam locomotives on the railroads. Yet many inventors worked hard at trying to produce a locomotive.

One day, in 1830, an unusual race took place on the little railroad between Baltimore and Ellicott's Mills. An inventor named Peter Cooper was going to test a steam locomotive he had made. He called his machine the *Tom Thumb*.

The locomotives of a hundred years ago were much different from those of today.

The *Tom Thumb* was to pull a wagonload of passengers. On a set of rails next to those used by the *Tom Thumb*, a horse was also to pull a wagonload of passengers. The horse and the locomotive were to race the thirteen miles from Ellicott's Mills to Baltimore.

The horse got off to a faster start than the locomotive. As the steam engine built up its power, however, it picked up speed. The *Tom Thumb* soon pulled ahead of the horse. It looked as if the *Tom Thumb* would easily win the race. But a belt broke on the machinery and the locomotive had to stop for repairs. In the meantime, the horse-pulled car passed by on the other track and won the race.

Even though the *Tom Thumb* lost a race, it still proved that steam power was faster than horsepower. More people began to believe that when the steam locomotive was improved, it could take over much of the work of the horse and do an even better job. In December of that same year, the locomotive *Best Friend* was used regularly to pull passenger cars on a short line into and out of Charleston, South Carolina.

It cost a great deal of money to build railroads, so the first ones were only short lines. These often ran from cities to nearby factories or mills where people from the cities went to work each day. Little by little, better locomotives were built and rails were laid over longer distances.

The rails in those days were made of hardwood. A thin strap of iron was fastened on the top of the rails.

Passengers on the early railroad trains often said, at the end of their journey, "Never again!" Cinders and bits of burning wood flew from the stack of the locomotive right back to the passenger cars. The first cars usually had no roofs, so the sparks and cinders fell right on the passengers, often burning holes in their clothes. Some of the cars did have roofs. They looked a little like stage coaches. These were a little better, but even they banged and crashed into each other whenever the train stopped. The connections between the cars were just chains. Passengers were thrown about as the trains started and stopped. Sometimes an iron strap would pop loose from the wooden rails and come up through the floor of a car.

Inventors and planners kept working, and as time passed, big improvements were seen in trains and railroads. By 1835, there were more than a thousand miles of railroads that reached over eleven states.

Leaders in the city of Chicago knew that they must find really good transportation for bringing farm products into their city. They had the choice of building good roads, more canals, or railroads. They chose railroads, and took the first step toward making Chicago the railroad center of the Middle West.

The invention of the telegraph helped to tie the nation together.

How did communication grow?

Until the year 1844, the fastest kind of transportation was also the fastest kind of communication. Mail and papers of any kind were carried in the same ways as passengers and goods. In 1844, the inventor Samuel Finley Breese Morse made it possi-

Passengers and mail were carried in western stagecoaches. Some went all the way across the mountains to the coast.

ble to send messages faster than people could ever dream of traveling. This was the year in which he tested his electric telegraph.

Many Americans had been interested in electricity since it had first been discovered about 1740. Much more was known about electricity by the time Morse became interested in it. He saw that it would be possible to use it in communication.

After getting permission from the government, Morse strung the wires he needed from Washington, D. C., to Baltimore, Maryland. Over these wires, he sent clicking sounds that could be heard through a receiver at the other end of the line. The clicking sounds were the dots and dashes of a code Morse had worked out. When the dots and dashes of this first message were changed into letters and words, the message read, "What hath God wrought?"

Soon telegraph wires were being strung from city to city. In less than twenty years, the telegraph reached as far west as the Mississippi River. As more and more Americans moved to California and the west coast, it became clear that telegraph lines all the way to the Pacific were needed. But this was a huge undertaking. In the meantime, other ways of communicating had to be used.

In 1858, John Butterfield opened his Overland Mail line from the end of the railroad in Missouri to San Francisco, California.

Butterfield cut the time for sending a message from Missouri to California down to less than three weeks. He set up a chain of stations all across the country. Fresh teams and drivers were kept at each station.

Years earlier, a man named Alexander Majors had opened a wagon freighting line across the Great Plains. He used wagons much like the Conestoga freighters of the East. His company, Russel, Majors, & Waddell, took another step forward in speeding communication to the west coast when they opened the Pony Express mail route between St. Joseph, Missouri, and Sacramento, California.

On April 3, 1860, the first Pony Express rider, on a fast horse, sped away from St. Joseph. On the same day, another rider left Sacramento and headed eastward along the trail. There were stations spaced all along the trail where the riders could change horses. Every so often, both horses and riders were changed. The fresh horses and riders would continue the ride to the next station.

The Pony Express cut the time of carrying a message across the country to ten days. The riders carried on bravely through such dangers as Indian attacks and stormy weather, over mountain trails and across open country. Their route followed the wagon trail along the Platte River valley to Utah and then on to the Sierra Nevada Mountain passes that led into California. The Pony Express performed a great service for the country, but it was used for scarcely longer than a year. In the summer of 1861, telegraph wires had been stretched all the way to the Pacific. Communication from the Atlantic to the Pacific Ocean was cut to just seconds.

Communication During the Middle 1800's

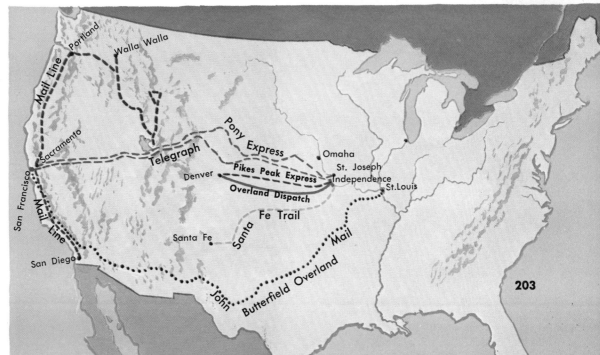

Words to Know

corduroy (kôr′dŭ roi) 198

Cotton Kingdom (kŏt′′n kĭng′dŭm) 193

Cyrus McCormick (sī′rŭs må kôr′ mĭk) 193

Erie Canal (ēr′ĭ kå năl′) 197

harvesting (här′vĕst ĭng) 193

locks (lŏks) 196

macadam roads (măk ăd′ăm rōdz) 198

National Road (năsh′ŭn ăl rōd) 199

plowshare (plou′shâr′) 192

reaper (rēp′ĕr) 193

scythe (sīth) 193

sickle (sĭk′′l) 193

towpath (tō′păth′) 196

turnpike (tûrn′pīk′) 199

Questions

1. How did the wheat farmer harvest his crop before the year 1834?

2. What great improvement was made in ocean travel after 1838?

3. What was the *New Orleans?* What part did it play in the improvement of transportation?

4. What two cities did the Erie Canal connect?

5. What was a corduroy road? Why was this kind of road not very good? Why weren't more macadam roads built?

6. How did turnpike roads get their name?

7. How were the rails of the first American railroads made?

8. Why was the race between the *Tom Thumb* and a horse important in the history of American transportation?

9. What kind of transportation did the leaders of Chicago decide to build up around their city?

10. What was the Pony Express? Why was it not continued beyond the year 1861?

You See for Yourself

Read what your encyclopedia tells you about the National Road. Trace its route on the map. What major cities did the road tie together? What rivers did it cross? About how much money did the federal governments spend in the building of this road? What modern highway follows the route of the National Road?

The Nation Divides

How did slavery cause problems?

One of the messages carried by the Pony Express early in 1861 was the news that some of the southern states had decided not to be part of the United States any longer. They were forming a new nation, called the *Confederate States of America*. The news did not come as a great surprise to most people. This act of the southern states came as a result of some very old problems.

From the very first days of the nation, the leaders of America had known that the question of slavery was bound to cause trouble. For any man to buy and sell another did not seem to fit the idea that "all men are created equal." People hoped that the laws against slavery in the Northwest Territory and against slave ships entering American harbors would bring slavery to an end. But they were wrong. The use of slaves was growing greater.

When the chief product of the south became cotton rather than tobacco, the southern planters found they needed field workers even more than before. The only way to get these workers seemed to be to buy more slaves.

The work of slaves was very important to the owners of large cotton plantations.

The planters cared for all the needs of their slaves. Most planters treated their slaves well, although there were some who did not. Sometimes a slave would run away. A runaway slave usually headed northward to a *free state*, one in which slavery was against the law.

The southern states often felt that laws passed by Congress favored the northern manufacturers but worked against the southern planters. Almost always, the northern representatives and the southern representatives in Congress split on voting.

For a number of years, while there were eleven free states and eleven slave states, the voting was even.

Trouble in Congress came when the new states Missouri and Maine were to enter the Union at about the same time. Maine, a northern state, would certainly be a free state. It was important to the southern states that Missouri should be a slave state in order to keep the voting in Congress even. The northern representatives wanted no more slaves to be taken into Missouri after it became a state. They also wanted the children of slaves to be given their freedom. The southern states would not agree to this.

A senator from Illinois offered an idea that ended the trouble. He suggested that Missouri should be a slave state, but that any other new state north of a certain line would be free. This line was the southern border of Missouri. Both North and South accepted this plan in 1820. It was called the *Missouri Compromise*.

Troubles over Slavery

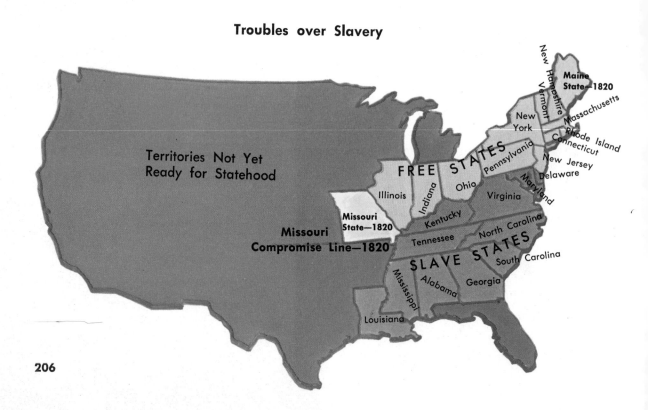

In 1860, Congress voted to have the Compromise Line reach all the way to California. This helped to settle further arguments of which states should be slave and which free when several western states were ready to enter the Union.

The North and South argued about another important question concerning slavery, too. Did a runaway slave win his freedom by escaping to a free state, or should he be returned to his southern owner? Most southern people thought the slaves should be returned. Most northern people thought they should be free.

Some northerners even helped slaves to run away. They had secret passages and hidden rooms in their houses. They allowed the runaway slaves to hide in these places until their southern owners had given up looking for them. Sometimes the northerners hid slaves under loads of farm products in their wagons to help them move unseen from one hiding place to another. This way of helping slaves to escape was called the *underground railroad*. It was especially strong in Ohio, but people of other states were also part of it. Many of the slaves tried to go all the way to Canada.

In 1852, a New England lady, who had once lived in Ohio, wrote a book about the underground railroad. Her story was about a young slave woman, who with her child ran away from the South.

Some slaves ran away from the plantation.

White members of the underground railroad helped runaway slaves. They sometimes hid the slaves in wagons and in secret rooms.

The book about the underground railroad told much of the cruelest side of slavery. The name of the book was *Uncle Tom's Cabin*. The author was Harriet Beecher Stowe.

Uncle Tom's Cabin became a very popular book in the North. It made people of the North more excited about stopping slavery than ever before. People became either strongly for or strongly against slavery.

The question of slave or free state came up every time a new state was to enter the Union. Kansas came in as a free state in 1861, after years of trouble. In 1856, men who favored slavery, most of them from Missouri, had attacked people who were against slavery. They burned the town of Lawrence, Kansas, and killed some men. John Brown, a Kansas settler, then began leading attacks against people who favored slavery. He felt that he had been chosen to lead a war against slavery.

He went East to raise an army. He found only eighteen men willing to serve in his "army." In 1859, they marched down to Harper's Ferry, Virginia, to capture the United States arsenal there. An *arsenal* is a place where guns and other war supplies are stored.

Brown and his men surrounded the arsenal and took sixty men prisoners. Later, Colonel Robert E. Lee and a small force of United States Marines arrived. There was a battle in which ten of Brown's men were killed and the rest captured. A Virginia court hanged Brown for crimes against the government. This angered the North.

The North was further angered by an 1857 court ruling that favored slaveowners. A slave named Dred Scott moved with his master from Missouri to the free state of Illinois. Later they returned to Missouri. A group of people from the underground railroad told Scott he should have been freed in Illinois. They took the case to court. It finally reached the United States Supreme Court. This Court decided that a slave was property, just as a cow or a mule, and could be taken anywhere and held. People took this to mean also that a runaway slave would also still belong to his owner by law.

The boy Abe Lincoln lived on the Kentucky frontier.

Young Lincoln held several jobs in New Salem, Illinois.

Honest Abe had a successful law practice in Illinois.

What caused the southern states to leave the Union?

By 1858, Abraham Lincoln, the son of poor frontier parents, was a successful lawyer in Illinois. Lincoln had always been interested in *politics*, the work of running the government. During the 1840's, he served in the state legislature of Illinois and in Congress. Lincoln did not become very popular during his term in Congress. One reason for this was that he spoke out strongly against slavery. Lincoln was sure that the people of Illinois would not again elect him to Congress. He decided to give up politics and to build up his law practice instead.

Lincoln's strong feelings against slavery, however, drew him back into politics after a few years. He became a member of the new Republican political party. The Republicans were very much against slavery. Lincoln worked hard for the Republicans, and in 1858, the party asked him to run for the United States Senate. The man running against Lincoln for a different party was Stephen Douglas. During the days before the voting took place, Lincoln and Douglas appeared before the voters of Illinois many times. They spoke and argued back and forth in the form of debates.

Lincoln and Douglas usually made their speeches outdoors from wooden platforms. Slavery was often the subject they talked about. The two men disagreed strongly on this point. Lincoln said that slavery was wrong. Although he did not want to take the slaves away from those who already had them, he was very much disturbed by the spread of slavery into territories and new states.

Douglas said that the United States need not think about whether slavery was right or wrong. He felt that if the people of any state wanted to allow slavery, they had the right to do so. He said the federal government had no business telling states whether to permit slavery or not.

Although Lincoln's voice was high and shrill, he was still a powerful speaker. He had always had a clever way of saying things. Even more important was the strong belief he had in everything he said.

Lincoln served in the state and national legislatures.

Lincoln was elected President in the election of 1860.

Americans honor Lincoln with a shrine in Washington, D. C.

The Lincoln and Douglas debates on slavery drew attention throughout the nation.

People of Illinois who knew Lincoln as a lawyer knew him to be completely honest. He was often called "Honest Abe." Honest Abe became known throughout the whole country after the Lincoln-Douglas debates. Large crowds of people came to the debates. Many more read about them through the newspapers all over the country. People admired Lincoln for his clear thinking.

The voters of Illinois chose Douglas to go to the Senate. But Lincoln was not forgotten. He was asked to speak before many large and important groups of Republicans in other parts of the country. In 1860, the Republicans asked him to run for President of the United States.

Lincoln won the election of 1860. Almost all his votes came from people in the northern states.

Biography Outline
Abraham Lincoln
1809-1865
American
Statesman
President of the United States from 1861-1865—opposed the withdrawal of the Southern States from the Union—felt the Union should be maintained even at the cost of war.

Biography Outline
Stephen A. Douglas
1813-1861
American
Politician
Member of the United States House of Representatives and Senate—well known for his debates with Abraham Lincoln on the question of slavery.

Lincoln did not take office until March of 1861. During the months between the election and his taking office, seven southern states withdrew from the Union. They formed a separate country of their own. There had been talk of this action for many years in the South. The election of Lincoln caused seven states to leave the Union almost at once. Four more southern states left soon afterwards. These eleven states felt that the only way they could have a government planned to meet their needs was to be a nation by themselves. Jefferson Davis was chosen as president of the Confederate States. The United States was united no longer.

How did war start?

Never had a President taken office at a worse time. Abraham Lincoln firmly believed that no state had the right to leave the Union. He refused to recognize the southern states as a separate nation. To him, these states were still in the Union. Many people hoped that he would not use force to carry through with this belief. Even some northerners felt that states should have the right to leave the Union if they wanted to do so.

The Confederacy took over the federal forts in the South as quickly as they could get together enough troops to take care of them. By the time Lincoln took office, only two forts in the South still flew the Union flag. One of these was Fort Sumter,

Northern armies wore blue uniforms and fought under the Union flag.

in the harbor of Charleston, South Carolina. Lincoln told the South that he was sending additional Union supplies to Fort Sumter. On April 12, 1861, the Confederacy opened fire on Fort Sumter. The Union and the Confederacy were at war.

Southern armies wore gray uniforms and carried the Confederate flag.

211

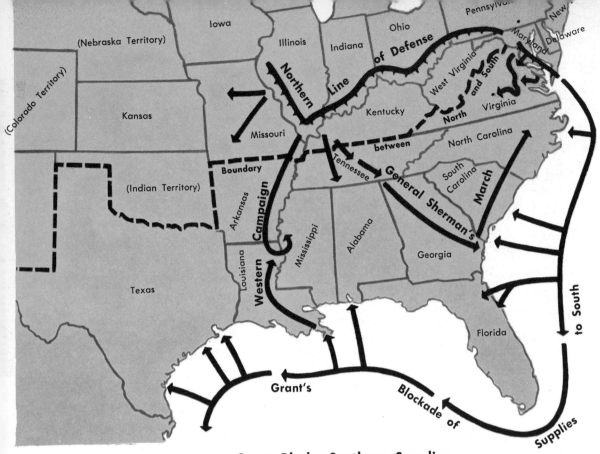

Grant Blocks Southern Supplies

What was the war like?

The *border states*, those between the northern and southern states, had to choose which side they would follow. In many of the border states lived families who felt the South was within its rights. Others agreed with Lincoln. Sometimes even the members of one family could not agree. One brother might join the Union Army and another would join the Confederate Army.

The governments of the border states had to decide whether or not to leave the Union. Missouri, Kentucky, West Virginia, and Maryland all decided to stay with the Union.

Most of the fighting took place in the southern and border states. Many battles were fought in Virginia.

At first, the South had many things in its favor. The people themselves were ready to work and fight hard to win. Many European countries believed the South was right. They helped the southern states by sending them manufactured goods. Since there were few factories in the South, the Confederacy had to buy goods from other places. There were many well-trained officers in the Confederate Army. One of these officers was Robert E. Lee of Virginia who headed the southern armies.

General Grant and General Lee met in the McLean house in a small town named Appomattox Court House on April 9, 1865. There they agreed on terms of the South's surrender.

At first, Lincoln could not find a really strong leader for the Union Army. With its better generals, the South won many of the first victories of the war. But this began to change after Lincoln chose *Ulysses S. Grant* to command the Union forces.

The men of the South fought bravely. Their army was far smaller than that of the North. At first, ships from Europe brought help to them. But one of Grant's plans was to keep these supply ships from entering southern harbors. Northern ships stopped the European supply ships before they reached the southern coast. The North had most of the country's shipyards and food-producing farms. It was only a matter of time until the Confederacy, with supplies cut off, would have to give up.

The war brought great sadness to President Lincoln. He still looked upon the southerners as United States citizens and disliked ordering them fired upon.

Biography Outline
Ulysses S. Grant
1822-1885
American
Soldier and politician
Commanded the Union troops during the War Between the States—President of the United States.

Biography Outline
Robert E. Lee
1807-1870
American
Soldier
Commander of the Confederate troops in the War Between the States.

Lincoln felt that the war should put an end to slavery throughout the country. During the war, he tried to make plans for the changes that the end of slavery would bring.

After much thought, Lincoln wrote an announcement saying that the slaves in the Confederate states were forever free. This was the *Emancipation Proclamation*, signed in the year 1863. In the months that followed, most of the border states passed laws that made slavery against the law in those states, too.

As the war was drawing to a close, Congress passed the thirteenth amendment making slavery against the law anywhere in the United States or in territories under its protection. The fourteenth and fifteenth amendments made Negroes citizens of the United States and gave them the right to vote.

The War Between the States came to an end early in April of 1865. By then, many of the southern plantations were ruined. Many fields had become battle grounds; others had been trampled by the boots of marching soldiers and by horses' hoofs; still more had been burned. Union soldiers had taken things from many of the finest homes and buildings of the South. After they took what they wanted, they often burned the buildings to the ground.

Grant brought the fighting to an end by splitting the Confederacy into two parts, as well as by keeping the southern harbors closed to ships. Even the brilliant General Lee could not hold on in the face of these hardships. He surrendered to General Grant at Appomatox Court House in Virginia.

What were the years after the war like?

The United States was a torn nation, badly in need of mending at the end of the war. Some people of the North wanted to punish the South.

General Lee believed General Grant to be quite fair in what he asked under the terms of the South's surrender. Lee had been an outstanding soldier of the Union Army before the War Between the States. He joined the Confederacy soon after the war began.

President Lincoln was shot and killed by an actor
named John Wilkes Booth.

Lincoln thought the war had been punishment enough for the South. He began to plan how the southern plantations could be rebuilt.

President Lincoln didn't get a chance to carry out his plans for helping the broken South. On the evening of April 14, 1865, only five days after Lee's surrender, President and Mrs. Lincoln went to the theater. A bitter, half-crazed actor, named John Wilkes Booth was at the same theater. He slipped up behind Lincoln as he sat watching the play. Booth shot a bullet into Lincoln's head. Lincoln died the next morning.

After Lincoln's death, Vice-President Andrew Johnson became President. President Johnson did his best to lead the nation through the difficult days after the war. But he did not have the backing of the people. One problem after another arose.

After the war, many Negroes moved to northern states. Most of them had no idea of how to live with their new freedom. Most of them had never had to look out for themselves. They did not know about simple everyday things, such as the value of money. Many had no last names. Too often, people of the North took advantage of them.

Instead of following Lincoln's plan to rebuild the South, Congress voted to keep soldiers in the southern states.

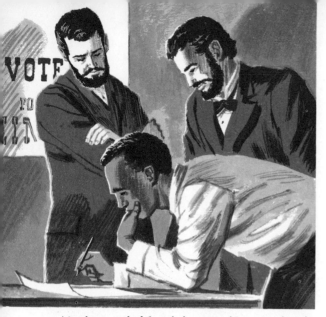

Northerners led freed slaves to the voting booths after the war.

Congress also voted to punish any southerners who had fought against the Union by taking away their right to vote. Feelings became very bitter as Union soldiers led Negroes to the voting booths. They voted even though they usually could not read what was written on the ballot.

These feelings led to the forming of the *Ku Klux Klan*. This was a

Covered by sheets, members of the Ku Klux Klan caused trouble in the South.

group of southern whites who wanted to frighten Negroes away from the voting places. They dressed up in sheets and pretended to be ghosts of soldiers who had died in the war.

Sometimes other people, in addition to the members of the Ku Klux Klan, dressed in white sheets and rode through the night. Hidden by the sheets, these people murdered and did other crimes that resulted from their bitterness and hatred.

What was "Seward's Folly"?

While Johnson was President, something completely separate from the war troubles took place. The United States bought Alaska from Russia. Since the Russian fur traders had already killed off most of the valuable fur-producing animals, many Americans thought this was a big mistake.

When Russia offered to sell Alaska, Secretary of State William H. Seward became interested at once. He thought the United States should buy it in order to get one more foreign power out of North America. He agreed to pay the Russian government $7,200,000. The United States needed money badly to help mend the torn nation. Many people called the purchase of Alaska "Seward's Folly."

In 1868, General Grant, running for the Republican party, was elected President of the United States.

Questions

1. What two laws made some people think that slavery would slowly come to an end? Were they right?

2. Why did southern representatives often feel displeased with laws passed in Congress? Why was it so important to the southern representatives that Missouri be a slave state?

3. How did Harriet Beecher Stowe help stir up feelings against slavery in the North?

4. How did Stephen Douglas think the federal government should deal with slavery in the states?

5. What finally caused the southern states to withdraw from the Union?

6. How did President Lincoln feel about the right of southern states to withdraw from the Union?

7. What was the Emancipation Proclamation? What did the fourteenth and fifteenth amendments do?

8. How did President Lincoln want to treat the southern states at the end of the war?

You See for Yourself

Many people, not only Americans but people all around the world, place Abraham Lincoln among the truly great men of history. Read about his life in other books. Think how you would answer this question: What made Lincoln a great man?

Robert E. Lee is another man whom Americans love and admire. Read about his life in other books. What job did Lincoln want to give to Lee? What things would you say made Lee a great American?

Stories and pictures in McGuffey's books made learning more interesting for many children in American schools.

Progress After the War

The men who wrote the Constitution saw that democracy would not work unless the voters knew a great deal about their government and about the things they were voting for. Thomas Jefferson believed that this meant the voters must be educated.

At the close of the War Between the States, there were many schools and colleges in the United States. Public schools were open to almost everyone, at least in the lower grades. Students at high schools and colleges usually had to pay to attend. Part of the planning for the new states was to provide for public schools, including colleges.

Who were some leaders in education?

There were several Americans who began working for better schools even before the War Between the States. One of these men was Horace Mann. He spent his life studying the problem of how to make schoolwork more interesting through better ways of teaching and better books.

William McGuffey, who grew up on the Ohio frontier, was another leader in education. As a boy, he went to school in log houses. When he was a young man, he went to a frontier college, carrying his extra clothing, a pair of sox and a shirt, in his saddlebags with his books.

Biography Outline

Horace Mann

1796-1859

American

Educator

Made important contributions to public education—established the elementary school system—founded the first state teachers' college at Lexington, Massachusetts.

Biography Outline

William McGuffey

1800-1873

American

Educator and clergyman

Published illustrated reading books for children for the first six grades—ordained Presbyterian minister.

McGuffey became a teacher in a Kentucky one-room school that had once been a smokehouse. Later he taught at Miami University in Oxford, Ohio. While he was there, McGuffey wrote a set of readers that were soon used to teach children to read. The readers were used in all parts of the United States, especially in the schools of the Middle West.

McGuffey tried to make the stories in his readers so interesting that girls and boys would enjoy their school work at the same time they were learning. Many of the boys who marched away to fight in the War Between the States had learned to read from McGuffey's Readers. When they came home after the war, their children also used McGuffey's books. For more than fifty years, American children grew up reading McGuffey's stories about brave heroes and truthful heroines.

Booker T. Washington worked in a coal mine after the War Between the States.

At night, he studied until he learned to read and write.

What progress was made in the education of Negroes?

The War Between the States gave the Negroes the right to vote. Yet since most of them could neither read nor write, voting meant very little to them. Most of them did just as they were told on voting day, not knowing for what or for whom they were casting their vote.

A Negro who was growing up right after the war saw what a sad thing this was for his people and for his country. The boy was born in 1859, on a back-country plantation in the Blue Ridge foothills of Virginia. His name was Booker Taliaferro Washington. He was nine years old when the slaves were freed. The plantation on which he lived was ruined during the war, so he had to find some place else to live and work.

Still just a boy, Booker went to work in the coal and salt mines of West Virginia. Somehow in the few hours left to him at the end of the long working day, the boy learned to read and write.

One of the women of the community took Booker T. Washington into her home to be a houseboy. She encouraged him to go on with his studies. She also taught him some other valuable lessons: the value of keeping clean and neat and how to take care of his money and other things that belonged to him. She encouraged him to work hard and to believe in himself.

Booker was about fourteen years old when he set out for a school he had heard about. It was a school at which Negroes could get some education. The name of the school was Hampton Institute, located only a few miles from the place where the first English-American colony had struggled at Jamestown long before. It was while he was at Hampton that Booker got the idea to go out and help train his people to be good citizens.

From Hampton Institute, Booker was sent to be a teacher at a new Negro school at Tuskegee, Alabama. When Booker arrived at Tuskegee, he found there was really no school at all. There wasn't even a building

for it. But this boy did not give up. He begged for the use of an old church and a shack for his first school buildings. Then he searched the countryside to find pupils. On the Fourth of July, 1881, the new school, named *Tuskegee Institute*, opened. Booker taught his pupils to read, write, and do simple arithmetic. He also taught them all he knew about farming and business, plus the lessons in hard work and believing in oneself that he had learned.

Other people saw the value of what Booker was trying to do. With their help, he built up his school. When the school was fourteen years old, it had 800 pupils, 55 teachers and other helpers, and more than $200,000 worth of farmland and buildings. Tuskegee Institute is still open today.

One of the teachers at Tuskegee Institute was George Washington Carver. His parents had been slaves in Missouri. Carver was born just before the end of the war. When he was old enough, he traveled north to Iowa and Michigan, where he worked and studied to get an education.

Carver saw the fine farms of the northern states. When he went to teach at Tuskegee Institute, he was very much interested in improving farming in the state of Alabama.

Most of the Negroes who had stayed in the South after the war, were trying to make a living by farming. They usually worked land they did not own, which meant they had to share their crops with the land-owners. Each man, with the help of one mule and little else, could not grow enough cotton to provide the money he needed to live on. The farmers and the land were both becoming worn out.

George Washington Carver knew that some crops return to the soil the food that other crops take out. The two main crops of the South were cotton and tobacco. No farm or plantation could be sown in these crops year after year without many plant foods being removed.

Carver showed the farmers how they could enrich their soil by growing peanuts, peas and sweet potatoes. He worked hard to find new uses for the peanut, too. In this way, a peanut crop would bring money as well as enrich the soil. He also learned how to grow a better peanut plant.

Carver's work in caring for soil helped the people all over the South as well as those in Alabama.

What was the work of Clara Barton?

Clara Barton worked in education of a different sort. She began her working years as a school teacher. But before the start of the War Between the States, she went to work in a government office in Washington, D.C. When a battle of the war was fought not far from Washington, Miss Barton visited the battle-field. There she saw wounded and dying men lying on the ground with almost no one to help them.

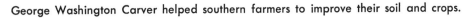
George Washington Carver helped southern farmers to improve their soil and crops.

After seeing that battlefield, Clara went where the armies went. She brought care and help to the wounded, Confederate and Union alike. She became known as the "Angel of the Battlefield."

After the war, Miss Barton helped families find out if their men who had not returned were dead and where they were buried. She saw to the marking of many graves of fallen soldiers.

It was Miss Barton's work of later years, however, that became even more important to the American people. On a visit to Switzerland, she learned of the International Committee of the Red Cross. This was a group of Europeans who were drawing up a set of rules for the merciful

Clara Barton

Biography Outline
Clara Barton
1821-1912
American
Nurse
Served as a nurse on the battlefields during the American War Between the States and the Franco-Prussian War—founder of the American Red Cross.

care of men of all armies when they fell in battle. Nations who joined the plan agreed to let persons carrying the white flag with the red cross enter enemy territory unharmed.

Miss Barton learned that the United States had refused to join the plan and sign the agreement. She came back to the United States and spoke to Congress and the President about the matter. She did not give up until the United States agreed to join the plan and to allow her to organize an American Red Cross.

She set up the American Red Cross in such a way that not only soldiers but also the peacetime victims of any disaster could receive the help of the Red Cross. She saw that Red Cross workers were on hand to help when yellow fever struck many people in Florida in 1887. When Johnstown, Pennsylvania, was swept with floods in 1889, the Red Cross was sent to help the sick and homeless. From then on, the Red Cross was ready to help whenever and wherever it was needed. Miss Barton died in 1912 when she was ninety years old. She had served as the first president of the American Red Cross for almost thirty years.

Horace Mann, William McGuffey, Booker T. Washington, George Washington Carver, and Clara Barton were only a few of the many Americans who worked to make the United States a better place in which to live.

How did the nation's wealth grow?

As the War Between the States drew to a close, the use of new machines and inventions was widespread. The growing number of factories was making use of minerals, lumber, and fine farm products. No one worried about how long it would be before all the trees of the forests were gone, or whether the soil could go on forever producing large crops. Nature seemed to have given America an endless supply of these things. The United States was rich in *natural resources*, all those things found in nature that can be used by man to better his life.

In its early days, the United States had to buy from other countries more goods than it had for sale. But as the nation grew, so did its products. By the time the nation was nearing its one-hundredth birthday, its people were producing many more goods than they could use themselves. The extra products were sent out of the country to be sold in other countries.

Goods shipped into a country are called *imports*. Goods shipped out are called *exports*. The value of the United States' exports became greater than the value of its imports. When any country's exports are greater than its imports, that country will usually grow richer. This is what happened to the United States. It grew wealthier and stronger with each passing year.

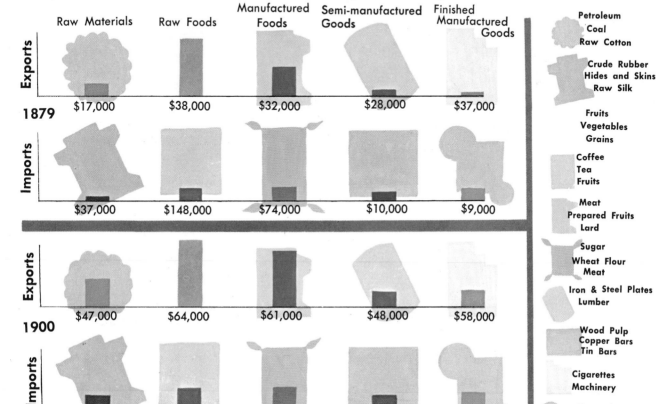

Growth in American Exports and Imports

	Raw Materials	Raw Foods	Manufactured Foods	Semi-manufactured Goods	Finished Manufactured Goods		
1879 Exports	$17,000	$38,000	$32,000	$28,000	$37,000	Petroleum / Coal / Raw Cotton	Crude Rubber / Hides and Skins / Raw Silk
1879 Imports	$37,000	$148,000	$74,000	$10,000	$9,000	Fruits / Vegetables / Grains	Coffee / Tea / Fruits
1900 Exports	$47,000	$64,000	$61,000	$48,000	$58,000	Meat / Prepared Fruits / Lard	Sugar / Wheat Flour / Meat
1900 Imports	$75,000	$176,000	$142,000	$48,000	$42,000	Iron & Steel Plates / Lumber	Wood Pulp / Copper Bars / Tin Bars

The United States was growing in population also. *Population* is the number of people who live in a country or other special area. More people meant more workers and more products. Many people from other lands came to live in America. In addition, large families were common in those days.

People from other countries who came to live in the United States were called *immigrants*. On each of the new steamships that came into the eastern harbor cities, especially New York, Boston, and Philadelphia, were people who had left their homes in Europe to live in America. During the 1870's, jobs and money were scarce in America. But things were even worse in European countries. Irish, German, Norwegian, and Swedish people came in great numbers. A few years later, a great many people from countries in southern Europe began coming to America.

Into the west coast cities, particularly San Francisco, came many Chinese people. They had heard of the money that could be made in helping to build the western railroads. In 1880, there were 75,000 Chinese in California alone. Other workmen of the western states were not happy about the arrival of so many Chinese workmen. The Chinese were willing to work for very low wages.

Even though many American lives had been lost during the War Between the States, the population jumped from 31 million people in 1860 to over 50 million in 1880.

The United States, as it approached the end of its first one hundred years, was the "Land of Opportunity." It was becoming the "Great Melting Pot," as people from more and more different nations lived together as one nation.

The United States was rich in natural resources and human strength. It offered freedom to people under its government. It seemed a land in which anyone who was willing to work could be happy.

The Arrival of Immigrants

	England	Ireland	Northern Europe	Germany	Poland	Russia	Italy

1880, 1860, 1840 pictograph rows

5,000 people

Words to Know

exports (ĕks'pōrts) 223

immigrants (ĭm'ĭ grănts) 224

imports (ĭm'ports) 223

natural resources (năt'ụ răl rĕ'sōrs ĕs) 223

population (pŏp'ū lā'shŭn) 224

Tuskegee Institute (tŭs kē'gē ĭn'stĭ tūt) 220

Questions

1. In what state did William McGuffey live and work? For what work in education is he best remembered?

2. Why did young Booker T. Washington have to leave his home on a southern plantation? Where did he go?

3. How did Booker T. Washington start his school at Tuskegee, Alabama?

4. How did Clara Barton become interested in helping wounded men during the War Between the States?

5. What group of people did Clara Barton learn about while she was visiting Europe? What did she do when she returned to the United States?

6. Why did George Washington Carver encourage the southern farmers to grow peanuts, peas, and sweet potatoes?

7. How did the value of American imports and exports change during the first one-hundred years of the nation?

8. Tell reasons why the population of the United States grew during the 1800's.

9. Why is the United States often called the "Great Melting Pot"?

10. In what part of the United States did many Chinese people settle? What work did many of them do?

11. Why did Thomas Jefferson and many other leaders in government feel that public schools were especially important in the United States?

You See for Yourself

Find the word "conservation" in your dictionary and study its meaning. Do you think early Americans thought much about this word as they made use of the country's natural resources? What man in this unit was interested in conservation of soil?

Americans Move to the Plains

Even before the end of the War Between the States, many signs of important coming advances could already be seen. It was during the war years, for example, that telegraph lines were stretched all the way to the Pacific Coast. The news of the southern states' withdrawing from the Union had been carried to the West by Pony Express. The news of General Lee's surrender was sent by telegraph.

How did the railroads grow?

While he was President, Lincoln had met with many of the men who were planning to build railroads. It was Lincoln's dream that all the major cities in the United States would someday be linked together by the railroads. If this dream were ever to come true, rails would have to stretch across the many miles between Missouri and California.

By the time the war started, several railroads had been built as far west as the Mississippi River. Building of railroads west of the river had just begun. The longest one was in Missouri and reached from Hannibal to St. Joseph. Mail from the East could be carried by train as far as St. Joseph. The Pony Express or stagecoach lines took it farther west. In California and Texas, there were a few short lines. Aside from these, there was not a mile of railroad track between Missouri and California.

During the war, railroads that were already in use could not carry on with their regular work of peacetime transportation. The trains were used to carry troops and supplies of war.

Work on the first railroad to reach the west coast was carried out during the 1860's. Many Chinese immigrants to this country joined the work gangs to lay the tracks.

Many locomotives and cars had iron plates fastened to their sides to stop the bullets from the guns of soldiers trying to capture the railroad. Sometimes wooden bridges were burned so that a train would have to stop and could then be attacked. It was of great help to either army to be in control of a railroad.

The building of railroads farther west was slowed by the war, but it was not stopped. By 1863, tracks had been laid almost as far as Omaha, Nebraska. At that time, plans were also being made to start building at Sacramento, California, and come eastward to meet tracks being built westward from Omaha. This would be the greatest railroad building job of all time. There were over 1500 miles to cover, through the unsettled plains and over the Rockies and the *Sierra Nevada* Mountains.

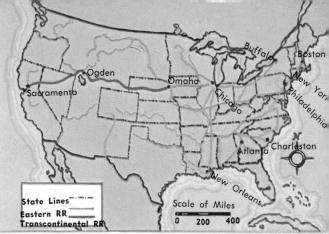

Rails to California

Hundreds of men shared in the work, from the drawing of plans to the driving of spikes. Some workers, drove teams of mules to scrape out a level roadbed. Others, among whom was Buffalo Bill, hunted buffalo on the plains to supply meat for the workers. Some of the Chinese workmen risked their lives hanging over cliffs in big baskets while they chipped out a shelf of rock on a mountainside so that tracks could be laid.

After six years of work, the two lines met at Promontory, Utah, north of Great Salt Lake. On May 10, 1869, the last spike, a golden one was driven. Many people came to the ceremony at which this spike was driven. The railroad was ready to handle transportation from coast to coast.

What were the homesteading days?

At the same time railroads were being built through western Kansas and Nebraska, the federal government decided to open the Great Plains to American settlers. The Indians were moved farther west to make room for the new settlers.

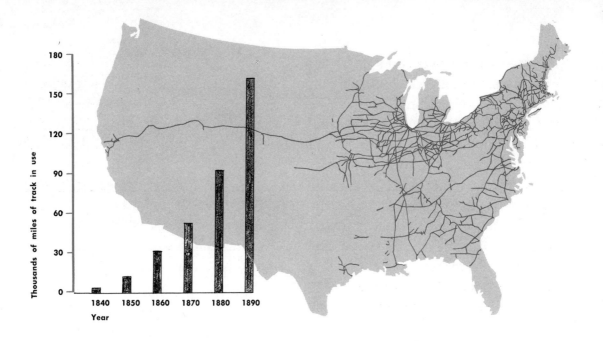

Railroad Growth Between 1840 and 1890

One of the laws signed by President Lincoln was the *Homestead Act*. This law made it possible for almost anyone to get a farm for a low price.

All a new settler needed to do to get one-hundred-sixty acres of land was to pay a small fee at a government land office. His *claim*, the land he had chosen to farm, was then recorded in the government office. If he lived on the land and farmed it for five years, it was his.

By the time the Homestead Act was passed, Americans had realized that the Great American Desert was not useless, as they once believed. Indeed, it was far from useless. The forest lands of the eastern states, had proved to be good farmland once the trees were cleared. Ohio and Kentucky were fine farming states. The farther west the settlers went, the fewer trees they had to clear. At the same time, they found the soil to be richer. They discovered that the soil of the grasslands on the Great American Desert was especially good for growing grain crops.

The Homestead Act sent a new wave of settlers westward. Some traveled as earlier pioneers had traveled, by wagon or by steamboat, taking with them their tools and furniture. Others packed just their clothes into a small trunk and went West by railroad. They planned to buy the furnishings they would need in one of the new towns that had grown up around the railroad stations.

Settlers on the western plains faced much more difficult lives than the settlers in eastern regions.

Perhaps the worst problem of the western settlers was the lack of water and trees. During the summer, there was often no rain for a long period of time. Even the streams dried up. The only trees the settlers saw were the thin groves growing along the banks of the streams. Of course, the first settlers chose land close to the streams in order to have water. But these lands were soon gone. Most of the settlers had to take lands that were far from streams.

The first job of the settler was to find a water supply. This meant digging a well. Often, the homesteader dug down twenty or thirty feet and still found no water. Sometimes it took many tries before he found underground water and was sure of a good well. In the meantime, he could do nothing about farming his land. It took a strong team of horses, mules, or oxen to pull the breaking plow, and animals could not live without water. The *breaking plow* cut into the thick, matted grass roots. The grass had to be plowed under before the farmer could plant his grain crop. Settlers of the Great Plains were called *sod-busters* because they broke up the sod. *Sod* is earth that is covered with grass and holds the roots of the grass.

The homesteaders also needed houses and fuel. Settlers in the eastern regions had used trees for both home-building and fuel. But the homesteaders had almost no trees. Lumber shipped in on the new railroads was very costly. Most homesteaders could buy only a little for home-building. Settlers along the streams collected driftwood from the banks of the streams and sold it for fuel. Sometimes they sold a whole tree from their land for lumber.

Those who hunted for them could still find a few buffalo chips where the great herds had once been. These *chips* were chunks of dried manure. Wagon travelers years before had used them for fuel. But it was clear that neither driftwood nor buffalo chips would last for long. The railroads would soon have to bring carloads of coal from eastern states to the Great Plains.

Many of the first homes on the Great Plains were much like the Indians' houses that had been partly dug out of the earth. These were called dugouts. To build a dugout, the homesteader used pick and shovel to dig a hole four or five feet deep.

Sod block

Breaking plow

The first home of the sodbuster was often made of sod blocks.

Breaking up the sod, covered by tough prairie grasses was hard work.

Using a sod-breaking plow, the homesteader would cut out large blocks of sod to build walls two or three feet high around the hole. He left two or three spaces for windows and put a door at one end. The steps leading down into the home were simply cut into the earth. To make the roof, the homesteader laid wooden poles across the top. Then he added a layer of corn stalks, marsh grasses, or any other dried material he could find. This was topped with another layer of sod.

Some houses were built entirely above ground with sod blocks. The greatest trouble with the sod houses came with a period of heavy rains. The roof was sure to leak, and the walls often started to lean. The owner had to prop up the walls to keep them from falling. His wife learned to cook and hold an umbrella over the stove at the same time. She also had to learn not to mind the bugs that crawled out of the sod blocks. During the first winter especially, the warmth from the stove inside the house brought out bugs by the hundreds.

The homesteaders were a group of rugged and hard-working pioneers. Most of them came from the eastern regions of the United States, but there were hundreds who came from European countries, particularly Germany, Norway, and Sweden. These immigrants had to learn not only how to live in a new country, but also how to brave the hardships of changing the wild grasslands into a gentle homeland.

Locusts and grasshoppers were among the hardships faced by the homesteaders.

In time, the homesteaders were able to change the grasslands into a homeland.

The sodbusters lived through long dry seasons that baked the earth hard. They felt driving winds that blew away much they had built. They carried on through hot summer winds that never seemed to stop and through the bitter cold of winter blizzards. Grasshoppers ate their crops; a lack of water killed the young trees they planted; prairie fires raced uncontrolled across their land. Through it all they held on.

In time the homesteaders nursed the young seedlings into sturdy trees that could break the endless wind. Slowly the sod houses were replaced by homes of stone, brick, or lumber. And in the end, they brought from their fields some of the largest and richest grain crops ever known to man.

What were the great cattle drives?

During the War Between the States, there were great herds of wild cattle feeding on the plains of Texas. These animals stemmed from the herds of the Spanish-Mexican ranchers farther south. The cattle had long horns, and lean tough meat.

Raising these cattle for meat seemed hardly worth while. The meat would certainly spoil before it could reach eastern cities. In the years after the war, however, some of the Texans got the idea of how they could get beef to the faraway markets. They decided to raise the cattle in Texas and then drive the live animals to the nearest railroad. The railroads could carry the animals to the eastern cities, where they could be butchered.

The Texas cattlemen rounded up herds and then hired a crew of cowboys to drive the animals north and east. They went mile after mile through Oklahoma, which until the 1880's was still Indian territory. The first herds had to be driven all the way to Sedalia, Missouri, for this was the nearest railroad shipping point. There the tired animals were loaded into the cattle cars and began their journey to the Chicago meat-packing houses.

As the railroads reached farther and farther west, the cattle drives were shortened. Several towns in Kansas became shipping points, so the cattle drives could end there. Kansas City became an important meat-packing center. Abilene and Dodge City became shipping points.

These towns were also the places where tired cowboys drew their pay and could then celebrate the end of the long drive and hard work. These "cowtowns" needed strong lawmen, not only to control the celebrations of the cowboys, but also to protect them from gamblers and thieves who were ready and willing to take the hard-earned money of the cowboys.

In time, the long cattle drives no longer took place. As the Great Plains were turned into farms, there was no grass along the trail to provide feed for the animals during the long drive.

Cowboys drove Texas longhorn cattle many miles to reach a railroad shipping point.

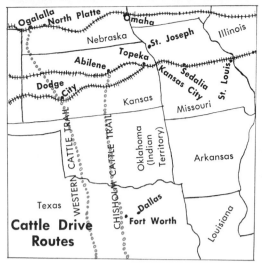

Cattle Drive Routes

As the railroads began reaching farther into Texas territory, the cattle drives became unnecessary. Cattlemen began to work at breeding better and better meat animals in place of the tough longhorns. The steaks became tender and juicy. The railroads and city meat-packing houses did an even better business.

Why did wagon trains continue to travel westward?

The end of the California Gold Rush did not bring an end to the wagon trains moving westward. Many later travelers headed for the mining sections in the Rocky Mountains. Some of the mines were rich in gold and silver. Young and old alike dreamed of finding quick riches.

Among the wagons in the trains were those of people planning to settle on the Great Plains. These wagons dropped from the train somewhere along the trail. Groups of men, traveling without families, made up most of the wagon trains that went all the way to the mountains.

In 1859, many of the wagons going to Colorado had "Pike's Peak or Bust!" painted on their canvas sides. Sometimes the same wagons were seen returning the following year. Just one word was written on the canvas: "Busted!"

Towns, such as Cripple Creek, Colorado, sprang up overnight as supply and amusement centers for the miners. Cripple Creek and others like it were boom towns. As soon as the miners moved on to another area, the towns faded away to almost nothing. They became "ghost towns" with only empty buildings to show where there had once been a town.

Other mining centers such as Denver, lasted and continued to grow. The railroads were built to them, and other industries besides mining grew up around them. Often other minerals in addition to gold and silver were found in the mountains.

Many people joined in the rush for gold in the mountains of Colorado.

Why were soldiers sent to the Great Plains and the mountains?

The railroad builders, homesteaders, and cattlemen made many changes in the Great Plains. The Plains Indians and all those who had been pushed farther west by settlers on the eastern frontiers watched as the white men took their last hunting grounds. The great herds of buffalo that had once meant the living of the Plains Indians grew smaller each year. Many of the great animals had been hunted and killed for food and sport. Many more were dying because their grassland feeding grounds were becoming ranches and farms of settlers.

As the eastern Indians had done, some of the western chiefs called their braves together to try to win back some of their lands. Their anger spread from tribe to tribe, and soon many of them were riding against the white man.

After the War Between the States, Indian attacks became worse. Many of the same soldiers who had fought in the war were sent West. Some new forts were built. But the government also bought many of the old fur-trading posts to house the troops.

Many Indians were killed in those years. Some died in the fighting, but others were killed by sicknesses the Europeans had brought to America. Often a village or camp was almost completely wiped out by sickness.

In the middle of the 1870's another gold rush came. This time it was into the Black Hills of South Dakota. Years before, the United States government had signed a treaty with the Sioux tribes in this area. It was agreed that this area should be kept for the Indians. But the treaty did not keep the miners and gold-seekers out of the territory. The Sioux were deeply angered when white men began breaking the treaty. Led by Chief Sitting Bull, Indian warriors gathered to attack any and all white men they found. Soldiers from the northwestern posts were ordered to quiet the uprisings.

In July of 1876, General G. A. Custer planned an attack on Sitting Bull's warriors. He and 264 officers and men met the Indians near the Little Big Horn River in Montana.

Growth of the United States

1789

1825

1850

234

0   100   500   1000

Many people flocked to see the "Wild West Shows" that once toured the country.

Among the 2500 chiefs and warriors Sitting Bull had gathered, was Chief Crazy Horse. Crazy Horse led the Indians in a battle during which Custer and all of his men were killed.

It was hunger that finally put an end to the trouble caused by the Indians. The white settlers had taken the Indians' means of getting food, clothing, and shelter. The last Indian uprisings were those of the Apache tribes in Arizona and New Mexico. By 1890, most of the Indians had settled down to life on small areas of land called *reservations*, the government had set aside for them. On the reservations, the Indians received food and other necessary supplies from the federal government.

About all that was left of the "wild west" were the shows in which actors acted out western adventures and scenes. The actors and shows traveled all over the United States. Buffalo Bill had one of the most famous of these shows. In the cast were rifle marksmen, such as Annie Oakley, cowboys, and Indians. Sometimes even Custer's last stand was acted out. The American frontier had vanished. The American wilderness was conquered.

from Thirteen States to Forty-Eight

1875

1900

1913

Questions

1. For what work were the railroads used during the War Between the States?

2. In what year were the Atlantic and Pacific coasts connected by railroad? How did people celebrate when the work of taking the railroad to the Pacific Coast was finished?

3. What was the name of the law that made it possible for settlers to get land on the Great Plains for a low price?

4. How did a lack of trees make the life of the western settlers different from the lives of the eastern frontier settlers?

5. What was a breaking plow? Why was a strong plow so important to settlers on the Great Plains?

6. Why didn't the western settlers buy the lumber they needed?

7. How did the settlers build dugout homes?

8. Name three European countries from which many of the Great Plains settlers came.

9. Why didn't the Texas ranchers butcher beef cattle on their ranches? How did they solve this difficulty?

10. What was a "cowtown"?

11. Why were many people interested in going to the Rocky Mountains in 1859?

You See for Yourself

Buffalo Bill was one of the most interesting and colorful men in the West. Find out a few more things about him from an encyclopedia. What was his real name? How did he get the name "Buffalo Bill"? How old was he when he rode for the Pony Express? Where is his grave?

Read about the American buffalo in an encyclopedia. Learn all you can about the conservation of buffalo during the late 1800's.

Now You Know

In many ways the years of the 1800's were working and building years for the United States. The farmer's work became easier and his crops larger because of new inventions. Steamships, canals, the railroads, and the telegraph brought the people of the country together. The work of the people and the products from one part of the country could be enjoyed by people in other parts.

During the middle of the 1800's, the nation and the democratic ideas upon which it had been built were put to a bitter test. The southern states felt that they could have the kind of government they needed only by withdrawing from the Union.

Many people agreed that these states had the right to withdraw.

President Lincoln was one who believed that the South must not be allowed to withdraw. The War Between the States settled the question. After four years of fighting, the South returned to the Union.

After the war, leaders in government and education worked hard to give the country better schools and better books. Great Negro leaders worked to bring education and hope to their people. The Great Plains, the last American frontier, were settled during the last half of the 1800's. The population swelled with the arrival of many immigrants.

You Talk It Over

If you had been alive during the days of the first steamboats, what do you think you would have thought of them? Do you think men like Robert Fulton and Peter Cooper used their imaginations? Do you think they had courage? Explain.

If you had been President Lincoln, would you have recognized the Confederacy as a separate nation? Who started the War Between the States?

Do you think this country could have grown as rich and as strong as it did without the slaves? What do you think southern farmers would have done with their slaves if they could have bought today's machinery to use in their fields?

Unit Questions

1. Why did it become necessary for people who wanted the pioneer life to move west across the Mississippi River?

2. What is a scythe? What is a sickle? Why did the wheat farmer stop using the scythe or sickle?

3. In what part of the country were steamboats first used? What was the first steamboat to travel down the Ohio and Mississippi rivers?

4. What is a canal? How did canals bring better transportation?

5. What was a corduroy road? A macadam road?

6. How were many of the first macadam roads paid for?

7. How were the early railroad tracks made?

8. Describe a ride on one of the early locomotive-pulled trains.

9. What was the Pony Express? Between what two cities did it run?

10. Who invented the telegraph? In what year did the telegraph reach all the way to the Pacific Coast?

11. What American idea did slavery seem to be against?

12. What was the Missouri Compromise? In what year did it become law?

13. What was the underground railroad?

14. What was *Uncle Tom's Cabin?* What part did it play in the trouble over slavery?

15. Who was Dred Scott? What was the Supreme Court's decision on the law case which concerned him?

16. How did Lincoln and Douglas disagree on the idea of slavery in the United States?

17. Why did Booker T. Washington feel that he should help his people after the War Between the States? How did he help them?

18. How did George Washington Carver help southern farmers?

19. Explain how a coast-to-coast railroad was important to each of these three groups of people: (a) cattlemen (b) grain farmers (c) city businessmen.

20. What caused the population to grow during the 1870's?

Puzzlers

The man pictured here is a manufacturer of leather goods in Fall City. He sells his goods in each of the other six towns and cities shown on the map. Using the table of rates and the scale of miles, decide how much it will cost the manufacturer to send a shipment of leather goods to each of the other towns. Why do you think the freight-wagon trail does not lead directly from Centerville to Cedar Springs?

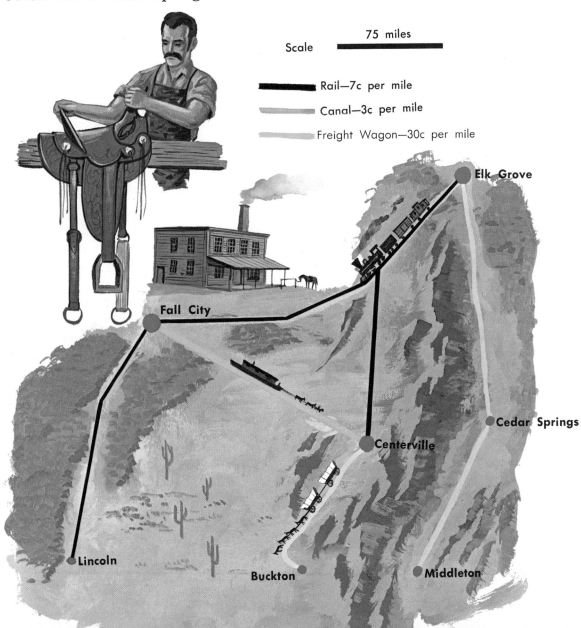

Scale   75 miles

Rail—7c per mile

Canal—3c per mile

Freight Wagon—30c per mile

Elk Grove

Cedar Springs

Fall City

Centerville

Lincoln

Buckton

Middleton

Unit Activities

You Make a Sod House

Choose a corner of your classroom or a large table on which to construct a homestead family's house. Begin your project with a sturdy pasteboard carton, which you will use to make your sod house. Cut a door and several windows in the box. Then take large sheets of blotter paper, such as that used for covering desk tops, and staple them to the outside walls and roof of your house. Use a dark color of blotter paper so that it will be something like the color of soil. Spread a thin layer of mucilage glue or rubber cement over the blotter paper. While the glue is still moist, sprinkle grass seed or bird seed over the blotter paper. Using a wet sponge or an eye dropper, water the seeds carefully each day. In about a week, grass and other plant growth should begin to cover your house just as it did the sod houses of the homesteaders. You may want to place some artificial flowers here and there over your house. The homesteaders often planted flower seeds in their sod roofs and walls.

If your house is large enough, make some construction paper furniture to place inside it. The sodbusters sometimes used greased paper instead of glass for their windows. You could do the same for your house, using construction paper and any kind of cooking grease.

When your house is finished, dress some dolls in costumes that look like clothes worn by the homesteaders. Place the dolls outside your house, or inside if your house is large enough.

You Play the Part

Pretend that you are one of the people who really lived or could have lived during the 1800's. Prepare a costume that would be suitable for the person you have chosen to be. Also write a short talk in which you tell what the person you represent did to help in the building of our country. Have a "Builders-of-America Parade" in which you wear your costume and give your talk for the rest of your classmates or for another class in your school.

You Plan a Pageant

A pageant is a program in which a story is told in word and song. Write a short paragraph for each event and learn to sing the songs listed below. Give your program for another class.

Event	Songs
Building of canals	Erie Canal
Building of railroads	I've Been Workin' on the Railroad
Gold Rush to Colorado	Sweet Betsy from Pike
Slaves on the plantations	Set Down Servant Steal Away
Western Cattle drives	The Old Chisholm Trail Home on the Range

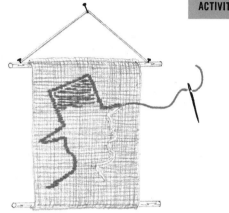

You Make a Tapestry

Using a piece of burlap material, colored yarn, and a darning needle, make a picture that represents something you have studied in this unit. Draw your picture on the burlap with a piece of chalk. Then weave the colored yarn in and out the burlap over the chalk lines. When you have finished, roll the top and bottom ends of the burlap around smooth rods and staple them in place. Tie another piece of yarn to the top rod so that your tapestry may be hung on the wall.

Some suggestions for what you might show in a tapestry are given here. But you may have better ideas of your own.

Head of Lincoln	Riverboat
Confederate flag	Stagecoach
Union flag	Covered wagon

The Second Hundred Years

As the United States approached its one-hundredth birthday, Americans were busy with plans for a celebration. They had decided to have a fair in Philadelphia, the city in which the United States was born.

The fair was called the *Centennial Exposition* of 1876. All the products of America's farms and industries were to be shown. A special hall was set up to show the many new things that American inventors had made. Many other countries of the world were invited to show their products and inventions, too.

Millions of people visited the fair. They could see that the United States was already on its way to becoming a leader among nations.

A model of the hand and torch on the Statue of Liberty stood outside one of the exhibit halls at the Centennial Exposition.

243

At the Fair

What American products were shown at the Centennial Exposition?

People who visited the Centennial Exposition were surprised to see that Americans had been able to accomplish so much in just one hundred years. The United States was still a very young nation compared with the nations of Europe.

The southern states sent cotton, rice, and tobacco to be shown at the fair. Citrus fruits, such as oranges and lemons, were sent from Florida. Fine samples of corn and wheat came from the Great Plains states. Iron, copper, gold, silver, and other minerals came from the mines in the north and the west. Lumber companies showed fine samples of the many beautiful types of wood taken from American forests. Many of the manufactured goods came from the mills and factories of the northeastern states.

This machine could produce nails very rapidly. Each of the nails was better than any that had ever been made by hand in the years before this machine was invented.

A stove used for heating homes was among the display of American inventions. Benjamin Franklin invented one of the first heating stoves used in earlier days of the country.

Visitors could see how Eli Whitney's cotton gin separated the seeds from the fibers.

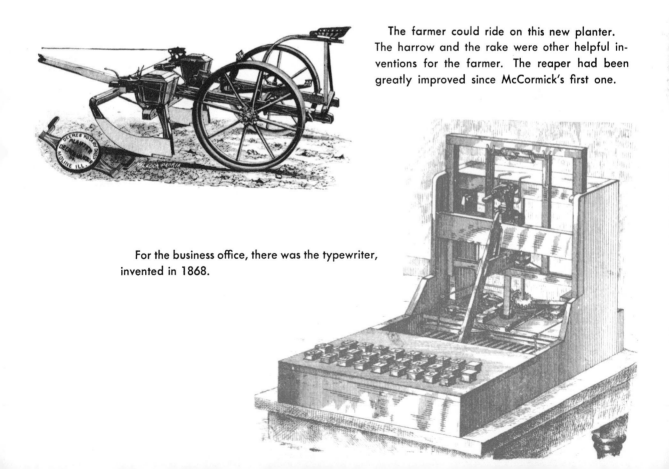

The farmer could ride on this new planter. The harrow and the rake were other helpful inventions for the farmer. The reaper had been greatly improved since McCormick's first one.

For the business office, there was the typewriter, invented in 1868.

A new kind of printing press could turn out
newspapers much faster than the older presses.

The invention of the sewing machine quickly
changed the way clothing was made. Clothing
factories opened soon after Elias Howe invented
it. By the year of the fair, a few homes already
had machines like the one on display.

Fine silver pieces, such as
this engraved coffee urn, came
from American silversmiths.

The Baily gun, an early type of machine gun, was already being used by soldiers fighting the Indians in the far west.

The Colt revolver and the Remington repeating rifle could fire several bullets before being reloaded.

The air brake was among the new inventions that made railroad travel safer and more comfortable. The newest locomotives burned soft coal instead of wood. Passenger cars were more comfortable. There was even one in which the seats could be made into beds. This was the Pullman car, invented by a man named George Pullman.

Watson heard Bell calling to him through the telephone receiver. Their attempts to send voice sounds over a wire were successful at last.

How did the use of the telephone grow?

Young Alexander Graham Bell had been in the United States for only five years at the time of the Centennial Exposition. He was born in Scotland, where his father was a teacher of the deaf. Bell helped his father in this work. He studied the workings of the human voice. Later he became interested in combining his knowledge of the voice with the use of electricity.

The Bell family moved to Canada in 1870. In 1871, Alexander Graham Bell moved to Boston to become a teacher in a school for the deaf. At night, he carried on his experiments with the human voice and electricity.

Bell was ready to test his invention, the telephone, two months before the Exposition opened. He and his partner, Thomas Watson, ran wires through the rooms of a building. Bell had the mouthpiece in one room, and Watson had the receiver in another. On March 10, 1876, Bell spilled some acid on his skin and clothing. "Mr. Watson," Bell called, "come here. I want you." Watson heard Bell's voice clearly through the receiver.

After several more months of work, Bell and Watson succeeded in building a telephone through which voices could be carried back and forth over the same wire. This telephone went on display at the Exposition in June. Scientists could see that the telephone was a great advance in communication. By August of 1877, there were about 800 telephones in use. By 1892, it was possible to make a long-distance call from New York to Chicago.

Biography Outline
Alexander Graham Bell
1847-1922
Scotch-American
Scientist and educator
Inventor of the telephone—opened a school for teachers of the deaf and spent many years serving the deaf—did a great deal of work on other communication devices.

How did Edison help in the progress of communication?

One of the men who helped improve the telephone was Thomas Alva Edison. As a boy, Tom Edison liked to watch the telegrapher at work in the railroad depot. One day, Tom saved the small son of the telegrapher. The child had wandered onto the tracks in front of a speeding train. The father asked Tom what he would like as a reward. Tom said, "Teach me to use the telegraph."

Young Tom was a good pupil. He not only learned to send and receive messages, but began thinking of ways to improve the telegraph. He worked out an improvement that was soon put into use throughout the entire country.

Edison worked in the entire field of electricity. His best known and probably most widely used invention was the electric light bulb. Although other inventors had worked with electric lighting, it was Edison whose work made it useable.

Edison enclosed wires in a glass bulb and then sent electricity into the bulb. His greatest problem was in finding a material for the wires which would not burn out quickly. In 1879, he succeeded in finding a material that burned hour after hour. The material was ordinary cotton sewing thread that had been burned to ash. Many changes have been made in light bulbs, but they have all been built on Edison's work.

Edison tried many different materials for the wires in an electric light bulb.

Besides improving the telegraph and the telephone, Edison made the first really workable motion picture camera. He invented the phonograph, which led the way to the modern record player of today. He worked out the idea of a machine for making copies of printed matter that became the mimeograph. His idea of enclosing wires in a bulb led to the many kinds of tubes needed in radio and television sets of later years.

Biography Outline
Thomas A. Edison
1847-1931
American
Inventor
One of the greatest inventors in history—known for the invention of the phonograph, and the electric light bulb.

The Passing Years

The same things that were to make the United States a leading nation in its second hundred years also brought problems.

What were the problems between big business and labor?

Soon after the Centennial Exposition, the growth of new business and industry brought one of the nation's biggest problems. The government had to make many new laws, laws that the writers of the Constitution never could have thought of.

Men who built and owned the railroads saw how much the farmers and other shippers needed their service. They raised the price of shipping. They knew the farmers would have to use the railroads no matter how high the rates were. The high shipping costs meant that the railroad owners made enough money to build still more railroads. It also meant that the farmers had to settle for less profit from their crops.

The same idea was true for other businesses. Owners of factories, mines, and oil wells paid low wages to their workers and had them work up to twelve hours a day. The workers often had to work in unclean and unsafe places. In these ways the owners kept their costs low and their profits high.

Sometimes one group of rich men would buy up all the companies they could find that were in the same business. They made one giant company of the many small ones. This was called a *trust*.

The trust companies often set high prices on their products. People who wanted to use their products or services had to pay whatever price the company set. There were few or no smaller companies left to offer the same product at lower prices.

Two things happened. Both the farmers and the *laborers*, mine and factory workers, formed groups to fight for their rights. The farm groups were usually called *granges*. The granges fought to get fairer rates from the railroads.

The labor groups formed *unions*. The unions saw the power they had if the members all went "on strike," or refused to work. The mines and factories could not stay in business without the labor force. Labor strikes could make the business owners improve working conditions and pay higher wages.

Most Americans believed that small businesses should have equal rights with large ones. Price-setting should not be allowed. Instead, business should go along on the "law of supply and demand." This meant that when there is plenty of any one thing, its price will be low. When something is hard to get, its price will be high.

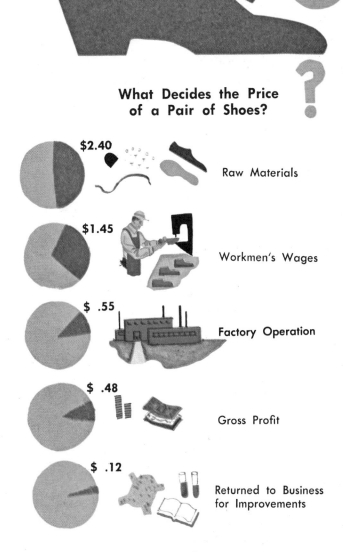

$5.00

What Decides the Price of a Pair of Shoes?

$2.40   Raw Materials

$1.45   Workmen's Wages

$ .55   Factory Operation

$ .48   Gross Profit

$ .12   Returned to Business for Improvements

People also believed that a manufactured article should be priced according to the cost of making it. The cost of making it includes fair pay for the laborers, the materials used in making it, and a reasonable profit for the company owners. Part of the profit should go into helping the factory get better machinery and in planning better products.

When was the Spanish-American War?

As United States merchant ships steamed into ports all over the world, problems with foreign countries were bound to arise.

Many ships went to the ports of Cuba, which was still owned by Spain in the 1890's. Many of Spain's other colonies had become free nations, and Cuba wanted independence, too. Many Americans felt that countries who wanted to govern themselves should be allowed by Spain to do so.

Cuba was trying to get its freedom in 1897. President William McKinley sent the United States battleship *Maine* to Cuba. The *Maine* was to offer protection to American citizens who were in Cuba while the fighting between Cubans and Spaniards was going on. On February 15, 1898, the *Maine* was in the harbor at *Havana*, Cuba. Suddenly the ship blew apart, killing 260 people.

Spain was blamed for the explosion. By April, the United States was at war with Spain. The American navy took ten Spanish ships in the Philippine Islands, which had belonged to Spain since Magellan's day. There was also some action on land, especially in Cuba. Theodore Roosevelt, then a member of the United States cavalry, won fame leading his "Rough Riders" up *San Juan Hill* in Cuba. Puerto Rico was taken by American troops, too.

The Spanish American War ended before the year 1898 was over. Cuba was granted its freedom from Spain. The islands of Puerto Rico and *Guam* were signed over to the United States. Puerto Rico is near Cuba, but Guam is an island in the Pacific Ocean almost as far west of the United States as the Philippine Islands. One reason the United States was interested in islands in the Pacific Ocean was to get coaling stations for her steamships.

The Philippine Islands were put under the protection of the United States. At about the same time, the Hawaiian Islands were made a United States territory. For the first time, as the 1890's drew to a close, the United States held land outside the continent of North America.

Many Americans thought that this was wrong. Freedom and independence for all nations was one of the things in which they strongly believed. Others wanted the United States to hold far-off lands, thinking it would give the nation more strength. Arrangements were made, however, for the people of the Philippines to get their freedom as soon as they were ready to govern themselves.

Biography Outline

Theodore Roosevelt

1858-1919

American

Politician and soldier

President of the United States—greatly influenced the place of the United States in world affairs—brought about many business reforms—did much to help conservation in the United States.

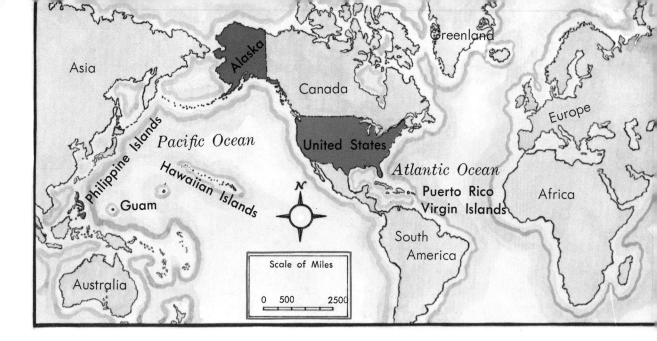

American Holdings in 1898

What were the early 1900's like?

During the early years of the 1900's, the nation was busy mostly with its own affairs. Many of the problems in business were settling down. The federal government had passed laws forbidding trusts.

Lawmakers had taken an interest in the problems of the working people, too. They passed laws dealing with the working conditions in the factories, shipping rates on railroads, and on other matters important to good conditions in business. Many of these laws were passed after Theodore Roosevelt became President in 1901.

In general, Americans found life good. People spent summer evenings sitting on their front porches. The young folks may have been singing such songs as "East Side, West Side" or "A Bicycle Built for Two."

Sometimes some of the bicycle riders went by. The peace might have been disturbed by a rattling, chugging automobile, raising a cloud of dust as it tore down the street at a frightening ten miles an hour.

The people may have talked about the World's Fair being held at St. Louis to honor the one-hundredth anniversary of the Louisiana Purchase, or the foolish thing the Wright Brothers were trying to do. Perhaps they talked about the first baseball World Series, or the new invention, the motion picture.

People were shaking their heads over the troubles in building the Panama Canal. They argued over the new business and labor laws. They discussed President Roosevelt's warnings that the coal, minerals, and forest lands of the country must be conserved.

When did the automobile arrive?

During the last half of the 1800's, inventors and scientists in both Europe and America were interested in building an engine that could burn fuel inside its own walls. Steam engines, with their big boilers, were fine for running big machinery such as riverboats. But they were too big and heavy for many smaller uses. Gasoline was one of the fuels that inventors worked with.

Inventors in France, Germany, and Austria were experimenting with automobiles, too. One of them made a gasoline engine. In the United States, two brothers, Charles and Frank *Duryea* of Massachusetts, built an automobile with a gasoline engine early in the 1890's. From then on, inventors in all parts of the country worked on automobiles.

The automobile bodies were much like the buggies in which people had been riding for many years. They were often called "horseless carriages." The horseless carriages were noisy and frequently broke down. Many a driver, dressed in his cap, goggles, and big gloves, had to either get out and under the car to fix it, or ask a farmer to bring his team of horses to pull the machine.

In the early 1900's, automobile factories began to center around Ohio and Michigan. Each manufacturer built one car at a time, in a small shop. These automobiles were very high priced because it took so much time and work to build them.

The early 1900's were peaceful days for Americans.

In this Ford assembly plant of 1914, the chassis and engine parts were assembled on the ground floor. This section of the automobile was wheeled to the bottom of the outdoor ramp. The bodies, assembled on the second floor, were pushed down the ramp and onto the frames waiting below.

In a few years, Henry Ford, who had been making automobiles almost from their beginning in the United States, used a new idea that made it possible to sell automobiles at a much lower price. Ford's idea was the *assembly-line* factory.

According to the assembly-line idea, the parts of one automobile would be exactly like the parts of every other automobile he made.

Biography Outline

Henry Ford

1863-1947

American

Industrialist

Founded one of the largest industrial companies in the world—pioneered in assembly-line manufacturing methods.

Workers were placed at stations along the line, a kind of moving belt. Each worker placed a certain part into each new automobile as it reached his station.

Ford's idea changed the automobile from a rich man's "toy" into an everyday means of transportation for many people. The assembly line set a new pattern for other kinds of manufacturing, too.

The growing use of the automobile gave rise to many other new industries. Tire-making, road-building, the making of automobile parts, service stations, parking lots, truck and bus transportation, motels, and other businesses came about through the automobile. The automobile made a great change in the lives of Americans throughout the country.

This picture was taken during the War Between the States. The Union is about to send up a man in the balloon to survey southern army movements from the air.

What was the first aircraft like?

Men had been interested in flying for many years before anyone ever succeeded in building a craft that would stay in the air. From time to time, inventors in different parts of the world would try out ideas they had for aircraft. One of the first types of aircraft was the balloon. Several American inventors had built rather successful balloons as early as the War Between the States.

Interest in balloons continued after the war. People also became interested in the flying of gliders. A *glider* looks like an airplane but floats through the air without the use of an engine. As the 1800's drew to a close, some people had gained a great deal

of skill in flying balloons and gliders. A flight in either a glider or a balloon was quite dangerous. Only those people who were willing to risk their lives took much interest in these early flying ships.

Who were Orville and Wilbur Wright?

In the year 1900, two brothers, Orville and Wilbur Wright, talked often of the latest news in glider flights. They both decided that they would like to try piloting a glider themselves. After they felt they had studied enough, they planned to build a glider. They left their bicycle shop business in Dayton, Ohio, and journeyed to Kitty Hawk, North Carolina. The United States Weather Bureau had told them that the steady winds and open country near Kitty Hawk made it a good location for the testing of gliders.

Biography Outline

Wilbur Wright — Orville Wright

1867-1912   1871-1948

American

Inventors

Invented and built the first successful airplane—first flight was on December 17, 1903, at Kitty Hawk, North Carolina—flight lasted 12 seconds—signed a contract with the United States Department of War in 1908 for the first military airplane—formed the Wright Company to build airplanes in 1909—Orville continued working to improve airplanes after Wilbur's death but sold his share in Wright Company—first airplane now in National Air Museum in Washington, D. C.

This photograph of Wilbur Wright at the controls to one of the brothers' early planes was taken in the year 1908.

The Wright brothers' first glider did not fly very long. To improve it, Orville and Wilbur spent hours near their Dayton home studying the way soaring birds tilted their wingfeathers as they glided along. They built a model glider and a wind tunnel to see how changes in the way the glider was made influenced its flight. Back at Kitty Hawk some time later, they built an improved glider. In this glider, they could stay in the air longer than anyone before them.

But just to glide was not what the Wright brothers wanted. They thought that if an engine were put in the glider to turn a big propeller, the air movement of the propeller could help keep the glider in the air.

In the summer of 1903, the Wright brothers built an engine something like the ones used in automobiles. Their engine, however, was made of aluminum in order to make it lighter than automobile engines. In December, they were again at Kitty Hawk, ready to try their glider with the engine in it. They ran a belt from the engine to a propeller, which they placed behind the wings.

This was the first airplane. Wilbur Wright flew 852 feet in that plane. He was in the air for fifty-nine seconds. He lay on his stomach and was strapped into place. He used hand levers to tilt the wings. From that beginning, the Wright brothers went on to build better and better airplanes. At first, Americans looked upon their work as only a stunt. The Wrights went to Europe and found more interest in their work there. After almost ten years, they were able to show that their idea was more than a stunt. The Air Age got its start at Kitty Hawk in 1903.

When was the Panama Canal built?

By the time the United States was beginning its second hundred years, steamships had replaced most of the sailing vessels on the oceans. But one problem that had faced the first New World explorers still troubled those who sailed the oceans. There was no way to take a ship from the Atlantic Ocean into the Pacific Ocean without going all the way around the tip of South America. For many years, men had dreamed of digging a canal that would connect the two oceans. Such a canal could save over five thousand miles for many ships.

The best place to build the canal seemed to be through the narrowest strip of land between North America and South America. The United States and England had studied the problem for quite some time. But it was France that took action first.

France began work at cutting a canal through Panama, a country of Central America, in the 1880's. The project turned out to have more problems than the French government expected. Money set aside for the work was soon used up, and France gave up the idea soon after the work was begun.

In 1902, Congress gave President Theodore Roosevelt permission to buy the French property in Panama. At that time, Panama was part of Colombia, South America. The United States and Colombia signed a treaty which gave the United States the right to control a strip of land ten miles wide. This was to be the Canal Zone. It was also agreed that all countries should be allowed to send ships through the canal. The ships would have to pay a fee for using the canal.

Routes through the Panama Canal

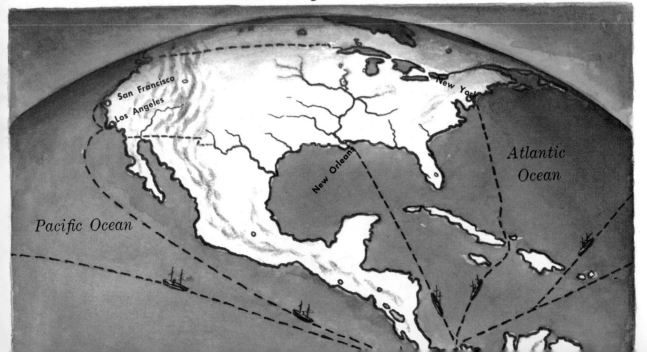

Pacific Ocean

San Francisco
Los Angeles
New York
New Orleans

Atlantic Ocean

President Roosevelt put Colonel George W. *Goethals* in charge of building the Canal in 1907. This was after two other Americans had already tried to direct the project. Both had given up the job as impossible.

According to Colonel Goethal's plans, a dam was built in the *Chagres* River to make a lake. A passageway was cut through the mountains. Locks were built to lift and lower ships in the water.

Colonel Goethal's work could not have been finished without the help of someone to fight the diseases that killed so many workers in the early years of the canal-building. Colonel William C. *Gorgas* took charge of the health problems in 1904. He was faced with *bubonic plague*, yellow fever, and malaria. He drained the swamps where mosquitoes lived, for mosquitoes carry malaria and yellow fever germs. He worked to clean up the places where rats lived. Rats are carriers of bubonic plague. Gorgas also brought in drugs and medicines.

With the work of both leaders, the Panama Canal was finally completed. On August 15, 1914, a ship made the first complete trip of about fifty miles through the canal. The dream of hundreds of years was realized. A passage from the Atlantic to the Pacific Ocean was built. A ship going from New York to San Francisco could cut the 13,000 mile journey to less than 8,000 miles.

Colonel George Goethals was in charge of building the Panama Canal.

Colonel William Gorgas helped fight disease and other health problems in the area.

Panama and the United States agreed that ships of all nations could use the canal.

When was World War I?

The peaceful days ended in 1917, when the United States entered the war that had been going on in Europe since 1914. Germany, Austria-Hungary, Turkey, and Bulgaria seemed to be trying to overpower all of Europe. England, France, Russia, and some of the smaller nations were trying to hold them back. The United States joined this group, known as the *Allies* in 1917, when German submarines began attacking American ships at sea.

Soon America's young men were in training camps, getting ready to go to France to "do their bit." Boys and girls as well as adults put their savings into "war savings stamps" and "Liberty Bonds." Through the stamps and bonds, people loaned money to the government to make guns, battleships, airplanes, and other war equipment.

Big troop transport ships left New York harbor. The rails were lined with soldiers in khaki uniforms. People sang "Over There" and "Keep the Home Fires Burning." They read newspapers for news of the war.

The war ended on November 11, 1918, with the Allies the victors. The people believed there would never be another war. They made November 11 a national holiday. Most of the soldiers came back home, but there were some left in France. Long rows of white crosses marked their graves. Thinking of those graves and seeing the men who came home missing an arm or a leg made people realize that war was more than parades and songs. It became clear that nations must live together in peace.

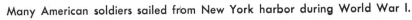
Many American soldiers sailed from New York harbor during World War I.

Questions

1. What was a business trust? How were trusts bad for people who wanted to use their services or products?

2. How did the Philippine Islands come under the protection of the United States?

3. How was the practice of forming business trusts put to an end?

4. Who were Charles and Frank Duryea?

5. Why were automobiles owned by only rich people at first? Whose ideas of manufacturing made it possible for more people to have automobiles? What were these ideas?

6. What was the first kind of aircraft with which Orville and Wilbur Wright worked? How did this lead to the airplane?

7. In what way was the Panama Canal a great help to ocean-sailing ships?

8. What were some of the problems faced by the builders of the canal?

You See for Yourself

Theodore Roosevelt was a very influential man during the early years of the 1900's. He was also a very colorful person. Read more about his life from books in your library. What did he do during the years he spent in the western part of our country? Who were many of the soldiers in his army of "Rough Riders"? What were some of his ideas on conservation of natural resources?

You have learned that the United States planned for the independence of the Philippines right from the beginning. Find out in what year these islands elected their first president.

From War to War

During the Roaring Twenties. . .

Airplanes saw wider use.

Passenger service between major cities began to be seen as a great possibility. The first flight across the Atlantic was made within ten years after World War I was over.

During the war, American women in great numbers had taken jobs out of the home. Some had taken over the work of the men who had gone to fight the war.

People could buy new items for the home.

As is usually the case, the war gave an extra push to the growth of industry and invention. It changed people's thinking, too. After World War I, Americans could not go back to the quiet days of the early 1900's.

How did the nation change during the 1920's?

Airplanes, used in the fighting of the war, had proved useful and not just for stunting. They were improved rapidly after the war. Soon mail was being carried regularly by air. When closed cabins were put on planes, people began to look to airplanes as a new means of transportation, faster than any kind before it.

Some of the women put on coveralls, tucked their long hair inside caps, and went to work in the factories. Most of the factories, of course, were producing guns and other war supplies. After working hours, the women wore their dresses shorter than ever before, about halfway between the ankle and the knee.

After the war, women refused to give up the new freedom they had known during the war. In 1920, the nineteenth amendment was added to the United States Constitution. This amendment gave women the right to vote. Until then, only men could vote.

Women cut their hair short for the first time during the 1920's. They wore a new dress style called the "flapper." They danced the lively "Charleston" and took part in the generally gay life that made up the years of the "Roaring Twenties."

What ended the Roaring Twenties?

Business in general enjoyed a greater growth and bigger profits than ever before. People all over the

Women enjoyed a new freedom.

country bought stock in companies. *Stock* is a share in a company. A person who buys stock gives a company money to help run its business.

This person then receives part of the profits of the company in which he holds stock. Companies that have stock for sale list their stocks on the *stock market*. People interested in buying stock can choose which company they want to invest in by reading the stock market listings.

During the twenties, many people who bought stock hoped to sell it at a higher price than they had paid for it. In this way, they could make money on the buying and selling of stocks rather than on the profits of the business whose stock they held.

Other people bought stock on *margin*. This meant that they paid only part of what the stock was worth, but they promised to pay the rest if the company needed it. Sometimes people bought more stock than they could possibly pay for. They thought they could hold the stock long enough to share in the profits of the business, and then sell the stock before they were asked to pay its full value.

Credit buying was popular.

There were many new things in the home. Electric refrigerators were new. The washing machine was greatly improved. Women wanted electric vacuum cleaners, coffee makers, waffle irons, and clothes irons. A man named Marconi had carried on with the same work Edison had started. Marconi's work led to the invention of the radio. By the 1920's, many families could enjoy radio programs in their homes. Many also bought their first automobiles.

Some of these things were bought on credit. *Credit* is the promise a customer makes to a store owner to pay later for the goods he buys. It looked as if good times had really come to stay.

Late in the 1920's, business began to slow down. Fewer and fewer businessmen were willing to sell goods on credit. Herbert Hoover became President in March of 1929. His business advisers told him that credit buying was getting out of hand. President Hoover tried to take steps to slow it down, but few people were willing to listen to his warnings.

In October of 1929, the Roaring Twenties came to an end. The value of stocks fell suddenly. People who had bought on margin could not pay the money they had promised. They tried to sell quickly, hoping not to lose the little they had invested. But almost all the people lost their stock investments. Many industries and businesses had to close.

What was the Depression?

The 1930's were called the Depression years. Jobs were hard to find, and people had to get along with almost no money. Often several families shared a house, while other houses and apartments stood empty. President Hoover put into action several plans to help people who had no jobs or money. But to rebuild the nation's business would take time.

Late in 1932, Franklin Delano Roosevelt was elected President. He introduced a government plan which he called the "New Deal." Through the New Deal, Roosevelt hoped to rebuild the nation's business strength. The federal government opened many new offices, such as the Works Progress Administration. The WPA gave jobs to many people who could not find work.

Biography Outline
Herbert Hoover
1874-
American
Businessman and politician
Successful and wealthy businessman and public official—President of the United States when the Depression began.

Biography Outline
Franklin Delano Roosevelt
1882-1945
American
Politician
President of the United States from 1933-1945—President longer than any other man—led the United States through its worst depression and war.

When did the United States go to war again?

Just as it seemed that the nation's problems were beginning to smooth out, the American people received a bad shock. On Sunday, December 7, 1941, their radios broadcast the news that the Japanese had attacked and sunk many of the American ships in the Navy base at Pearl Harbor, Hawaii. The next day, Congress declared war against Japan.

There had been wars and trouble throughout the rest of the world for a number of years before the United States went to war. One-man rulers, called *dictators*, had taken over the governments of Germany and Italy. Adolf Hitler, Germany's dictator, and *Mussolini*, Italy's dictator, were trying to force other European countries under their control.

Several European countries, including England and France, were already at war. They were trying to keep Hitler and Mussolini from marching into their lands. Japan's army leader, Hideki Tojo, had ideas much like those of Hitler and Mussolini. The attack on Pearl Harbor was the first step in his plan to conquer the United States.

In less than a week, the United States was at war with Germany and Italy as well as with Japan. American troops had to go both east and west, into many different parts of the world. Before long, almost every nation in the world was at war. Some

Thousands of American soldiers went to foreign countries to fight World War II. These soldiers are watching for enemy soldiers in the ruined streets of a German town.

were on the side of the *Axis*, of which Germany was the main nation. Others joined the Allies.

The fighting of World War II was more terrible than history had seen before. Scientists had learned how to make large bombs that could be dropped from bomber airplanes. Factories and cities were destroyed in this war. Many people other than soldiers were killed.

The American general, Dwight D. Eisenhower, was made leader of the Allied armies in Europe. Slowly, and with the loss of many lives, the Axis armies were pushed back. Mussolini stepped down as head of the Italian government in 1943. Hitler took his own life in April, 1945. War in Europe ended soon afterward, but the war with Japan lasted until August.

Just before Japan surrendered, United States' bombers dropped a new kind of bomb on two Japanese cities. Scientists had been working for years to learn how to divide the atom, long thought to be the smallest possible bit of matter. By the summer of 1945, scientists had learned the secret of splitting the

The whole world realized the power of the atom when two atomic bombs were used against Japan in World War II.

atom and how to use that knowledge in making a bomb almost too powerful to imagine. The bombs dropped on *Nagasaki* and *Hiroshima* were the first atomic bombs. Within a month, Japan surrendered.

World War II made it clear that nations had to learn to work together. With this thought in mind, fifty-one nations set up an organization known as the United Nations. In the United Nations, countries could try to meet and settle their problems without turning to open warfare. Today there are more than one-hundred member nations in the U.N.

What new troubles followed the War?

World War II was over, but real peace was slow in coming. Russia and China both fought on the side of the Allies during the war. After the war, China, then under a dictator joined dictator-ruled Russia. These dictators favor communism instead of democracy. They try to force other nations to adopt the ideas and become members of the Communist party.

In the small Asian country of Korea, the Communist party members helped by China made war against the people of their country who did not wish to be Communists. For three years, between 1950 and 1953, United States troops helped fight back the Communists in Korea. Other countries in the United Nations also sent soldiers to fight the Communists in Korea.

World War II brought many new machines and much knowledge that could be used in peaceful ways. So much progress had been made in communication, for example, that television could be brought to the public almost immediately.

Atomic power was seen as a new source of fuel. It could perhaps take the place of such natural resources as coal and oil, both of which were being used at a fast rate. Today, some electric power plants are run by atomic power. Submarines and other ships have atomic engines. Scientists are continually trying to make atomic power useful to workers in many fields.

Words to Know

Axis (ăk'sĭs) 265

credit (krĕd'ĭt) 264

dictator (dĭk tā'tĕr) 265

Hideki Tojo (hē dĕ kē tō jō) 265

Hiroshima (hē'r̥ shē'ma) 266

margin (mär'jĭn) 263

Mussolini (mōōs'sŏ lē'nĕ) 265

Nagasaki (nä'ga sä'kē) 266

stock (stŏk) 263

stock market (stŏk mär'kĕt) 263

Questions

1. How did the lives of women change during World War I? What did the nineteenth amendment do for American women?

2. What does it mean to buy stock on margin? During what years of American history did many people buy stock on margin?

3. When and what were the Depression years? What was the New Deal?

4. How did war between the United States and Japan begin?

5. What helped to make World War II the most terrible war in history?

6. What action did the United States take shortly before Japan's surrender?

7. Why was the United Nations begun?

8. Why was the war in Korea fought?

You See for Yourself

Read about Charles A. Lindbergh in an encyclopedia. For what is he best remembered? What was the name of his airplane?

Alan B. Shepard, Jr.
November 18, 1923
U. S. Navy
Made first U. S. suborbital
flight on May 5, 1961.

Alan Shepard

Virgil I. Grissom
April 3, 1926
Mitchell, Indiana
U. S. Air Force
Made second U. S. suborbital
flight on July 21, 1961.

Virgil Grissom

Living in the Space Age

The study of improved fuels and progress in air travel pointed the way for the jet-powered airplanes and giant rockets. With the use of jet engines, the propeller on the airplane became unnecessary. The jet engines, which work something like rockets, gave airplanes far greater speed than they had ever had.

Rockets carried satellites into space. The satellites travel around and around the earth, above the blanket of air that surrounds the earth. "Space" begins beyond this blanket of air. The satellites send back weather and other information.

Satellites have also been used to send television signals over long distances. The satellites catch television beams, that would otherwise be lost in space, and send them back to the earth. The returning beams are picked up by receiving towers that are far from the sending station. The first satellite to do this work was *Telstar*, put into space by the United States in July of 1962.

When did man enter space?

At the same time that the jet engine was being tested for use in airplanes, scientists were working on

American Astronauts made their flights into space
in capsules like this one.

John Glenn

John H. Glenn, Jr.
July 18, 1921
Cambridge, Ohio
U. S. Marine Corps
Orbited earth three times on
February 20, 1962.

M. Scott Carpenter
May 1, 1925
Boulder, Colorado
U. S. Navy
Orbited earth three times on
May 24, 1962.

Scott Carpenter

the next step in transportation. This was the step that would take man himself into space.

In 1959, seven young men began their training as space travelers for the United States. They were called Mercury *Astronauts*. Each day the Astronauts went through special training exercises.

Each of the seven men was eager to take part in the first space flights. Yet none of them made the first space flight in the history of man. This was made by a Russian named *Yuri Gagarin*, on April 12, 1961. Less than a month later, American Astronaut Alan B. Shepard, Jr., journeyed into space. During the next two years, five more American Astronauts made space flights. The seventh Astronaut, Donald Slayton, from the state of Wisconsin, was unable to make a space journey because of a slight heart disorder.

Walter Schirra

Walter M. Schirra, Jr.
March 12, 1923
U. S. Navy
Hackensack, New Jersey
Orbited earth six times on
October 3, 1962.

Leroy Gordon Cooper
March 6, 1927
U. S. Air Force
Orbited e a r t h twenty-two
times on May 15-16, 1963.

Gordon Cooper

An artist's drawing gives us an idea of how the inside of a space capsule looks.

The X-15 rocket plane is carried into the air by a mother plane. Shot from the mother ship in the air, it can travel at great speeds and high altitudes.

What work has been done to build airplanes for space flights?

Scientists and inventors never stopped trying to build planes that could fly higher and faster. Jet-engined planes began to be used for regular passenger service in 1958. They traveled at between 500 and 650 miles per hour and about five to seven miles high in the air.

Work continued on more new kinds of winged aircraft. Some were rocket planes, which were carried high into the air by a "mother" ship. The rocket plane is shot from the mother ship in the air. The rocket plane speeds along the same way in general as the jet plane, but with great-

er power. The rocket plane can rise higher and go faster than any other winged aircraft. It is thought that one model in particular, the X-15, may one day be able to rise to 100 miles above the earth and travel at speeds up to 4,000 miles an hour.

In 1962, Air Force Major Robert White piloted the X-15 rocket plane to a distance of 59.6 miles above the earth. Other pilots have flown the X-15 to greater heights since Major White's flight.

Military and government leaders have worked with Presidents Harry Truman, Dwight Eisenhower, John Kennedy, and Lyndon Johnson to carry forward the Space Program.

How does water transportation fit into the Space Age?

The work of today's pioneers, the pioneers into space, is interesting and exciting. Their findings may make great changes in man's way of living. Still the great waterways of North America have not out-lived their importance. The age-old dream of a "northwest passage" has been realized during the Space Age.

Even after the European explorers finally learned that there was no water passage through the continent, they still wanted to use the waterways to travel from the Atlantic Ocean to the westernmost Great Lakes. The building of a canal around Niagara Falls made this possible for most lake steamers and for small ocean-going ships.

The old canals had to be widened and deepened. New locks and dams were needed at several places. It took years to complete the work, but in June of 1959, the St. Lawrence Seaway was opened. Canada and the United States had worked together to build it.

The St. Lawrence Seaway made ocean ports of such inland cities as Cleveland, Toledo, Detroit, Chicago, Milwaukee, Buffalo, and Erie.

For a number of years, the great Missouri-Ohio-Mississippi River system that had meant so much to the country's early growth, was not used much. Railroads handled the work once done by boats on rivers.

As years went by, some people began to see the value of using great flat barges to ship things that weighed a great deal or that took up much space. Now the rivers are becoming busier each year. Powerful tugboats push long lines of barges along the great waterways. The barges carry such materials as oil, coal, ore, chemicals, and grain to the river cities. They carry away some of the finished products of these cities, such as large machinery.

These two barges are passing the city of Cincinnati as they make their separate ways along the Ohio River. Such barges have brought new importance to river transportation.

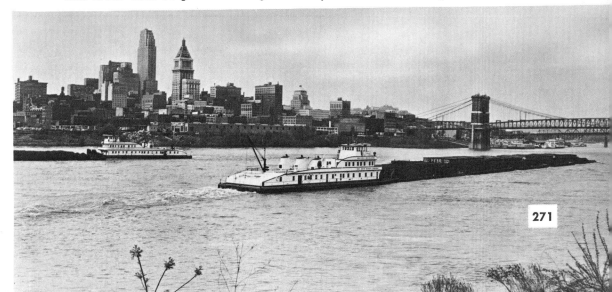

Saint Lawrence Seaway and Lake Ports

Questions

1. What changes did jet engines bring to the airplane?

2. What is Telstar?

3. What did the Astronauts have to do for several years before they made their flights into space?

4. Who was the first man to enter space? From what country did he come? When was his flight?

5. For what special use was the X-15 rocket plane built?

6. Why is the St. Lawrence Seaway important to Great Lakes cities?

7. What kinds of things are today sent over the Missouri-Ohio-Mississippi River system?

You See for Yourself

Learn as much as you can about space and space travel. What is meant by weightlessness? What did our Astronauts have to say about weightlessness when they returned from their space flights?

Now You Know

The Centennial Exposition of 1876 helped to show the progress that Americans had made since the beginning of the nation in 1776. The many machines and inventions shown at the fair were great advances in communication, manufacturing, and other fields of work.

Business and industry grew rapidly during the 1800's. As the 1800's drew to a close, problems between labor and business arose. The federal government began passing laws to limit the power of business and industry owners in this country. This law-making continued into the early 1900's.

The airplane and the automobile were the biggest advances in transportation during the early 1900's.

In more recent years, the possibility of space travel has opened a new field for pioneers in new transportation methods.

The telephone, radio, television, and space satellites have all marked great advances in communication during the 1900's.

The United States took part in two world wars during the 1900's. Perhaps the United States' most serious problem as a leader among nations is to help prevent any more such wars from taking place. The use of atomic power in warfare has greatly added to the necessity for keeping peace. The United Nations, formed at the end of World War II, has given the nations of the world a place to discuss their differences peaceably.

You Talk It Over

You have learned that at one time in our country's history certain business owners became selfish in the way they offered their goods and services to the public. Pretend that you own a very large company that does millions of dollars' worth of business each year. What things would you think about in deciding how best to make use of the company profits? What things would you think about in regard to the people who worked for you? What things would you think about in regard to the people who used the goods or services of your company?

Unit Questions

1. What invention changed the method of making clothing in the United States? Who invented this machine?

2. What were some of the main products of the United States at the end of its first one-hundred years?

3. What inventions of the 1800's were of special help to each of these groups of people: farmers, soldiers, office workers?

4. How did Thomas Edison learn to be a telegraph operator? What did he do with the telegraph besides learning to operate it?

5. List as many of Edison's inventions as you can.

6. What is meant by the "law of supply and demand"?

7. Why did some people think that the United States should not hold the Philippine Islands? Why did other people think it was a good idea?

8. What is an assembly line? Where was one first used?

9. How is a glider different from an airplane?

10. Why did the Wright brothers first work with gliders?

11. Why were many countries interested in building a canal through Panama? What country built the Panama Canal? What were some of the problems faced by the men building the Panama Canal?

12. In what year did the United States enter World War I? In what year did the war end?

13. What influence did World War I have on the lives of American women?

14. What is credit? During what years in the nation's history did credit buying get out of hand?

15. Against what three leading countries did the Allies fight during World War II? What were the names of the dictators of these countries?

16. Who are the Astronauts? Who was the first man to enter space?

17. How is a rocket plane different from other planes?

Puzzlers

Most important inventions of today are worked out by groups of people working together in laboratories. They use the inventions of the past and make improvements on or additions to them.

Here are ten pictures of things commonly seen today, all of which began with earlier inventions and inventors. For each of the "today" pictures, give the letter of the earlier invention and the name of the inventor who laid the groundwork for today's inventions.

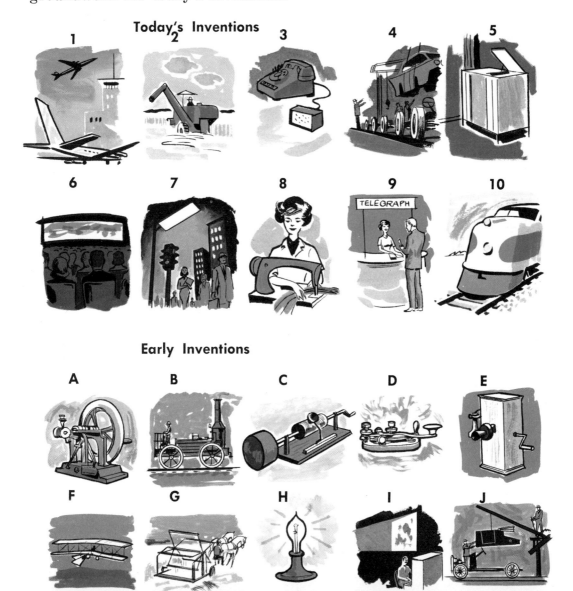

Today's Inventions

1 2 3 4 5

6 7 8 9 10

Early Inventions

A B C D E

F G H I J

Unit Activities

You Play a Word Game

You have studied a number of new and important words in this unit. Ask your teacher to make up a list of words that she thinks you should remember from your study of this unit.

Divide the class into two groups. Then divide each group into teams of two pupils each. When you are ready to play, team one from each group should be seated in front of the room. Your teacher will write one of the words from her list on a piece of pa- per and show the word to one member of each team. The pupil who sees the word will give his or her partner one-word clues that will help the partner to guess what the word is. Each team will have ten chances to guess the word. If one team guesses the word on the first try, it means ten points for their group. If a word is guessed on the second try, it gives that team's group nine points, and so on. The group with the highest score after every team has had a chance to play, wins the game.

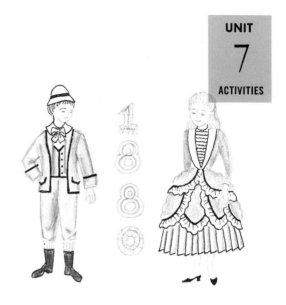

You Make a Scrapbook

Collect all the pictures and other information you can find about the United States Space Program. Paste them into a scrapbook. Try to keep them in order so that the earliest pictures and stories come first in your book and the latest developments come last.

You Draw a Time-Line

Find pictures of early models of automobiles and of the changes that have been made in automobiles since the early days. Make your own drawings from these pictures. Arrange your drawings along the chalkboard or on a long strip of wrapping paper so that the earliest model is shown first and the most recent model is shown last. You may even be able to find some pictures of what manufacturers think automobiles of the future will look like. Include a drawing of one of these in your time-line. Below each drawing write the year in which that particular model was made.

Encyclopedias and the big dictionary in your library will show you pictures of many of the early automobiles. You may make your drawings from the pictures you find in these books.

You Give a Fashion Review

Men's and women's fashions have changed greatly since the nation was one-hundred years old. Find as many pictures, old and new, as you can showing women's fashions since 1876. You will want to divide the years into particular periods. The list below shows one way you might arrange the time periods. Draw several large poster pictures showing the popular fashions for each period.

The year 1876
The 1880's
The 1890's
From 1900 to 1920
World War I
The Roaring Twenties
The 1930's
World War II
The 1950's
Today

UNIT

7

ACTIVITIES

Section Two

The Northeastern States

The eleven Northeastern States are in that part of our country where the New England farmers chopped trees and cleared rocks from the thin, rocky soil. It is where the Sons of Liberty pointed the way to freedom. Slater's Mill, America's first factory was built here. The city of Philadelphia, where the Declaration of Independence was signed, is here.

The Northeastern States are part of the great "Eastern Woodlands." Visitors are usually surprised to see how much woodland still stands. Of course, it is not the same forest that stood when the Indians held the land. It is second growth where the trees were cut down. The climate and the soil allow the growth of many trees.

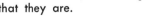

Great cities that line the Atlantic coast help to make the Northeastern States the manufacturing center that they are.

279

Location of Northeastern Section

CANADA

St. Lawrence River

Maine

Bangor

River

Penobscot River

Augusta

Kennebec

Montpelier

New Hampshire

Vermont

Connecticut River

Portland

Portsmouth

Concord

Lake Ontario

Rochester   Syracuse

Buffalo

New York

Albany

Hudson River

Lowell

Massachusetts   Boston

Springfield   Worcester

Lake Erie

Cape Cod

Providence

Hartford

R.I.

New Bedford

Connecticut   Newport

River

New Haven

Capitals

State   Federal

Allegheny

West Point

Scranton

River

Long Island

New England States

Middle Atlantic States

Pennsylvania

Susquehanna River

New York

Newark

0   25   50   100   150

Pittsburgh

Harrisburg

Allentown

Reading

Delaware River

Trenton

New Jersey

Philadelphia

Monongahela River

Gettysburg

Wilmington

Maryland

Baltimore

Dover

Washington, D.C.

Annapolis

Delaware Bay

Potomac River

Delaware

Chesapeake Bay

Me.

Vt.

N.H.

N.Y.

Mass.

Conn.

R.I.

Penn.

N.J.

Md.

Del.

Atlantic Ocean

Megalopolis

0   400

The Northeastern States

What is the climate of the Northeastern States like?

The states at the northern end of the Northeastern section have long cold winters and short cool summers. The states farther south have a milder climate. The average winter temperatures for Maryland and Delaware are above the freezing mark. Their summers are long and warm. This milder climate is not only because the states are farther south, but also because there are so many arms of water reaching into the land. The nearness of the water keeps the air from becoming extremely cold or extremely warm. At the same time, it adds dampness to the air. The dampness often makes it seem cooler or warmer than it really is.

The climate of the Northeastern States is fine for growing the crops that do not need a long growing season. It is the soil and land surface that prevent farming in some places. In the valleys and along the coastal plains, however, the soil is good enough and the land level enough for farming to be important.

You will remember that the earliest settlers in this section looked to farming to make a living. They later turned to manufacturing and other work. Today, by far the largest number of people in the Northeastern States live in cities.

What is Megalopolis, U.S.A.?

If you were to list the ten most densely populated states in the United States, you would find that eight of them are in the Northeastern States. A *densely populated* area is one in which large numbers of people live on each square mile of land. Areas in which few persons live on each square mile of land are said to be *sparsely populated*.

A large part of this dense population is found in a long strip of land that stretches along the coastal plain from Boston to Washington, D.C. This strip, five hundred miles long, is sometimes called *Megalopolis*.

"Megalopolis" means a very large city. Megalopolis, U.S.A., really includes a number of large cities. But these cities have grown so large that their boundaries often touch.

The heart of Megalopolis is Manhattan Island in New York City. Here are most of New York City's skyscrapers, including the Empire State Building, the tallest building in the world. Besides its skyscrapers, Manhattan Island has famous churches, museums, libraries, universities, and colleges.

Densely Populated States

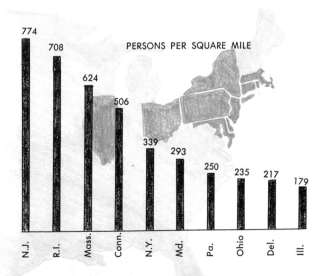

PERSONS PER SQUARE MILE

774 N.J.
708 R.I.
624 Mass.
506 Conn.
339 N.Y.
293 Md.
250 Pa.
235 Ohio
217 Del.
179 Ill.

Ocean passenger liners and freighters from many parts of the world dock at the fine harbor of New York City.

Manhattan is also home for many people, most of whom live in apartments. Some live in beautiful buildings where a doorman helps them from their cars, and elevators carry them swiftly to their richly furnished rooms. Others climb dark, narrow stairways to sooty apartments where a large family is crowded into two or three rooms.

Boroughs of New York City

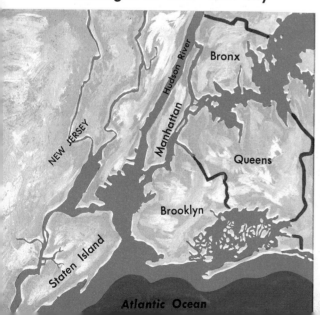

The rest of New York City spreads out from Manhattan. It stretches across several rivers and includes four more boroughs besides Manhattan. The *boroughs* are the sections of land into which New York City is divided. The other four boroughs are Queens, Brooklyn, the Bronx, and Richmond, better known as Staten Island. Beyond these boroughs stretch the suburbs. They blend into the suburbs of New Jersey cities to the south and west and into Connecticut cities to the north and east. Many people who work in New York City do not live there. Their homes are in the suburbs, in the cities of New Jersey or Connecticut, or miles away along the Hudson River in New York State. These people pour into New York City each morning over a number of different transportation routes that lead into the city.

The workers ride in a network of subway trains that travel under the city streets. They ride crowded railroad trains or come by bus or automobile over streets and great new expressways that sweep through crowded towns.

The transportation system of Megalopolis does not end with taking people to and from work. Ocean ships keep the docks from Boston all the way to Baltimore, Maryland, busy. Railroads bring freight cars into yards along the steamship docks. In these yards, are great warehouses that cover acres of land. Trucks, too, come and go, day and night.

Airports near all the Megalopolis cities are busy transportation centers. Big jetliners make regular trips back and forth across the Atlantic Ocean, to South America, or to any part of the United States. Smaller planes often carry businessmen from one city to another.

Not all of the great cities of the Northeastern States are part of

Many cars cross the George Washington Bridge as they enter and leave New York City each day.

Megalopolis. Albany and Syracuse, New York, and Pittsburgh, Pennsylvania, are a long way from the coast.

The city of Buffalo, New York, makes use of the Niagara Falls to supply electric power for homes and industries there.

Lumber from this forest in Maine will provide materials for manufacturing.

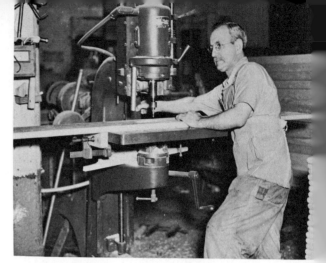

The Northeastern States have the people to work at the many jobs in manufacturing.

Why are the Northeastern States a good place to carry on manufacturing?

American manufacturing had its beginning in this section of the country. Today, New York State does more dollars' worth of manufacturing than any other state in the Union. Pennsylvania, New Jersey, and Massachusetts are among the nation's top ten manufacturing states. Throughout the section, one can find mills and factories that make almost everything. But the products that bring the most money to Northeastern manufacturers are clothing, machinery, which includes much electrical equipment, foods, metals, and textiles. *Textiles* include the materials used in making woven fabrics and the woven fabrics themselves.

There is a very good reason why the Northeastern States are so important in manufacturing: all the things that are needed for manufacturing are found there.

You have already seen that a great number of people live in the Northeastern States. You have also learned that transportation of all kinds has been developed. But without materials, power, and markets, manufacturing could not be carried on.

What materials for manufacturing are found in the Northeastern States?

The materials factories need to make their finished products are called *raw materials*. The natural resources of the Northeastern States provide many raw materials for factories. Logs from the forests furnish wood for boxes, furniture, and other wood products. Factories that prepare food use much fish from the nearby fishing banks and some of the farm products of the area.

In addition to the raw materials close at hand, other raw materials from distant states and countries are brought in over the excellent transportation systems.

Railroads and coal help give the Northeastern States power and transportation.

The many kinds of stores in the cities are among the markets of the Northeastern States.

Where do Northeastern factories get the power to do work?

The first factories were run by the muscle power of men or work animals. The word "manufacture" is taken from Latin words meaning "to make by hand." Muscle power is still used for some types of manufacturing, but the factory of today uses machines whenever possible. But machines would be useless without power to run them. Almost all factory machines of today are run by electric power.

Electricity can be found anywhere, but special machinery is needed to put it into usable form. A machine that does this is called a *generator*. But it takes power to run a generator, too.

Most of the generators in the Northeastern States are powered by steam engines. Steam engines need large amounts of both water and fuel. Water has always been a plentiful natural resource in the Northeastern States. The necessary fuel, too, is close at hand. Much of it comes from the rich coal fields in the state of Pennsylvania.

In recent years, the power of the atom has been put to use in steam engines for the electric generators. The first electric power plant to put the atom to work was built at Shippingport, Pennsylvania. It began furnishing electric power in December of 1957. This was still another "first" in the work of manufacturing for the Northeastern States.

The widespread use of atomic power for making electricity could help to solve one of the nation's problems. The coal, oil, and gas found in the earth are being burned at a rapid rate today. It is possible that the country could one day be left without these important fuels. If atomic power could take over some of the work now done by these fuels, it would help greatly in saving these precious natural resources.

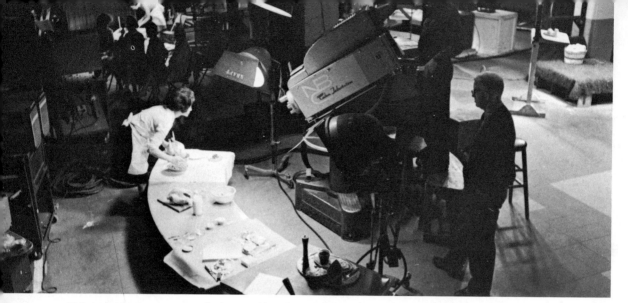

This television commercial, being filmed in New York, is part of the advertising industry, which has its center in the Northeastern States.

Where are the markets for products of the Northeastern factories?

Since so many people live there, many of the products from the factories of the Northeastern States are also sold in that area. But many more products are sent to other parts of the United States and to foreign countries. The fine transportation system leading into and away from the Northeastern States is an important part of marketing.

The markets themselves are the hundreds of different kinds of stores and shops that sell goods to buyers all across our country and throughout the rest of the world. Other businesses also take part in marketing. The great warehouses of the cities store manufactured products until they are needed on the market. Many of these warehouses are near railroads, trucking offices, and steamship docks.

Advertising, the business of making a product known to possible buyers, is a very large and important part of marketing. The main offices of advertising firms of this country are in Northeastern cities.

How do people live in New England?

(Maine, Vermont, New Hampshire, Massachusetts, Rhode Island, Connecticut)

Although the manufacturing industry gives more jobs to people than any other industry, there are still many people who make their living in other ways.

New Englanders have always faced problems given them by nature. From the very earliest days of settlement, the rough and hilly land and rocky soil made life difficult for the farmer. The long winters are bitterly cold. Although the summers are pleasant, they are too short for the growing of many crops.

Yet facing these problems seemed to bring out the strength of the New Englanders. They learned to make the best of their poor soil and short growing season. They found crops that could be grown on their land and learned to market them in the way that would bring the most profits.

Today, many of the New England farm products are foods that are eaten while they are fresh, such as dairy products and fruits and vegetables. These foods are usually sent quickly to markets in nearby cities.

The glaciers of ages past left many lakes, ponds, marshes, and swamps, throughout this section of the country. New Englanders make use of the wet lands called *bogs*, by growing cranberries. Most of the cranberries eaten in the United States are grown in Maine and Massachusetts.

Vermont maple trees produce more maple syrup and sugar than any other area in the United States. Potatoes grown in Maine's sandy soil are shipped all over the country.

Another farm product shipped out of New England is the tobacco grown in the lower valley of the Connecticut River, which divides the White Mountains from the Green Mountains. Many of the tobacco growers build cloth shades over their crops to protect them from the sun and weather. This shade-grown tobacco is the most costly tobacco grown in this country. Unlike the early Virginia tobacco growers, the Connecticut farmers have learned to *conserve* their soil. This means that they feed the soil heavily so that they can use the same ground over and over again without wearing it out.

Connecticut tobacco growers place canvas shades over their fine crops.

The sea, pounding endlessly against New England's rocky shores, may seem to be an enemy in times of storm and bad weather. But to New Englanders, the sea has been a helper in a number of ways. Shipbuilding began there in earliest times and still continues. Big ocean liners, tugboats, fishing boats, pleasure boats of many kinds, and even atomic-powered submarines are built in New England shipyards.

The life that grows in the sea has also given many New Englanders a living. The waters off the coast have always been rich in fish. The nets and traps of the fishermen bring in fine catches of codfish, haddock, rosefish, flounder, lobsters, and crabs.

Although whaling is not as important today as it once was, whaling boats still travel far from the coast. Today's boats are equipped with har-poon guns that shoot the harpoon directly from the deck of the ships. The harpoon carries a charge of explosive that kills the whale when the harpoon hits it. The oil of the whale is used in making soap and certain explosives, for dressing leather, and for oiling machinery. The meat and some of the ground bone make fertilizer and cattle and chicken feed.

From the stone quarries, especially in Vermont and New Hampshire, come fine building stones. Granite, marble, limestone, and slate are among the leading types of stone quarried in that area.

Many tourists come to New England to see the lovely color of the maple trees in autumn, the rolling hills and sparkling lakes, and the many miles of seashore. Many New Englanders make a living by providing food and lodging for these visitors.

Many fishing villages can be found along the shores of the New England States.

Besides showing visitors many beauties of nature, New Englanders can point out many places where important events in American history took place. They can tell of life during colonial days and show interesting old inns and houses. They are proud of the ways New England led the nation. There, the first printing press was set up, and the nation's first newspaper printed. The first American public high schools, libraries, and colleges were opened in New England. During the 1800's, it was the home of many leading American authors, including Henry Wadsworth Longfellow, Ralph Waldo Emerson, John Greenleaf Whittier, Oliver Wendell Holmes, and Henry David Thoreau. It is still a center of art and education and home to many writers, artists, and leaders in all fields of work.

How do people live in the Middle Atlantic States?

(New York, New Jersey, Delaware, Maryland, Pennsylvania)

Since the earliest days of settlement, the Middle Atlantic region has drawn people from all different countries and walks of life. The Dutch brought in people from Denmark, France, Germany, Ireland, and Norway to help farm the land in their colony, which was to become New York. William Penn invited many people besides English Quakers to live in Pennsylvania. Delaware, New Jersey, and Maryland, too, drew people of different backgrounds.

East Corinth, Vermont, is among the many lovely New England villages.

This quarry is in Graniteville, Vermont.

These tourists in New Hampshire are enjoying one of the state's beautiful lakes.

The steel industry had an early start in the city of Pittsburgh, Pennsylvania.

soft coal, which is much needed in the making of steel.

In addition to coal, this region has iron ore in small amounts, limestone, and water also needed in the steel-making industry. The steel industry here got its start during the 1800's. Today, the steel mills in such cities as Pittsburgh make the Middle Atlantic States an important steel-making region. Some of the iron ore needed by the steel industry is shipped across the Great Lakes from the iron ranges in Minnesota. Some comes from even farther away, including other countries. The steel mills are usually located near the coal supply, since iron ore can be shipped more easily than coal.

The steel industry helped the growth of other nearby cities, too. Many plants that make tools, machinery, and hardware of many kinds from the products of the steel mills are located in these cities.

Like New England, the Middle Atlantic States also have textile mills and clothing factories. Chemicals are the main product of Delaware cities. Printing and publishing are important in Philadelphia and in New York. A number of coastal cities are shipbuilding centers.

Several important federal government offices are placed in this part of the United States. The United States Naval Academy is at Annapolis, Maryland. The Military Academy is at West Point, New York.

This mixture of people with different ideas and customs is one of the things that helped industry and business to grow so rapidly in this region. As in New England, many things needed for manufacturing were present, so mills and factories sprang up rapidly. This was true not only in the coastal cities, but also beyond the Appalachian Mountains in western New York and in Pennsylvania. Railroads and canals, the Great Lakes, and the Ohio River gave these cities the necessary transportation.

The Middle Atlantic States are rich in natural resources. In coal production, Pennsylvania stands second among all the fifty states. It is the only state where hard coal is mined. But most of the coal mined in Pennsylvania is a high grade of

With so many people to feed, most of the farmers of these states raise products that can be used to help feed the people in the nearby cities. Many are dairy farmers. Others grow fruits and vegetables. Poultry is important in all five states. Grain crops are grown, but much is used as feed for cattle and chickens.

Frozen food packaging makes it possible for some of the products of this area to be shipped all over the United States. Oysters and other seafood, especially from the Chesapeake Bay area and from Delaware and New Jersey, are enjoyed by people everywhere.

The Middle Atlantic States are as proud of their part in American history as New England is. Tourists can visit many places where important happenings in the story of the nation took place. In addition, there are many who go to the eastern coast of New Jersey for seaside vacations. The famous "boardwalk" along the edge of the ocean at Atlantic City is a favorite vacation spot.

With so many people and so many cities, the Middle Atlantic States have had many problems to solve. Almost all the cities are working on projects to replace old and dirty housing with new buildings.

Many are looking for ways to make their cities more beautiful, too. The steel mills add the special problem of too much smoke. Great study has been given to how to make the air cleaner and purer. Truck and automobile traffic is thicker here than anywhere else in the nation. The great network of expressways and clover-leafs where highways meet has been a building project of the past years. Everywhere, work is going on to make the cities better places in which to live.

The city of Philadelphia has replaced sections of old and unsafe housing with attractive buildings like these.

Words to Know

bogs (bŏgz) 287

advertising (ăd'vẽr tīz'ĭng) 286

boroughs (bûr'ȯz) 282

conserve (kŏn sûrv') 287

densely populated (dĕns'lĭ pŏp'u̇ lāt ĕd) 281

generator (jĕn'ẽr ā'tẽr) 284

Megalopolis (mĕg'a̤ lŏp'ō lĭs) 281

raw materials (rô ma̤ tẽr'ĭ ălz) 284

sparsely populated (spärs'lĭ pŏp'u̇ lāt ĕd) 281

textiles (tĕks'tĭlz) 284

Questions

1. How many states are included in the Northeastern section of our country? Into what two groups are these states often divided? Name the states in each group.

2. What is meant by a "densely populated" area? What is meant by a "sparsely populated" area?

3. What is Megalopolis, U.S.A.? Show where it is on a map of the United States. Is this region *densely* or *sparsely* populated?

4. Where do the largest number of people live in the Northeastern States?

5. What American city is made up of boroughs? How many boroughs does this city have and what are their names?

6. What five things important to the growth of manufacturing are found in the Northeastern States?

7. What are some of the natural resources of the Northeastern States that provide power and materials for manufacturing?

8. How have soil and climate influenced the size and kind of crops grown in New England?

9. What crop is grown in the valley of the Connecticut River?

You See for Yourself

Learn more about the making of steel and the important uses to which it is put. Why is steel more useful than iron? How long ago did man learn to make steel? How many products can you name that are made of steel or of steel parts?

Now You Know

The Northeastern States make up the leading manufacturing region in the United States. Manufacturing was begun during colonial days, and has enjoyed a steady growth ever since. Part of the reason for the growth of factories was the presence of the things necessary for manufacturing: large population, raw materials, power, transportation, and markets for the finished products. Another reason was that the soil and land are not suitable for farming in parts of the Northeastern region.

Many large cities are found throughout the Northeast. They are manufacturing centers.

The Northeastern States are often thought of as two separate groups, the New England States and the Middle Atlantic States. The New England States are located in the far northeastern corner of our country. In addition to its importance in manufacturing, New England is a favorite tourist spot.

The Middle Atlantic States enjoy a milder climate than New England because of their location farther south and because of the many water inlets along the coast. The manufacturing of steel and steel products is one of the most outstanding industries in these states.

Both New England and the Middle Atlantic States point with pride to the part their sections of the country has played in the history of the United States. Tourists to the states visit many historic sites.

You Talk It Over

You have read that the trees now standing in the Northeastern States are second growth since the days of the Indians. What happened to those trees of the early days? What things do you think could be done to help *conserve* the trees in our country's forests? Why is it even more important for people today to practice conservation than it was long ago?

Puzzlers

The map on this page shows some of the most important products of the Northeastern States. Study it carefully. For each manufactured product, tell where you think the raw materials come from. For the farm products, tell how the location helps in the growing of that food.

Unit Activities

State	Large and Important Cities	Natural Resources	Ways People Make a Living
Pennsylvania	*Harrisburg Pittsburgh Philadelphia	Coal Natural gas Water power	Publishing Factory Work Steel mill work Farming

You Make a Chart

Divide a large sheet of paper into four headings as shown above. Fill in the information for each of the states in the Northeastern section. The star in front of the name of the city means that it is the state capital. You may want to use an encyclopedia to find the population for the cities you name. If so, write the figures below the name of the city. The map on page 280, your reading of the unit, and encyclopedias will help you.

You Plan a Trip

Pretend that you are going to make a vacation trip to either New England or the Middle Atlantic States. Make a list of the places in each state that you would like to visit. Tell why these places are of particular interest to you.

Perhaps you or someone in your class has made such a trip to this part of the country. Bring snapshots, travel folders, or souvenirs that class members may have to show to the class. You may be able to get some free posters or folders from travel agencies in your community, too.

You Think about "Liberty"

One of the things most visitors to New York City wish to see is the Statue of Liberty. Find pictures of this famous statue. Read about it in books from your library. On a large sheet of construction paper, make a drawing of the Statue of Liberty.

Pretend that you have made a long trip to foreign lands and are on an ocean ship returning to the United States. Write what you think your thoughts and feelings might be as your ship passes the Statue of Liberty in the New York Harbor.

The Southern States

It is hard to tell what would have happened in the South if the War Between the States had not taken place. The people had to begin again—to work out new ways of living and new uses for the war-torn land.

Battles and marching soldiers ruined many plantation lands during the war years. But the land had suffered even before that. Cotton and tobacco had taken much of the richness from the soil. When rivers flooded, tons of soil were washed from the open plowed fields and carried away by the rivers.

Many of the tall pine trees of the southern woods were gone. Men cut them down as they chose, and no one gave much thought to their value.

The South has been the scene of much work in conservation, helped by the TVA and other organizations.

A tobacco field of the coastal plain.

A mesa of the western end of the section.

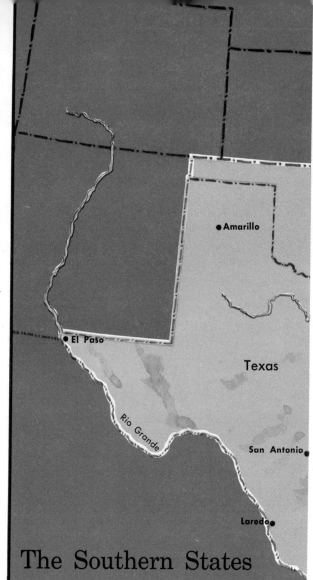

Amarillo

El Paso

Texas

Rio Grande

San Antonio

Laredo

The Southern States

A broad coastal plain covers the eastern end of the southern section of our country. This plain, with its many rivers and inlets, has been farmland since the earliest days of settlement. The great Appalachian Mountain chain marks the western end of the coastal plain. Here are the beautiful Blue Ridge, Smoky and Allegheny Mountains, all part of the long Appalachian chain.

During the early days of settlement, when communication and transportation were poor, the mountains formed a wall between the people of the coastal plain and those west of the mountains. It is not surprising that the people on the coastal plain developed a way of living quite different from that of their neighbors across the mountains.

Some of these differences lasted many years. The people living in the Ozark Mountains and in the Mountains of Tennessee, Kentucky, and

West Virginia developed a way of life much like that of hill people everywhere. They were somewhat cut off from other communities.

Their ideas and customs were rigidly strict. Much of this has changed and is still changing as better transportation and communication are set up. The building of new industries has also brought changes.

The people of Texas and Oklahoma, at the western end of the south-

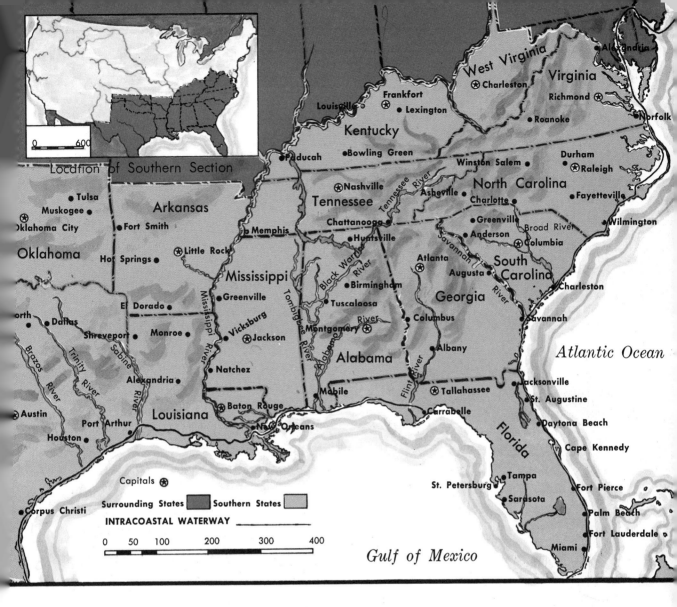

Location of Southern Section

Capitals ✪

Surrounding States ☐ Southern States ☐

INTRACOASTAL WATERWAY ———

0   50   100   200   300   400

Atlantic Ocean

Gulf of Mexico

ern section, are often thought of more as westerners than southerners. In their land is a touch of the broad open plains, the mesas, mountain ranges and deserts that lie farther west. A *mesa* is a flat-topped hill with sides that slope steeply.

Yet all the Southern States are alike in some ways. The climate throughout all the states permits the growing of crops that need a long growing season. From earliest days, farmers saw that tobacco and cotton were good money-making crops. In time, all the states faced the same problem of how to save their natural resources, especially their soil and forests. All started out as farming states, but in more recent years, they have turned to mining and manufacturing. Today, all the states are working to build up new industries.

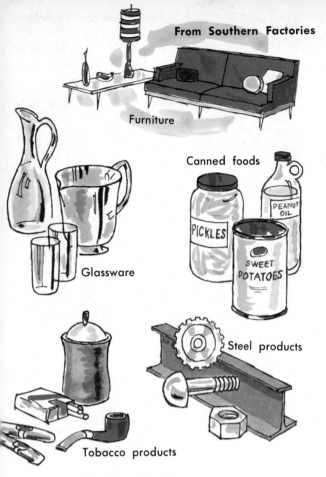

From Southern Factories

Furniture

Glassware

Canned foods

PICKLES

PEANUT OIL

SWEET POTATOES

Steel products

Tobacco products

Within fifteen years after the War Between the States, the South began to build some of its first factories. Before the war, all the southern cotton crops were sent to northern factories to be spun and woven into cloth. After the war, some people began to see that the South could help to rebuild itself by spinning and weaving the cotton in mills in its own cities. A few mills were built, marking the beginning of manufacturing in the South. You will remember that it was also after the war that the South learned some of its first lessons in soil conservation, through the work of George Washington Carver.

How has southern manufacturing grown?

With plenty of workmen who did not ask high wages, and with raw materials close at hand, the southern mills could make cotton cloth more cheaply than the New England mills could. Some of the owners of New England mills moved their businesses to the South. By the 1920's more cotton cloth was milled in the South than in the North. Today, almost all the nation's cotton mills are in the South, many of them in small towns. Raw materials, power, labor, transportation, and a growing market are all close at hand.

The Southern States have other important factories, too. All use raw materials found in the South.

Before the War Between the States, much southern farmland was in large plantations.

Land that was worn out or ruined by wind and water, was simply left. Farmers moved on to better fields.

Most of the battles of the War Between the States were fought on southern soil, destroying much good farmland.

Peanuts, sugar cane, fruits, vegetables, and some grain from southern farms are sent to southern factories to be made into finished products for market. Peanuts are especially important in Georgia. Much cooking oil is pressed from them in the factories. The growing of peanut crops has also helped the southern farmers to enrich their soil.

Southern forests provide raw materials, too, for southern manufacturing. The sap from the soft pine trees can be made into turpentine. *Rosin*, the thick yellow material left after the turpentine has been taken from the sap, can be used in many ways, including the making of paints, soaps, and varnishes. The soft pine lumber is used in southern box and paper factories. The hardwoods, such as cherry, oak, and walnut that grow on the mountain slopes, provide raw materials for factories making fine furniture in North and South Carolina, Virginia and West Virginia.

Although the Southern States do not manufacture as many dollars' worth of goods as the Northeastern States do, manufacturing has become very important to their people. Until World War II, more dollars were earned in the South through farming than in any other way. Today, as new factories are opened each year, more dollars are earned through manufacturing than through farming.

From Southern Factories

Paper products

Petroleum products

Cotton textiles

Paint

After the war, it was impossible to rebuild the old plantations. Too much of the Old South was destroyed.

Some of the southern farmland was given to the freed slaves so that they could become farmers.

Through the years, cotton mills plus other types of manufacturing have been added to the business life of the South.

Coal is a natural resource of West Virginia.

How have mines and oil wells added to the wealth of the South?

Perhaps the greatest help to the growth of industry in the South has been its mines. There is enough coal, iron, and limestone close at hand to make the iron and steel industry important, especially around Birmingham, Alabama. Cast-iron pipe from Alabama factories is widely used.

The hills, especially in West Virginia and on the western side of the Appalachians, are underlaid with soft coal. Its blackness can be seen almost any place that a cut is made into the ground. West Virginia leads the nation in the mining of soft coal. Much of it is used in steel mills and in electric power plants run by steam.

In years past, West Virginia supplied the coal for the furnaces in thousands and thousands of American homes. Since many home-owners of today have changed to gas, oil, or electric heating, there is far less demand for the coal once taken from the West Virginia mines. Many of the mines are now closed, and the miners who used to work in them have no jobs. Since almost all the men of a coal-mining community worked in the mines, the closing of the mines has brought serious problems to these communities. The government is trying to help these people learn new skills so that they can find other jobs. The government also hopes that new industries can be brought to these places to provide work for the jobless people.

Petroleum was discovered in Oklahoma in the year 1889. Since the growth of the automobile industry began just a few years later, this was a very important discovery. Gasoline as well as oil is made from petroleum.

Petroleum is the leading product of the state of Oklahoma. Compared with other states, Oklahoma is the fourth-largest producer of oil. Tulsa and Oklahoma City are the business centers of the oil industry there.

Other Southern States also have large and rich oil fields. Texas produces more petroleum than any other state in the Union. Louisiana ranks third-highest among the nation's oil-producing states. Arkansas and Alabama, too, have some oil wells.

The discovery of petroleum led to yet another manufacturing possibility in the South—the making of chemicals of many kinds. Texas, Tennessee, and Virginia are among the nation's top ten states in the production of many different chemicals.

Oil fields such as this one in eastern Texas can be seen throughout the state.

The early settlers worked long and hard to clear away the wilderness to get fields for farming. Yet, in so doing, they were opening the way for the soil to be washed away. The roots of the trees and brush were what held the soil in place when the waters of flooding rivers and heavy rains rushed across the land.

The rain and flood waters could carry soil to the nearest river. The river would carry the soil for a distance and then drop it. The Mississippi River has carried many tons of soil all the way to its mouth. The soil dropped here has built up to more than 15,000 square miles of land that once was not there. This land is called the Mississippi Delta. Delta soil is very good for growing crops.

Quarries from which come a number of different kinds of building stones are found in places throughout the South. *Bauxite*, from which aluminum is made, is found in huge amounts in Arkansas. Aluminum mills were opened there soon after bauxite was discovered.

The salt mines near the mouth of the Mississippi River are of special importance to Louisiana. Mine shafts are placed down into the salt, and tons and tons are mined.

How has conservation helped the South?

Conservation means making wise use of natural resources, avoiding waste, and keeping some back for future use. There is a need for different kinds of conservation all over the United States. The South has made use of many conservation practices.

Tons of rich topsoil have been piled up on the Mississippi Delta.

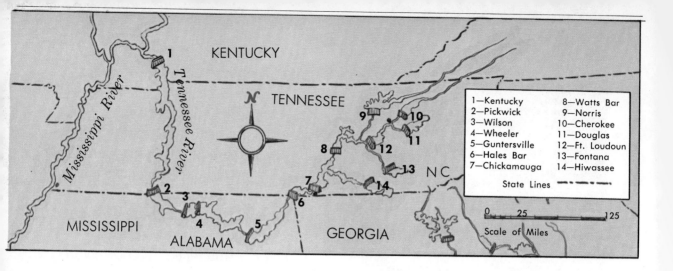

TVA Dams on the Tennessee River

Plans to control the flooding rivers and the washing away of southern soil were put into effect beginning in the year 1933. The federal government, through an act of Congress, set up the plan to control the waters of the Tennessee River and the smaller rivers running into it. It is known as the Tennessee Valley Authority, or simply the TVA. The TVA built twenty dams in the Tennessee River. Many more were built in other southern rivers through other plans. Behind each dam, a lake was formed.

When heavy rains come, much of the water is held in these lakes, called *reservoirs*. The reservoirs have done more for the South than just help conserve its soil. Allowing water to come through the gates and flow over the dams has given the South new power to run electric generators. Without these power plants, many of the South's new and growing industries would never have been possible.

The TVA did more for the South than control the Tennessee River. It put into effect a complete program of water, soil, and forest conservation throughout the Southern States. The pine forests were fast disappearing. For years, lumber companies had cut down all the timber in a forest section, young trees as well as old. The TVA set up a plan under which only certain trees could be cut.

Fontana Dam, 480 feet high, is the tallest of the TVA dams. It is on the Little Tennessee River in North Carolina.

The plan allowed for the thinning of forests, so that young trees had a chance to grow after older ones were removed. In addition, seedling pines were set out to make sure that more trees would grow to replace the timber that had been cut.

The TVA officers also taught the farmers how to feed their soil, and helped them get fertilizers with which to do it. During World War I, the federal government had built an ammunition plant at Muscle Shoals, Alabama. After the war, the plant was used to make fertilizer, which the government sold to the farmers at low cost. Another part of the soil conservation work was to teach farmers to choose crops which would help keep the soil in good condition. Farmers also learned to change the crops planted in the same field from year to year. Peanuts, sweet potatoes, and soybeans became important additions to the cotton, tobacco, rice, and sugar crops.

Farmers also learned that the direction in which they plowed their fields could help to control the washing away of soil. If they plowed straight up and down a slope, they were cutting little ditches through which water could wash right down, carrying away the valuable soil as it went. The farmers learned to plow their land crosswise to the slopes. This kind of plowing made little dams that held back the water and the soil, too.

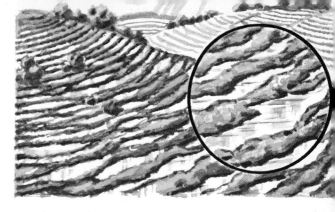

Plowing across a slope makes ridges of earth that hold back rain waters.

Plowing up and down a slope makes little ditches for the waters to follow.

Everyone in the South, and especially those people along the Mississippi River, have to guard against flooding rivers. Walls made of earth and wood and sometimes concrete have to be built along the banks of the river. These flood walls are called *levees*. When the river rises dangerously near the top of the levee, almost every able-bodied man from town or farm alike, helps stack sandbags on top of the wall to make it higher. Often this work holds back the flood waters and saves thousands of dollars' worth of property.

Cotton boll

Pipes carry water from the main ditch between the rows in cotton fields where irrigation is necessary.

What are the major farm products of the South today?

The Cotton Kingdom of one hundred years ago is still the Cotton Kingdom of today. (See page 193) Tobacco, too, is still a very important crop. Conservation, however, makes the big difference between the tobacco and cotton growers of one hundred years ago and those of today. Texas produces more cotton than any other state. It has become the leading cotton producer because its farmers have conserved water and irrigated their fields. Dams are built in rivers to hold back and save the water. It is let out as needed into man-made

canals. Irrigation ditches branch off the canals and carry water to the crops in the fields. Since Texas and Oklahoma do not have enough rainfall to grow cotton in many regions, irrigation becomes necessary. The strength of the soil is also conserved through the plant foods that are added to the irrigation waters.

Many citrus fruits are grown in the South, especially in Florida. Irrigation has also made it possible for Texas farmers to grow huge citrus crops. Many of the fresh vegetables bought in northern grocery stores during the winter months come from Texas farms, too. Georgia peaches are famous all over the country. In many places the foothills of the mountains have been planted in fruit orchards.

The cattle industry, which began in Texas after the War Between the States, kept on growing. Today it has spread to other Southern States. Where the Ozark Mountains and their foothills rise, in Arkansas, and southern Oklahoma, much of the land is suitable only for pasture. There are also great grazing areas in the lowlands set aside for the raising of livestock. Most of Florida's beef cattle are raised in the south central part of the state. Alabama, too, is an important cattle state now. Chicken-raising has become important to southern farmers.

What are some of the special products of the Southern States?

Just west of the Appalachian Mountains are the rolling grasslands that Daniel Boone found so lovely. A very special product of these lands today is the riding horse. The people here are proud of the fine animals they raise, and horse racing has always been a popular sport.

The nation's guided-missile and rocket programs have touched the Southern States in recent years, particularly in two places. One is Huntsville, Alabama, where much of the study that led to the sending of satellites into space took place.

On the eastern coast of Florida is a point of flat, sandy land reaching out into the Atlantic Ocean, known as *Cape Kennedy*. The United States government owns 15,000 acres of land there on which is the Cape Kennedy Missile Range. The space flights of the Astronauts are launched here, as well as missiles and rockets. The men who work at Cape Kennedy plus all the visitors to the test range, have brought new business to the area.

The people of many Florida communities make much of their living from the tourist business. Each year, over a billion dollars is spent there by vacationers. There are many hotels, restaurants, motels, trailer camps, and amusement places to meet the needs of those who come to enjoy the sunny beaches. There are also many communities in which retired people live. These are the older people who have retired from the jobs at which they worked during their lifetimes and who want to enjoy the mild climate of Florida.

How has the port of New Orleans held its importance?

The return to water transportation in recent years has again made New Orleans an important shipping point. Large and important railroads lead into the city. They carry goods to and from the 5,000 or more ocean ships that dock there each year. Many of the goods are moved by barges that travel up and down the Mississippi River. These barges also travel into the great long canal known as the *Gulf Intracoastal Waterway*. This canal cuts a path just inside the coast of the Gulf of Mexico all the way from Brownsville, at the southern tip of Texas, to Carrabella, Florida. Work on the canal was completed in 1949. Traffic on this waterway can travel protected from the rough waters of the Gulf of Mexico.

Words to Know

bauxite (bôks'īt) 303

Cape Kennedy (kāp kĕn'ĕ dĭ) 307

conservation (kŏn'sēr vā'shŭn) 303

Gulf Intracoastal Waterway (gŭlf ĭn'trȧ kōs'tȧl wô'tēr wā') 307

levees (lĕv'vĕz) 305

mesa (mā'sȧ) 299

reservoir (rĕz'ēr vwôr) 304

Questions

1. What event in history made it necessary for the people of the South to change their way of life?

2. Which of the Southern States are crossed by a broad coastal plain? In which states are there hills and mountains? Which states have plains, mesas, and mountains?

3. How did the location of cotton cloth manufacturing change during the years between the later 1800's and 1920? What was the reason for this change?

4. Why have Southern States turned to growing peanuts, sugar cane, fruits and other crops besides cotton and tobacco? What is done with many of these farm products?

5. What finished products are made from southern forest resources?

6. What mine products come from West Virginia? What problem have miners of West Virginia faced in recent years? Why did this problem arise?

7. Which Southern States are major producers of petroleum?

8. Which southern state has rich amounts of bauxite? What important material is made from bauxite?

9. Where is the Mississippi Delta? How was it formed?

10. How did the TVA help conserve the soil of southern farmland? How did it help conserve southern forests?

11. What has caused the towns near Cape Kennedy, Florida, to grow in the past few years?

12. By what two routes do river boats and barges enter and leave the port of New Orleans?

13. How have southern manufacturers produced much of the power needed for their factories?

You See for Yourself

The history of the state of Oklahoma is especially interesting. Read about it in one of the encyclopedias in your library. What were the five civilized tribes? What was the "trail of tears"? What was the Oklahoma land rush? When did Oklahoma become a state?

Now You Know

The Southern States have been and still are in a period of change. The climate and broad coastal plain gave rise to farming from the earliest days of settlement. The continued planting of tobacco and cotton, however, took much of the richness from the soil. The War Between the States destroyed much farmland. Even more of the soil was damaged by flood and rain waters in the years before the war.

One of the first steps taken was to build cotton mills so that the South could manufacture cloth from its own crops. By the 1920's, more cotton cloth was manufactured in the South than in the North. Steps were taken to help southern farmers re-place plant food taken from the soil. The TVA, set up by the federal government in 1933, took action to control the flood waters of the Tennessee River and taught other lessons in soil and forest conservation. The TVA dams brought a source of electrical power to the South. This helped the growth of more and more factories throughout the Southern States. Today their factories make use of the oil, coal, bauxite, salt, lumber, and other natural resources in the region. The factories also handle southern farm products, which today include much sugar cane, peanuts, sweet potatoes, fruits, vegetables, and livestock, as well as cotton and tobacco.

You Talk It Over

What are the advantages of having cotton mills in the South rather than in the North? Think of such things as transportation and labor as you give your answer. How would these things influence the prices of finished products, such as cotton dresses or shirts? Tell how the location of these factories in the South would help people other than those living in the South. Do you think the problems of the freed slaves after the war would have been so great if there had been factories in the South?

Puzzlers

Match the number of the industry or product at the top of this page with the correct letter given for areas outlined on the map of the Southern States.

Unit Activities

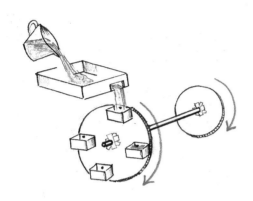

You give a demonstration report

You have learned that the TVA dams gave the South a great source of power for electric generators. From science books and encyclopedias, learn all you can about what turbines are and how they are used. You will be able to make simple models of wind turbines. Draw a large diagram showing how a water turbine can be placed in the flow of water from a dam.

Explain to the class how water flowing over a dam turns a turbine and how this turns the electric generators. When you give your report, you may also be able to show some pictures of dams and generator plants. If you like, ask several other classmates to work with you.

You make a display

Find as many products of southern farms and factories as you can. You will want to look for the manufacturers' names on the labels of your clothing, canned goods, and packages of sugar and rice. Arrange all these items on a table.

You tell the story of cotton

From an encyclopedia, learn all you can about the cotton industry in the United States. Plan a television program in which you give a report on what you have learned. Start your report by telling where cotton is grown in the United States. The next part of the report should tell of the work of the cotton farmer—how he plants his crop, cares for it, harvests it, and problems he faces.

On a strip of shelf or wrapping paper, draw pictures to show as many steps of your story as possible. Put the paper on rollers in your school TV viewer or in a cardboard box if your school has no viewer. Show the pictures as you tell the story to the class. You may work with several of your classmates, each of you taking a different step in writing the story and drawing pictures for it.

The North Central States

The great work of the North Central States is to provide bread and meat for the nation and to keep it moving by land, water, and air.

The Mississippi River divides this group almost down the center. The two main kinds of work—farming and manufacturing—are divided in almost the same way. East of the Mississippi, lie five states bordering the Great Lakes. Farming is important in each, but more money is earned through manufacturing than through farming.

In the states west of the Mississippi, more people live on the farms than in the towns and cities. There are cities, too, but more people work in farming than in manufacturing.

Machinery manufactured in North Central factories is used in the great work of farming throughout the North Central States.

313

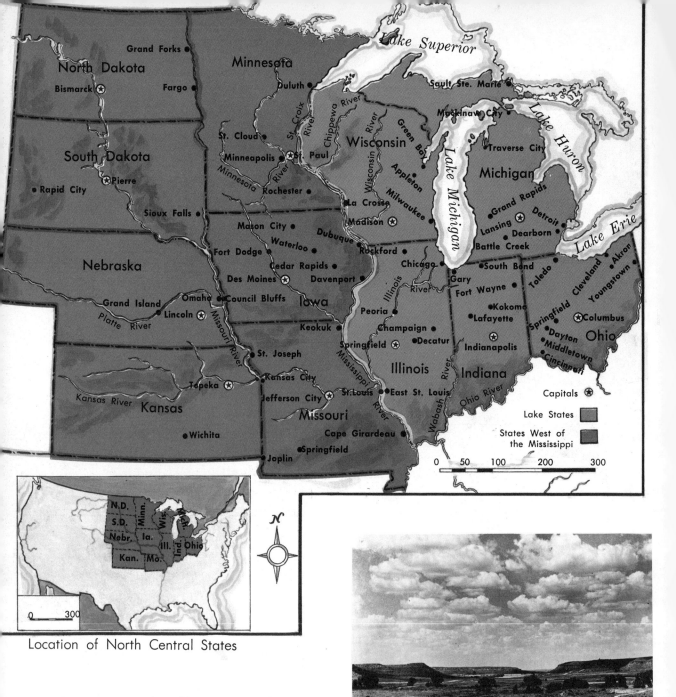

Location of North Central States

The North Central States

Great herds of buffalo once roamed the western
end of the North Central section. Today, only
a few animals are still alive and most of them
are protected in state or national parks.

What kind of land and climate do the North Central States have?

The North Central States have more square miles of fertile soil than any other part of the United States. *Fertile* soil is land on which crops can be grown. Only small sections of the area cannot be farmed. These sections are the Badlands of South Dakota and Nebraska; the Ozark Mountains in southern Missouri; and the forest areas of northern Wisconsin, Minnesota, and Michigan. Many people in the forest regions make a living through mining or lumbering.

The climate is the kind that makes it easiest for people to work at their best. The summers are generally pleasant, with occasional heat waves. The winters can be long and stormy in some parts, but they do not usually keep people indoors for any great length of time.

Almost all the land is open and nearly level. This made the building of roads and railroads fairly easy. The weather is generally good for flying, so there are many excellent airports. In addition, the waterways that helped the early pioneers to open this land are still very much in use. Most of the present-day shipping centers had their start during the years when the waterways were the nation's only highways. Almost every main city of the North Central States is located on either a river or one of the Great Lakes.

The Badlands are interesting rock forms.

Open pit mining of iron ore is carried on in northern parts of this section.

Most of the North Central section lies in a plains region and has been turned into farmland.

How has the use of machinery affected the North Central States?

Nature was unusually kind to this part of the country, but the ideas and hard work of the people have had much to do with its becoming such a rich and important region. The invention of so many wonderful machines that can greatly reduce the labor of man, have made the farm and factory production of the North Central States worth billions of dollars each year.

On the farms and in the factories, machines and the people who run them are a key part in the story of the North Central States. The first steel plow, with a blade to which the soil would not cling as it did to an iron blade, was made in Grand Detour, Illinois. Today, more farm machinery is manufactured in Illinois than in any other state. A large part of this output is sold to the farmers throughout the North Central States.

The North Central States are the automobile center of the nation. Even during the early days of the industry, many of the necessary raw materials were close at hand. Others could be gathered from other areas at low cost because of the excellent transportation into the region. The cities that had been marketing centers for farm products and the few manufactured goods of earlier days grew to centers of industry as well. Factories to produce the many different items needed in automobile manufacture were set up. Such things as glass, upholstery material, rubber, nuts, bolts, and hundreds of other items used in automobiles were manufactured. More people were needed for work at the thousands of machines set up in the factories, many

The steel blade for the breaking plow was one of the first great advances in farm machinery.

The reaper was a great aid in the cutting of wheat and other grains.

A great many kinds of machinery and electrical equipment are made in North Central factories. These refrigerators are on an assembly line in a Chicago factory.

of which produced machines for use in still more factories. With so many people to feed, those who stayed on the farms had a greater market for their products. They, too, needed machinery to increase their output. These states became an area of high production.

The threshing machine gave the grain farmer a machine that would separate the grain from the straw quickly and easily.

Today's modern machinery allows the farmer to cut and thresh his grain all in one step. This combine has its own engine; no tractor is needed to pull it through the field.

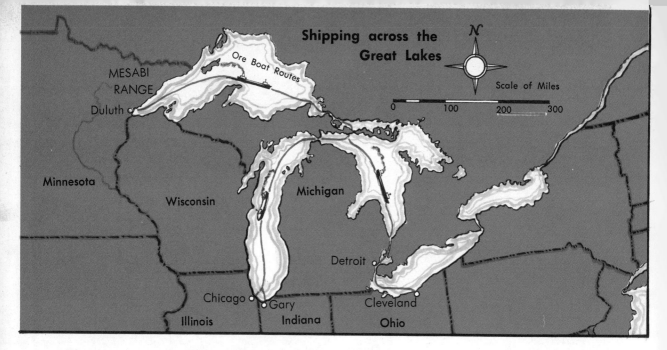

Shipping across the Great Lakes

MESABI RANGE

Duluth

Ore Boat Routes

Minnesota

Wisconsin

Michigan

Detroit

Chicago Gary

Cleveland

Illinois Indiana Ohio

Scale of Miles

0   100   200   300

What are the products of the five Lake States?

(Wisconsin, Illinois, Indiana, Ohio, Michigan)

Transportation equipment, especially the automobile, is the best known manufactured product. Yet this group of states is also the greatest steel-milling region of the United States. Coal and limestone are both close at hand. During the warm months, iron ore from the Mesabi Range in Minnesota and other regions can be shipped in by way of the Great Lakes. Long oreboats take the ore to Chicago, Gary, Detroit, and other important ports on the Great Lakes. Much of the steel from the mills of the Lake States is used in the factories that make automobiles or automobile parts.

Different automobile parts may go through several factories to be joined to smaller parts. Then these parts enter the assembly plants where the finished automobiles are put together. There are parts factories and assembly plants in all the major cities of the North Central States, but the center is around Detroit, Michigan.

This ore boat is leaving Duluth, Minnesota, for a trip across the Great Lakes.

Compare this assembly line in an automobile factory with the one shown in the picture on page 255. Cars and factories have changed much but the assembly line idea is still very much in use.

At Dearborn, Michigan, there is a rather unusual automobile factory at which all the parts and different items that go into the automobiles are made. All the manufacturing for all the parts is done at the same factory from which the finished automobile comes. This huge plant gives jobs to almost 40,000 people and operates twenty-four hours a day.

While Michigan's special product is the automobile itself, many of Ohio's factories make automobile parts. Automobile bodies, body paint, batteries, and nuts and bolts are made in Ohio factories. Many of the tires on cars today come from the city of Akron, "Rubber Capital of the World." Ohio is a leader in the whole field of electrical equipment, but electrical systems for automobiles are special products in this line.

More than 25,000 tons of steel come from Ohio's great steel mills each year. Cleveland, Youngstown, and Middletown are "steel cities," but there are mills in other cities, especially cities on the Ohio River and Lake Erie.

In addition to these products, Ohio factories turn out machine tools, conveyor belts for factory assembly lines, cash registers, scales, airplane parts, and countless small metal parts for machines. This state leads the nation in the manufacture of clay and tile products, which include everything from sewer pipes to fine china. The china-making center is in the southeastern part. One of the natural resources of that region is excellent clay. Ohio is second only to New York in the total value of manufactured products.

Indiana, too, manufactures automobiles and automobile parts, airplane engines, electrical machinery, and many other things. Yet steelmaking leads all other industries. Over 13,000,000 tons of steel leave Indiana mills each year. One of the world's largest steel mills is located in Gary, a city in the northwestern part of the state.

Manufacturing is done in many of the cities of Illinois, but the great manufacturing center for the state is in and around Chicago. Three-fourths of all Illinois factories are in Cook County, where Chicago is located. Machinery is the major product of these factories, but there are many other products, too. Factories that make almost anything from a giant locomotive to a candy bar can be found in the Chicago area.

Chicago is second only to New York in size, and in the printing and

The Corn Belt

publishing business. Besides Chicago's great industry, the city is noted for its beautiful lake front, great universities, beautiful parks, and fascinating museums.

The Natural History Museum is among the interesting places to visit in Chicago.

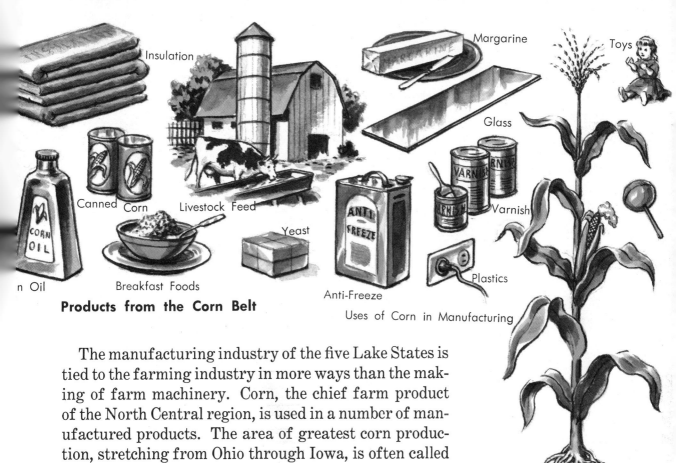

Insulation

Margarine

Toys

Glass

Canned Corn

Livestock Feed

Varnish

CORN OIL

Yeast

ANTI FREEZE

n Oil

Breakfast Foods

Plastics

Anti-Freeze

Products from the Corn Belt

Uses of Corn in Manufacturing

The manufacturing industry of the five Lake States is tied to the farming industry in more ways than the making of farm machinery. Corn, the chief farm product of the North Central region, is used in a number of manufactured products. The area of greatest corn production, stretching from Ohio through Iowa, is often called the *Corn Belt*.

Some of the corn from this area is grown as feed for livestock. It reaches market in the form of meat. The second most important farm product of the Great Lakes States is the hog. Chicago, Kansas City, Missouri, and East St. Louis all have stockyards which handle many hogs.

Dairy products are the leading farm output in Wisconsin. Of the five Lake States, Wisconsin does the least manufacturing. There is heavy industry around Milwaukee, where machinery is the main manufactured product. But almost every town, large or small, throughout the gently rolling land of southern Wisconsin, has a plant where dairy products are handled. Farther north, there are paper mills in many towns. These mills make use of the wood pulp from the northern woods. Wood *pulp* is a mixture of wood fibers and water.

The Lake States all started as farming states. Farms have not disappeared by any means, and farm products are of great importance. But the use of machinery has brought changes. Less workers are needed on the farms and more are needed in the city factories. In all these states, more people work at manufacturing than at farming. Here the value of manufactured goods is much greater than that of the farm products.

321

Spring wheat is planted in spring,

grows during summer,

and ripens in late summer.

Winter wheat is planted in autumn,

lies in the ground during winter,

and ripens in early summer.

How do people live and work in the states west of the Mississippi?

(Minnesota, Iowa, Missouri, North Dakota, South Dakota, Nebraska, Kansas)

The miles and miles of plains stretching westward from the Mississippi River, look level to the eye. Yet there is a steady rise to the land. The western sections of the Dakotas, Nebraska, and Kansas are about a half mile higher than the banks of the Mississippi River. Almost all parts of these states are higher above sea level than the Missouri Ozarks.

The climate at the western side of these states is dry. Some farmers here must irrigate their fields. As was done in the Southern States, dams have been built in the rivers. Farmers draw water for irrigation from the reservoirs formed behind these dams.

Wheat is grown in all of the states west of the Mississippi, but Kansas and North Dakota grow more than the others. They lead the nation in wheat production. Because of its warmer climate, winter wheat is grown in Kansas. North Dakota farmers plant spring wheat because the winters are too cold for winter wheat. Much *durum* wheat is grown in North Dakota. This is used for macaroni and other such products.

Many fields in North Dakota and some in South Dakota are a beautiful sweep of blue at certain times of the year. The blue is the flower of the flax plant, which farmers there grow mainly for its seed. Oil pressed from the seed is used in the making of paints and varnishes. After the oil has been pressed from it, the seed can also be used as livestock feed.

In the wheat-growing sections, every small town along railroad or highway has a grain *elevator*. This is where grain is stored until it is sold and shipped to a mill. Sometimes farmers as a group own the elevators in their community. This was one solution to the high storage rates once charged by the railroads that owned elevators.

Nebraska and South Dakota farmers have found the land and climate better for the raising of beef cattle than for growing grain. Some of their fields are planted to get winter feed for their cattle. But much is allowed to grow in natural grasses as it did in the days when buffalo grazed there. Cattle, hogs, and corn are the chief farm products, with much of the corn grown as feed for the hogs.

Corn, dairy products, and hogs come from the farms of Minnesota. This state produces more butter than any other. The flour, breakfast cereals, cake mixes, and other packaged mixes that come from the great mills

Many Kansas wheat farms store their crops in elevators such as this one.

of Minneapolis and St. Paul are sold all over the nation. Many grain crops from the farmlands of the North Central States are handled in these two cities.

Cattle and hogs, fed with grain from the North Central farms, are prepared for market in the great meat-packing houses of this section.

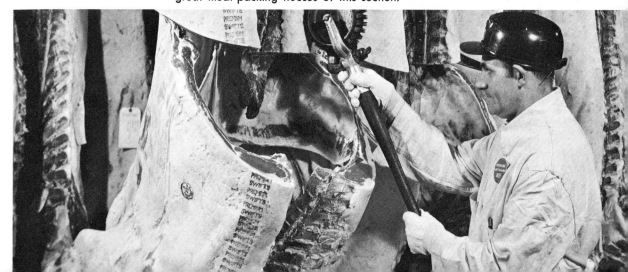

The beauty of the Ozark Mountains in southern Missouri has made them a tourist favorite.

Iowa's chief work is feeding the nation. About one-third of all the land of Iowa is planted in corn each year. Some of it goes directly into corn products, but much is used as feed for hogs. Meat-packing is the chief industry of Iowa cities.

There are hundreds of small towns and villages in Iowa, but only one city with more than 100,000 people. Des Moines and the smaller cities have factories that make all kinds of machinery from washing machines to farm equipment.

Kansas City and St. Louis, Missouri, have heavy industry, and many people work in the factories of these cities. Outside these cities, however, Missouri is more a farming than a manufacturing state. Northern

Missouri has good rolling farmland with fertile soil, especially on the plain north of the Missouri River. Much of the southern part of the state, in the Ozark region, is too rough and rocky for farming. Beef cattle are pastured on some of the land but much of it is woodland. Dairy cattle are raised, too, and dairy products are becoming an important source of income.

Just as the people of the hills in Tennessee and Kentucky have been troubled with flooding rivers, so have the people of the Ozarks in southern Missouri. Flood control dams have been built and more are being planned. The dams bring with them a source of electric power and a new tourist trade. Many people visit the reservoir lakes and beautiful hills.

More money is made through manufacturing in Missouri than through farming. The greatest product in dollar value is in the field of transportation. Aircraft, including some space travel equipment, automobiles, trucks, trailers, and railroad cars are among the things made in St. Louis and Kansas City.

Kansas shares in the manufacturing of transportation equipment, for several airplane makers have their factories in that state.

How do the waterways serve the North Central States?

Now that water transportation is again growing in importance, the Missouri-Mississippi-Ohio river system means a great deal to the North Central States. A number of diesel powered towboats have been put into service pushing long barges loaded with freight up and down the rivers. One towboat can push a whole line of barges. Sometimes as many as ten or twelve are lashed together. Each barge can carry about as much freight as eighty trucks or twenty-four freight cars. This means that the power operating the towboat is doing the work of many land transportation engines, making the water transportation much cheaper.

Some of the freight carried on the river barges includes fertilizer, livestock feeds, lime, sand, petroleum, gasoline, crushed rock, coal, lumber, ice, concrete blocks, and automobiles.

The growth of the North Central States began because of the easy transportation the rivers offered. Today, its transportation system on water, land, and in the air is highly developed. In many ways, transportation continues to be the key to the wealth and growth of the North Central States.

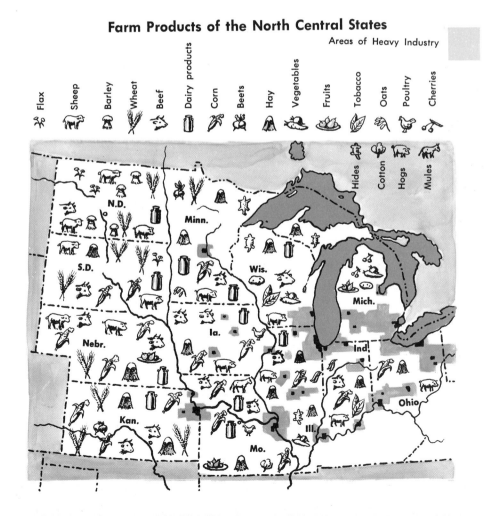

Farm Products of the North Central States

Corn Belt (kôrn bĕlt) 320

durum (dū′rŭm) 322

elevator (ĕl′ē vā′tẽr) 323

fertile (fûr′tĭl) 315

pulp (pŭlp) 321

Questions

1. How has the land of the North Central States aided the growth of farming in this region? How has it aided the growth of good transportation?

2. How were the rivers and Great Lakes important to the North Central States in their early days? What influence have they had on the growth of cities in this region?

3. In what field of manufacture is Illinois the leading producer? Where are many of these manufactured products used?

4. What is an automobile assembly plant? Where in this country are the major automobile assembly plants? Why is this a good location for them?

5. Of what importance are many Ohio factories in the manufacture of automobiles? Why is Ohio a good location for these kinds of factories?

6. Where is the manufacturing center of Illinois? What two industries in particular show that this city is in the midst of farmland?

7. How has machinery changed the five Lake States since their early days?

8. What two states are the nation's top wheat producers? How are the crops of these two states different?

9. What is the Corn Belt? What are some of the ways in which corn from this region is used?

10. In what ways do the North Central States "feed the nation"? In what ways do they "keep it on the move"?

You See for Yourself

Find out who Charles Kettering was. From what state did he come? How was his work important to automobile manufacturers? What kind of person was he?

Look closely at the country in the region of the Great Lakes States. What was this land called when it first belonged to the United States? You may want to review what you learned earlier in the book before you answer.

Now You Know

In many ways, the North Central States have changed a great deal since their early days. They all began as farming states, but today those east of the Mississippi River make more money from their manufactured goods than from their farm products. The states west of the Mississippi are still largely farming states, but machinery has brought many changes to this area, too.

The automobile brought great changes to the entire country and led to many new industries and businesses besides automobile manufacturing. The coming of the automobile probably left a greater mark on the North Central States than on any other region. The automobile factories themselves are located here. Many parts factories are here, too.

Cities grew larger as more factories opened. The farmers sought ways to increase their crops in order to help feed the growing population. This led to more factories and more machines to help the farmers.

Transportation in the North Central States is excellent. The lakes and rivers gave cheap and easy transportation in the early days. Since then, great railroads and highways have been built across the clear, level stretches of land. Good transportation continues to play a large part in the high production of these states.

You Talk It Over

Think of as many ways as you can in which the North Central States have changed since the early days of settlement. For example, you will remember that Cincinnati was once called "Porkopolis." What cities of today could be called "Porkopolis"? What reasons can you give for this change?

Although the farms of the North Central States produce larger and richer crops than ever before, there are still fewer farmers than there were years ago. How would you explain this? Why do you think farms are larger today than they were years ago? Why would it take much money to start a farm today?

Puzzlers

Look at the rows of finished products on this page. Then look at all the pictures in the center of the page. For each finished product, tell which of the things from the pictures in the center would be concerned in producing the finished product. Some of the things in the center of the page will be used several times. Others will be used only once.

Finished Products — Pork — Automobile — Flour — Paint

Grain elevators — Corn — Farmer — Rubber Factory — Battery — Steel mill — Wheat — Hog — Grass — Flax — Flax oil — Clay — Glass — Dairy cow — Forest — Iron ore — Factory worker

Finished Products

Farm plow — Cornstarch — China — Cheese — Butter — Paper

Unit Activities

You report on the cities

Choose one of the cities shown on the map on page 325 and make a report on it. Several of you may want to work together on some of the larger cities, such as Chicago, St. Louis, or Kansas City. Begin your report by telling what manufactured products come from the city. Include pictures or samples of the products.

Learn as much as you can about the early days of the city and what things helped it to grow.

You assemble an automobile

Using a long piece of burlap and scraps of material, show how the parts of an automobile travel the assembly line until the finished auto is put together. You will need to start with two lines—the chassis line and the body line. You will be able to find a great deal of information on the making of automobiles from encyclopedias and other sources. You will want to study these sources and make your assembly line as nearly complete as you can.

You learn about soil conservation

The farmers of the North Central States are deeply concerned with soil conservation. Using encyclopedias and other books, prepare a report on this important subject.

Be able to tell your classmates exactly what topsoil is, how it is formed, and why it must not be wasted or lost. Tell what problems are faced by the North Central farmers. What has already been done to protect the soil and some of the things that still need to be done. You will want to show pictures of what can happen to unprotected soil.

You have a tasting party

Find as many food products as you can that come from the North Central States. Bring them to class and read the labels. Tell as much as you can about how each product is manufactured. Are all the necessary materials for manufacture found in the North Central States? Which ones would have to be shipped in? Could you plan a healthful meal using only the products you brought to class?

The Western States

For a number of years in our nation's history, the West drew many people. Some were seeking wealth, and others wanted adventure. Today, the West still draws many people, even though the days of beaver-trappers and gold-seekers are gone.

Most of the people going to the West today want to see the fascinating country. Here is Mt. Whitney, the highest point in the country, outside Alaska. Here, too, is Death Valley, the lowest point.

There are stretches of land level as a boxtop and mountain walls too steep to climb. There are places where snow falls in August and places where summer temperatures are often over one-hundred degrees.

Interesting rock formations and unsettled land help to make up the strange and vast beauty of the Western States.

The Western States

Olympic National Park
Seattle
Olympia ⊗ Tacoma
Washington
Spokane●
Glacier National Park
Great Falls
Missouri River
Portland● Vancouver
Columbia River
Snake River
Salem ⊛
Helena ⊗
Butte
Montana
Eugene ●
Oregon
Idaho
Yellowstone River
Boise ⊛
Nampa
Yellowstone
National Park
Idaho Falls ●
Wyoming
North Platte River
Sacramento River
Nevada
Ogden ●
Salt Lake City ⊗
Laramie
Cheyenne ⊛
Reno ●
Carson City ⊗
Sacramento ⊛
Stockton ●
South Platte River
Berkeley ●
San Francisco ●
Oakland ●
Palo Alto ●
Modesto ●
Santa Cruz ●
Yosemite
National Park
Utah
Denver ⊛
Fresno ●
San Joaquin River
Las Vegas ●
Colorado River
Pikes Peak
Colorado Springs ●
Colorado
Arkansas River
California
Grand Canyon
Santa Barbara ●
Flagstaff ●
Santa Fe ⊛
Santa Monica ● Los Angeles ●
Long Beach ● Palm Springs ●
Colorado River
Arizona
Albuquerque ●
San Diego ●
Phoenix ⊗
New Mexico
Gila River
Rio Grande
Pecos River
Tucson ●
Pacific Ocean
Carlsbad ●
N

Mexico

Capitals ⊗

Pacific Coast States ☐

Rocky Mountain States ☐

| 0 | 50 | 100 | 200 | 300 | 400 |

Wash.
Mont.
Ore.
Idaho
Wyo.
Nev.
Utah
Colo.
Calif.
Ariz.
N.M.

| 0 | 500 |

Mountains along the west coast often trap rain clouds so that they cannot reach lands on the eastern side.

In some parts of the Western States, rain falls almost every day from October until spring with a total of more than eighty inches. On some of the mountain slopes, forty and fifty feet of snow may build up during the winter months. The desert regions, however, usually get less than five inches of rain each year. Death Valley once went without rain for more than two years.

Farms on one side of a mountain range have all the rainfall needed for crops. Farms on the other side must be irrigated.

Just as there are great differences in land and climate in the Western States, so there are great differences in population. There are more people living in California than in any other state except New York. Just east of California is Nevada, which has fewer people than any state except Alaska.

Some parts of California do not need to be irrigated in order to grow crops.

Cactus and sagebrush grow wild on the "dry" side of the mountains.

Visitors to Lassen Peak National Park can see many craters of volcanoes.

Why are the western lands so different from the rest of the country?

Part of the reason for the unforgettable scenery of the West is that this part of our country has not yet "settled down" in its land and water forms. Thousands of years from now it will not be nearly as rugged as it is today. It may look a great deal like the land regions around the Mississippi and in eastern states.

The land of the eastern part of North America was formed before the Rocky Mountains, the Sierra Nevadas, and the Cascades took shape. These three are the chief ranges of the Western States. In eastern North America, volcanoes erupted long before the Age of Dinosaurs, between 100 and 200 million years ago. It was only about 50 million years ago that volcanoes began erupting in the region where the Rocky Mountains are today. The earthquakes and shifts in the surface of the earth have continued through all those years. But the action of the volcanoes has slowly fallen off so that now only the last signs of the forming earth can be found in the West.

By the time the Ice Age began, about one million years ago, the western mountains had taken form, although there were still many volcanoes erupting. Today all the volcanoes of the West are dead except *Lassen Peak* in northeastern California. It, too, is dying.

Hot, liquid rock bursts from the earth when a volcano erupts.

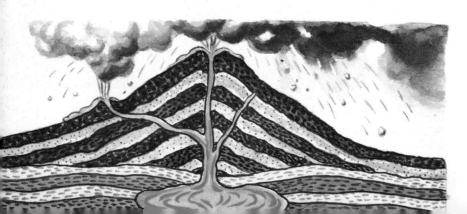

Most of the mountains of the Cascade range to the north of Mt. Lassen are old volcanoes. Gassy fumes still rise from some, but none of them have erupted since the days of exploration. Crater Lake in Oregon was formed in an ancient volcano. It is thought to be the deepest lake in North America, being 1,983 feet deep.

In the Western States, the restlessness of the earth can be seen and felt in other ways, too. There are still occasional earthquakes, especially around San Francisco. In 1906, there was one so bad that fires started and added to the damage that was done. Thousands of buildings burned down, and more than four hundred people lost their lives. The city had to be completely rebuilt.

The heat deep in the earth brings some of the underground water to the boiling point. This water forces its way upward in the still unsettled area of the West. In many parts there are boiling springs. Some of the water spurts up with such force that it rises in a column. This is called a *geyser*. The most famous geyser erupts so regularly, every sixty-five minutes, that it is called "Old Faithful." It and many other geysers are found in Yellowstone National Park, in the northwestern corner of Wyoming.

One cannot see how the land and rock formations of the West are changed from day to day or even

The buttes are formations of lava from volcanoes of long ago.

from year to year. But changes are taking place. The *buttes* that rise above the plains east of the Rockies were once surrounded by other rocks. These other rocks, softer than the hard lava rock of the buttes, have been worn away. Today, the buttes stand alone, like great stone tables for giants.

Old Faithful is the most famous geyser in the West.

Several things wear away the rocks and land forms on the surface of the earth. Frost, followed by thawing, can break up rocks. Water and wind *erode* the surface, or wear it away by rubbing. Water and wind carry tiny particles of dirt, rock, and other matter that rub against larger rocks and slowly but surely wear them down. The wind, carrying these particles, is still grinding away at the rocks, causing the buttes and strange-looking rock forms that rise from otherwise level land. These, too, are still slowly changing shape as the winds continue their work through many years. Some day, many years from now, they will have completely disappeared.

Many years ago, great rivers flowed through what is now dry land in many parts of the Western States. Carrying soil and rock particles as they flowed, the rivers cut channels for themselves. Most of the steep-sided canyons of the Western States were cut by rivers. The Grand Canyon in Arizona is the work of the great Colorado River through the ages. Now the Canyon is 217 miles long, from four to eight miles wide, and in places more than a mile deep.

What changes has man made in the West?

Nature goes on with its work of changing the West, but the changes are made so slowly that we do not notice them. People, however, are making changes that one cannot help but see. One of the greatest changes was made in order to conserve water so that the farmers on the "dry" side of the mountains could grow crops.

As is being done in many other parts of the United States, great dams are being built in the West. Their purpose is both flood control and water storage. Stored water is used during the long dry seasons. As in the Eastern States, the dams also provide electric power for industry and homes.

Each year, man brings irrigation farther into the lands that would otherwise be desert, or almost desert. The same desert areas that caused so much suffering for the early westward travelers are today good vacation lands. The desert blooms where irrigation ditches bring water to it. Because water can be piped long distances from the great reservoirs, communities can thrive where men once died of thirst.

Irrigation has turned many acres of Western land into useful areas.

The dams have brought plenty of electric power to the Western States. There is little need for steam engines, for the push of the water as it is allowed to pass through the gates of a dam can generate plenty of electricity. The states through which such great rivers as the Columbia and the Colorado flow, have grouped together to plan the wisest use of the water and the power from these dams.

The highest dam in the United States is Hoover Dam, on the border between Arizona and the southern tip of Nevada. Its reservoir, *Lake Mead*, holds more water than any other man-made body of water in the world. Hoover Dam's power plant provides electricity for the city of Los Angeles, about 250 miles away in the state of California. The water from Lake Mead and many other reservoirs makes farming important in land that would otherwise be desert or covered with tough grasses.

How do people make a living in the Rocky Mountain States?

(Idaho, Montana, Wyoming, Utah, Colorado, Nevada, Arizona, New Mexico)

It was mining that brought the first settlers and started many of the communities in the Rocky Mountain States. Although farming today brings in more dollars than mining, mining is still very important. It is much different, however, from that done in earlier days. Even the ores that are mined are different.

During the days of the gold and silver "rushes," it was every man for himself. When the gold and silver near the surface were gone, most of the miners either left the mining area or went into another kind of business. It took costly machinery to drill down to the veins deep in the earth. No man could do the work alone, and most did not have the money for machinery and workmen. Today, most of the mining is done by large companies that have the necessary money and workmen.

Modern mining methods are used in the Rocky Mountains today. This is a molybdenum mine in Colorado.

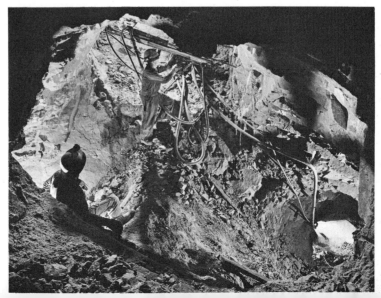

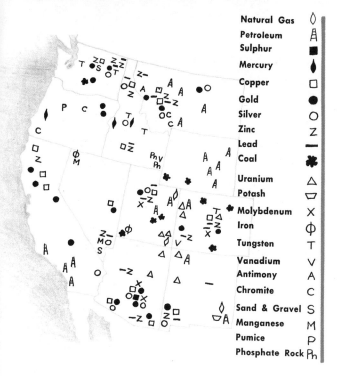

Natural Gas	◊
Petroleum	₳
Sulphur	■
Mercury	◆
Copper	□
Gold	●
Silver	○
Zinc	Z
Lead	—
Coal	✿
Uranium	△
Potash	▽
Molybdenum	X
Iron	Φ
Tungsten	T
Vanadium	V
Antimony	A
Chromite	C
Sand & Gravel	S
Manganese	M
Pumice	P
Phosphate Rock	Ph

From the Mines of the West

Gold and silver are still mined, but many of the veins have been worked out. Idaho is the leading state in silver-mining today. Copper is among the very important mineral products of some of the Rocky Mountain States, especially in Utah, Montana, and Arizona.

There are also beds of soft coal underlying much of the land in these states, but not all of it is easily mined. Drilling into the earth for petroleum and natural gas has been more profitable. All the Rocky Mountain States produce petroleum and natural gas, with New Mexico, Montana, and Wyoming leading.

Since World War II, another great mining interest and a new source of income has come to the Rocky Moun-

tain States, especially to Colorado and New Mexico. Both have rich deposits of *uranium*, which is the main source of atomic power.

The federal government has opened research and testing stations in several places. One testing ground is near Las Vegas, Nevada. Many young men are stationed there and at the government air bases in the wide open spaces of the Southwest. In New Mexico, the federal government has the largest payroll of any employer in the state.

The people of the Rocky Mountain States do not earn nearly as much of their living from manufacturing as do the people in the rest of the United States. They have the power from the electric plants of their great dams. There are not enough people, however, to provide a market nearby for finished products, and the cost of transportation is high.

There are few large cities in the Rocky Mountain States. None has over a million people. All the Rocky Mountain States together, even though they cover over one-fourth of the land of the whole United States, do not have as many people living in them as live in the state of Michigan.

Rocky Mountain manufacturers make mostly products that can be used near the factory or ones that are made from raw materials found in that part of the country. These raw materials would, of course, include the ores from the mines.

Many of the factories that are found in the Rocky Mountain States are food plants. They handle products from the farms and ranches in the area. Denver plants handle most of the food shipment, for this city has the best transportation for sending goods to market. Wheat grown in the irrigated lands, especially in Montana, and tons of sugar beets come to the mills of Denver. Other important crops that pass through this transportation center are Idaho potatoes, peas, beans, onions, and cantaloupes.

There are large packing houses and stockyards in Denver, too, as well as in some of the smaller cities. They receive the beef cattle and other meat animals raised on the ranches. Thousands of acres of the plains east of the mountains and many of the valleys and plateaus in the mountain areas are used as grazing land for both beef and dairy cattle and for sheep. The wool from the sheep, is, of course, another product from the ranches.

There is one area of the West that produces little of anything. Nature left the soil of this area almost unsuitable for growing plants, even when the land is irrigated. Covering much of Nevada and spreading out into the western corners of the neighboring states is a desert area often called the *Great Basin*. It is called a "basin" because almost all its rivers never reach the ocean. The rivers either flow into one of the lakes in the Basin or else just dry up.

Both sheep and cattle graze in the mountain valley pastures.

Here and there throughout the Great Basin are holes in the ground called *pockets*. The deeper pockets are called *sinks*. Others, such as Great Salt Lake, the largest of them all, have water in them. This water is usually very strong in minerals, including salt. This water is sometimes said to be *brackish*. The soil, too, is full of salt. This is called *alkaline* soil. Sagebrush grows plentifully here, but no paying crops.

There is one business, however, that does well in the desert. That is the tourist trade. Nevada, one of the desert states, has great beauty. There are low mountain ridges running through it, pretty lakes, and great snow-capped peaks surrounding the desert.

What are the Pacific Coast States like?
(Washington, Oregon, California)

The three Pacific Coast States are on the "wet" side of the mountains. All of them are affected in their climate by the Pacific Ocean, especially the regions north of San Francisco. The ocean keeps the summers cool and the winters mild. There is a long period in the summer when it seldom rains. In October, the "wet" season begins. Snow falls in the mountains, but along the coast, it is seldom cold enough for snow. Rain falls instead.

Ever since the first explorers reported the wonders of the Pacific Coast area, people have been drawn to this land. Settlers, among whom was John Sutter, journeyed thousands of miles to get to California or to beautiful Oregon. You will remember that in those days Oregon was the name for the land that today includes both Washington and Oregon. Fishing, the fur trade, and the gold rush brought many people. Even without the gold rush, it is probable that the millions of people who live in these three states would have gone there. The gold rush only brought them a little sooner.

Western dude ranches give easterners a chance to live "western style."

Lumber taken from the fir forests of Washington will be used in building projects throughout the country.

The land is generous in its offers to help people make a living. The forests of the Pacific Coast States include the pines and the tall Douglas firs in Washington, Oregon, and northern California. The fir trees provide wood used in the making of plywood and for many other building purposes. East of the fir forests are the pines, most common wood used in lumber for building, for pulp in paper making, and in the manufacture of rayon.

In northern California begin the forests of the giant redwoods and the *sequoias*. Some of these trees will be left standing for as long as possible. They are among the world's tallest trees with huge trunks. Some of the giant sequoias are well over one thousand years old.

Some of the redwoods are cut for lumber. Much of it is used for siding on buildings. This wood will not rot easily, and it can even be used without paint or varnish. Inside walls can also be covered with redwood.

Forest fires are seldom a problem in the redwood forests, and that may be one reason the giant trees are still standing. The bark is thick, deeply grooved, and difficult to burn.

Farther south, however, especially in the hills of Los Angeles, forest fires are a serious problem. At the end of the summer dry season, fires destroy acres of trees each year. Wild life of the forests is hurt, either through direct death in the fires or through the destruction of the animals' food supply and shelter.

All three states work steadily to prevent forest fires.

Seeds are scattered and the seedlings are well cared for in areas in which trees have been lost by fire or cut down for lumber in western forests.

The San Francisco harbor is in the sheltered area of San Francisco Bay. The San Francisco-Oakland Bay bridge, shown here, crosses the bay.

Nature gave these states a climate especially helpful for the growing of crops. This region is the country's leading fruit-producing area. Washington is famous for its apples. Cherries, pears, plums, apricots, peaches, and grapes are large fruit crops in all the states. The southern part of California grows many citrus fruits. Olives, dates, figs, and nuts are also California products.

California grows almost every crop that can be grown somewhere in the United States. Although farming is not the leading industry in California, the state makes more money through farming than any other state in the Union. Grains of all kinds are grown, and livestock and poultry are raised. Irrigation is needed in some parts of the state.

Nature also gave the Pacific Coast States excellent harbors. Shiploads of products from other nations are brought in, and the lumber, pulp, metal, hides, fruits, and other products of the western region are shipped out. Some of the out-going products are for trade along the Pacific coast, some for across the ocean, and some goes through the Panama Canal to eastern American ports.

Sea foods are an important product of the Pacific Coast food plants, especially those around Puget Sound and the Columbia River in Oregon. There are many people who work in the fishing industry, bringing in tuna, salmon, halibut, sardines, oysters, shrimp, and other sea foods. The canneries and freezing plants supply stores all over the country.

Fish ladders have been built beside many of the dams in the West. Salmon, swimming upstream to lay their eggs, get around the dams by using the ladders.

Conservation measures have been taken to see that the supply of salmon does not die out. Salmon always swim upstream to the shallow parts of the rivers to lay their eggs. When great dams were built, the salmon were blocked. The Columbia River is very important to the salmon. Part of the conservation work was to build *fish ladders*, watery steps up which the fish would be able to leap and so still make their way upstream.

With its fine harbors for transportation and raw materials at hand, the Pacific Coast States quickly developed manufacturing after the power plants at the dams were set up. The products are many, but transportation equipment is the most outstanding of all.

Airplanes, from large jets to small private planes, are manufactured in several locations in the Pacific Coast States. Los Angeles assembly plants turn out more automobiles than any other city except Detroit.

Nature helped, too, in the building of the industry for which California is famous the world over—the making of movies. The long rainless season of southern California allows the actors and other people to work outside with little trouble from the weather. The natural background for almost any scene, desert, mountain or ocean, is not far away.

Tourists come to see it all, from the movie-making business to the deep canyons. The call of the West does not seem to die.

343

Words to Know

alkaline (ăl′ká lĭn) 340

brackish (brăk′ĭsh) 340

buttes (būts) 335

erode (ė̇ rōd′) 336

fish ladders (fĭsh lăd′ẽrz) 343

geyser (gī′zẽr) 335

Great Basin (grāt bā′s′n) 339

Lake Mead (lāk mēd) 337

Lassen Peak (lăs″n pēk) 334

pockets (pŏk′ĕts) 340

sequoias (sė̇ kwoi′áz) 341

Sierra Nevada (sĭ ẽr′á nė̇ vădá) 334

sinks (sĭngks) 340

uranium (u̇ rā′nĭ ŭm) 338

Questions

1. What keeps the eastern parts of the Rocky Mountain States from getting much rainfall?

2. How does the population of California compare with the population of Nevada? Why is there such a great difference?

3. What is one reason for the unusual land and water forms found in the West? When were the lands of the eastern North America formed?

4. Why are gassy fumes often seen rising from the Cascade Mountains?

5. Why did the city of San Francisco have to be rebuilt in 1906?

6. What is a geyser?

7. How was the Grand Canyon of Arizona formed?

8. How have the great dams of the West helped the people who live there?

9. How does the mining of today differ from the mining done during the days of the gold and silver "rushes"?

10. Why is uranium an important metal?

You See for Yourself

Learn more about rocks and their importance in the formation of the earth. What is magma? What is lava? How is soil different from rock? What are igneous, sedimentary, and metamorphic rocks? Find as many different kinds of rock as you can around your school. Do any of them have shiny crystals?

Now You Know

In some ways, the western section of our country is "new." The action of volcanoes formed the lands of the eastern part of the United States more than fifty million years earlier than the land of the West began to appear. This is one reason why the land of the West is rugged and often strange-looking. Frost, water, and wind erosion are still at work changing the land and rock formations.

The coastal mountains have a great effect on the climate of the Western States. They trap most of the rain clouds that come off the Pacific Ocean so that they never reach the lands east of the mountain ranges. These lands are on the "dry" side of the mountains. Farmers here have to irrigate their lands to grow crops. The work of irrigation has been helped in recent years through the building of dams and reservoirs in western rivers.

On the "wet" side of the coastal mountains, some sections of the Pacific Coast States receive enough rainfall for a number of different types of farming. California, especially, has farms where everything from grain to fruits is grown.

Mining has always been an important industry, especially in the Rocky Mountain States. Little manufacturing, however, is done here because of the high cost of getting goods to market. In the Pacific Coast States, California does some important manufacturing, including the making of automobiles and airplanes. The tourist industry is important in almost all the Western States.

You Talk It Over

You have learned that one of the reasons manufacturing has not become important in the Rocky Mountains is that the finished products would have to be shipped to far-away markets. How does transportation affect the price of items you buy at the store? Where do you think oranges would cost more, in a Texas grocery store or a Michigan grocery store? Explain your answer. Why would it not be profitable for a Rocky Mountain businessman to manufacture cotton dresses or other clothing to be sent to market in stores of the Eastern cities?

Puzzlers

A list of industries found in the West is given below. Look at the pictures on this page, and decide which industry is shown in each one.

Mining
Farming

Tourist
Fishing
Ranching

Manufacturing
Lumbering

Unit Activities

You make a park booklet

More national parks and forests are located in the West than in any other section of our country. Below is a list of some of the most popular ones. From encyclopedias and other sources, find out as much as you can about each one. Give special attention to any unusual land forms for which the parks are known. Using a different sheet of paper for each park, write several paragraphs telling about each park.

Olympic	Bryce Canyon
Mt. Rainier	Zion
Crater Lake	Grand Canyon
Lassen Volcanic	Carlsbad Caverns
Yosemite	Mesa Verde
Sequoia	Rocky Mountain
Kings Canyon	Yellowstone
	Glacier

You make a chart

On a large sheet of paper mark off the headings and columns shown below. Using books from your school library and information from this unit, fill in the columns for each state in the Western section.

You make a peep box

Let each pupil in your class bring a large shoe box to school. Cut away most of the lid, and cover the opening with a piece of colored tissue paper. Let each pupil choose some view that a visitor to the West might see if he traveled through these states. Be sure that no two pupils choose the same scene. Each pupil should arrange this scene in his shoe box and cut a small hole in one end of the box through which the scene may be viewed. Choose whatever materials would work best for each particular scene. For example, someone showing the Grand Canyon could shape clay into the needed formations and then paint it different colors. Someone showing a cattle ranch could cover the bottom of the box with a piece of green cloth and place stand-up cattle made of stiff paper on the "grass."

This list gives you some suggestions of things to show.

Volcano	A redwood forest
Geyser	A large dam
Buttes	A western desert
Mountains	California vineyard

State	Capital city	Other large cities	Kind of land	Products

UNIT 12

Other States, Possessions, and Territories

Long ago, during the years the colonists were fighting for their independence, an English sea captain was making an important world voyage. His name was Captain James Cook. His purpose was to settle once and for all the old question of whether or not there was a sea route around North America. He found no such route.

Cook's voyage did, however, bring him to Hawaii and Alaska our forty-ninth and fiftieth states. Earlier European ships may have stopped at the Hawaiian Islands, but Cook is usually called their discoverer. Russian fur traders had already entered Alaska some forty years before Cook and his men arrived there.

Diamond Head crater, rising above the Waikiki Beach, is a famous landmark of the Hawaiian Islands.

349

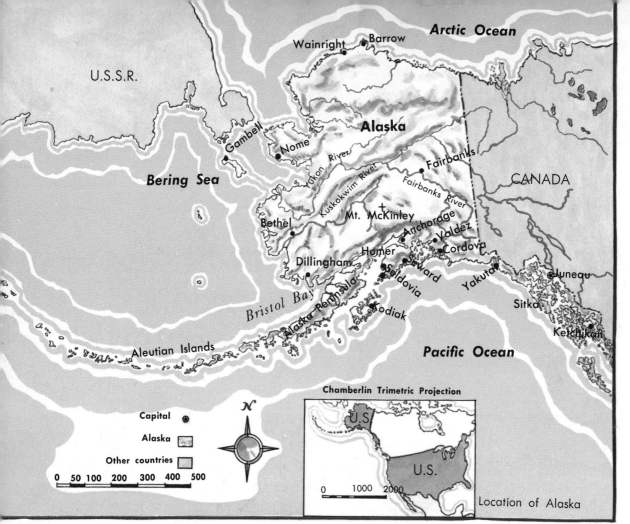

Alaska, the 49th State

When Cook and his men visited Alaska, they probably saw the *Aleut* Indians, who lived in houses made of sod and grasses and built skin canoes called *kayaks*. Moving about skillfully in these kayaks, the Aleuts used harpoons and poisoned spears to hunt seal and whale. Cook may have seen a number of Russian fur traders also. The Russian hunters had been going to Alaska since the 1740's. In 1784, they made a small settlement on *Kodiak Island*. From then on, the Russians pushed their claim to Alaska by opening a chain of fur-trading posts along the coast that reached south nearly as far as San Francisco Bay. The Russians took thousands and thousands of furs from this part of North America.

When United States Secretary of State Seward received Russia's offer to sell this land, the fur business was about ended. You will remember that this was in 1867, just after the War Between the States. Most Americans at that time thought of the purchase as "Seward's Folly."

1740
Russian fur traders
come to Alaska.

1778
Captain Cook
visits Alaska.

1867
United States
buys Alaska.

FISH CANNERY

1878
First salmon cannery opened.

1898
Gold discovered
in Yukon.

1900
Lumbering
industry begins.

1959
Alaska becomes a state.

What was done with Seward's Folly?

At first, the United States did little with this great piece of land, twice as large as Texas. No one had any idea that the fishing industry alone would some day be worth much more than the purchase price. The first salmon cannery was opened in Alaska in 1878. Today the town of *Ketchikan* at the southern end of Alaska is the "Salmon Capital of the World." Kodiak and *Sitka* are leading salmon-canning centers, too.

Gold was discovered in Alaska in 1898. This brought a gold rush into the *Yukon* River Valley, near the western Canadian border. Only the first gold-seekers to arrive in the Yukon became wealthy from this gold rush. Most of the mining was soon taken over by large companies.

Perhaps the most important thing to come out of the Yukon gold rush was the new interest that the United States began to take in this great territory of the northwest.

Farms such as this dairy farm five miles from Fairbanks help supply that city with fresh food.

Many fishing boats, used in the catching of salmon, are seen here in the harbor of Ketchikan, Alaska.

Alaska was found to offer a number of important resources besides gold. Among these were its forests, coal, and water power. In recent years, oil was discovered there. Drilling companies are searching for more rich pockets, which they feel sure are there.

The first oil discovery was made on the *Kenai* Peninsula, which is in south central Alaska. This is the place where most Alaskans live. A mountain range, which includes Mt. McKinley, the highest mountain in North America, shelters the Kenai Peninsula from the north. The climate is fairly mild in this part of Alaska. The cold parts lie north of the town of Fairbanks.

How did World War II bring changes to Alaska?

Although the value of its products had paid its cost many times over, the United States did little to build up Alaska until World War II. Then it was realized how near Alaska was to enemy nations in Asia. The United States set up military bases in the Aleutian Islands and has kept them there ever since. Today, a great many Alaskans work for the government. The building of military bases led to other projects that called for more workers. Transportation and communication systems had to be improved, and offices, supply depots, and houses built for the people who were sent to the bases.

The work of building a highway from the United States through Canada to Alaska was begun. Air strips were built in many locations in Alaska, for it became clear that small airplanes provided the best kind of transportation in a land so vast. Ocean steamer service from the United States to Alaska was also increased.

Alaskans saw the possibilities for their region, but they felt that the best way for them to develop their land was to become a state. Then they would have a governor and lawmakers elected by their own people and an equal voice with other states in the Congress. A large group of public-spirited Alaskans began to work toward this goal. In 1959, Alaska entered the Union as the forty-ninth state. It was the first state whose boundaries did not touch those of other states.

What is the state of Hawaii like?

Hawaii is thought by some to be the most beautiful state in the Union. It is certainly different from all the other states in its form, its climate, and its people. It is the only state made up completely of a group of islands. The Hawaiian Islands were built up from the eruptions of volcanoes in the Pacific Ocean. The largest island of the group, Hawaii, (the same name as the state), was formed by five volcanoes.

Fire and burning lava light up the sky during an eruption of Mount Kilauea.

Two of the volcanoes, both on the island of Hawaii, are still very active. Visitors may look down, from the Hawaiian Observatory which is built on its rim, and see the glowing metal rock. The *crater* is the hole around the mouth of the volcano. The other active volcano is the high mountain named *Mauna Loa* that erupts every few years.

Some of the volcanoes such as Diamond Head on the island of *Oahu*, died out before they built up to any great height. Oahu is the island most often visited by the thousands of tourists who go to Hawaii each year.

The climate of Hawaii is mild all year round. The average temperature of *Honolulu*, the capital city, is seventy-five degrees. The highest temperature ever recorded was only eighty-eight degrees.

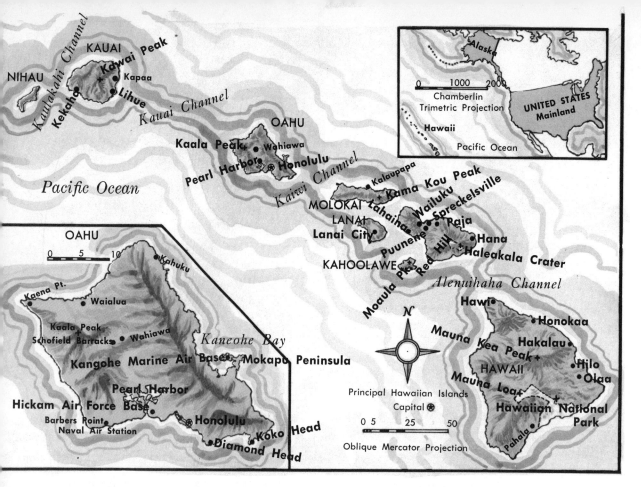

Hawaii, the 50th State

Who are the people of Hawaii?

The people Captain Cook found living in the islands were *Polynesians*, like the people of many islands in the South Pacific. Their forefathers had come to Hawaii across many miles of tossing seas in large, open canoes. After Captain Cook's voyage, many traders from all over the world began stopping at Hawaii to get sandalwood from the islanders. Some of these traders liked the land so well that they stayed there. Through the years, the population of the islands became a mixture of many different peoples.

Missionaries from the United States arrived in Hawaii early in the 1800's. Because of their work, the Hawaiian rulers began to do away with their old religious customs. Although the people were kind and generous in their everyday lives, their religion often included such savage customs as human sacrifice.

Some of the newcomers decided to set up sugar plantations in the islands. They brought shiploads of workers from China, Japan, and the Polynesian Islands, for the Hawaiians were not interested in doing field work.

In 1882, Captain John Kidwell of England brought 1,000 pineapple plants from Jamaica and began the first pineapple plantation. Outside the federal government and the tourist business, sugar and pineapple are the two main sources of income for Hawaiians today.

The Hawaiians continued their government under kings and queens for many years after outsiders, including many Americans, began living there. In 1891, the king died, and his sister, the new queen, decided to take more power for herself. The outsiders, especially the Americans, objected. The queen soon lost her power. The Republic of Hawaii was formed in 1894. Sanford B. Dole was elected president.

American businessmen were very powerful in Hawaii. They wanted the United States to take over protection of the islands. Congress voted to do this, and the islands became the Territory of Hawaii in 1900. Mr. Dole became the governor instead of president. Hawaii proved to be a good place for the United States to set up Army and Navy bases.

The Navy base at Pearl Harbor was attacked by the Japanese on December 7, 1941. The United States then joined in the fighting of World War II. When the war was over and the damage had been repaired, a new life began for Hawaii. Giant airships began taking people to Hawaii for vacations in far greater numbers than ever before. Now, jet liners can take tourists from California to Hawaii in only a few hours time.

Hawaiians, like the Alaskans, felt that becoming a state would help them. While he was President, Harry S. Truman urged Congress to allow Hawaii to enter the Union as soon as a suitable constitution had been drawn up. But it was not until a few months after Alaska had entered the Union in 1959, that Congress voted to allow Hawaii to become the fiftieth state.

What is a United States territory?

A United States territory is a section of land which may or may not be on its way to becoming a state. Alaska and Hawaii were the last territories that became states. The first territory the United States had was the Northwest Territory, from which five states were formed.

The people of a territory have certain citizenship rights. They do not have regular representatives in Congress as people of a state have, but sometimes Congress votes to let them send someone to speak for them in the House of Representatives. In this way their needs and problems come to the attention of the nation. They choose their own representatives to make the laws within their territory. The President of the United States chooses their governor. The people of the territory are protected by the United States.

What two territories does the United States have today?

The island of *Guam* has been a territory of the United States since August 1, 1950. Guam is one among a group of islands known as the *Mariana* Islands. There are 67,000 American citizens on Guam although most of them have never lived in the United States.

Guam is a little tropical island about thirty miles long and from four to six miles wide. The tropical forests that once grew over much of the island have been cut away to make room for the United States air strips and government buildings. But there are still great groves of coconut palms on the hilly sections. The climate of Guam is mild, but the tall palms often bend under the winds of tropical storms known as *typhoons*.

Magellan discovered Guam in 1521. From then until the end of the Spanish-American War, Guam belonged to Spain. At the end of that war, the island was signed over to the United States. The American citizens who live there usually speak English but with a Spanish accent. Many of the people raise most of their own food on small farm patches or work in the towns as tradesmen.

Guam is very important to the United States because it gives this country a place for Navy and Air bases far out in the Pacific Ocean. About four out of every ten citizens are either people who work on the bases or members of their families.

Territories in the Pacific

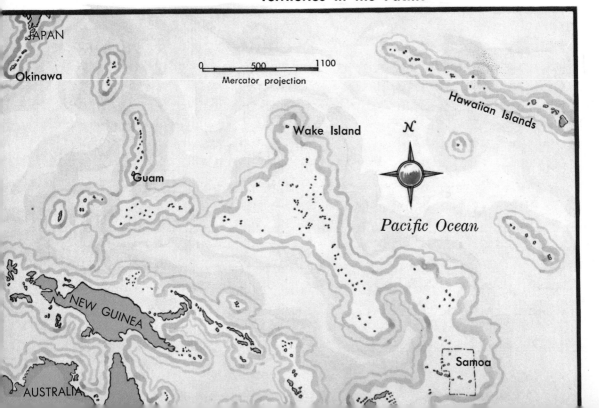

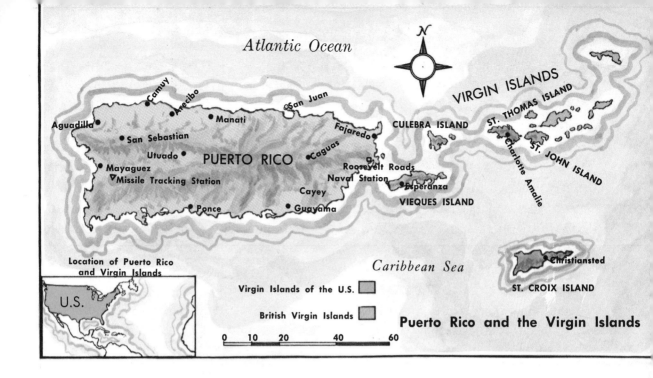

Virgin Islands of the U.S. ☐

British Virgin Islands ☐

0   10   20   40   60

Puerto Rico and the Virgin Islands

The only other regular territory of the United States is the Territory of the Virgin Islands, located where the waters of the Caribbean Sea blend with the Atlantic Ocean. Not the whole group of the Virgin Islands belongs to United States. The western half, which includes *St. Croix*, St. John, St. Thomas, and some smaller islands, are American. The rest are English. The United States, seeing the value of the islands as a protective base, bought them from Denmark in 1916. Congress gave the people citizenship rights in 1927.

Christopher Columbus discovered the Virgin Islands in 1493. In the years that followed, Spain, England, Holland, and Denmark were all interested in owning and settling the islands. They changed hands a number of times, but English became the language generally used.

Many slaves were brought to the islands to work on the sugar-cane plantations. Today, almost two-thirds of the citizens of the islands came from slave beginnings. Many of them still work at growing sugar cane, much of which is grown for export. Cattle are raised for beef, and many tropical fruits are grown.

Other income is from rum, the chief manufactured product. The taxes collected on the exported rum have paid the cost of the islands and still pay for their upkeep.

The tourist industry is very important to the Virgin Islands. Fine hotels and restaurants have been built for the visitors. There are good beaches for swimming and excellent fishing, too. Many tourists like to visit the coves in which pirate ships once hid and the castles built by the pirates who stopped there.

357

When did Puerto Rico become a self-governing island?

This island, won by the United States in the Spanish-American War, was an American territory for many years. Late in the 1940's, however, work was begun to allow Puerto Rico more independence. By 1952, the island became self-governing, and its name was changed to the Commonwealth of Puerto Rico. The governor is now elected by the Puerto Ricans, and he works under a constitution much like that of the United States.

The United States has Army and Air bases in Puerto Rico, and the laws of the United States are in force in Puerto Rico much as if it were a state. This is the choice of the Puerto Ricans. They may come and go in the United States as American citizens, but they do not have a vote in Congress. Neither do they pay federal income taxes.

Puerto Rico was also discovered by Columbus on his second voyage to the New World. As in the Virgin Islands, the Spanish fought and killed most of the unfriendly Indians they found there. The islands stayed under Spanish rule until the Spanish-American War in the late 1800's.

Puerto Rico is about 1,000 miles southeast of Florida and tropical in its location. The winds coming to the land help to keep it from becoming uncomfortably warm. It is eighty to one hundred miles long and up to thirty miles wide. It is a crowded island even though about four-fifths of its land is in farms. Well over 2,200,000 people live there. Its many towns are swarming with people. Much of the old and unhealthful housing in them has lately been torn down and new buildings put up.

Sugar-growing takes up much of the land and provides raw materials for the sugar mills and rum distilleries, both powered by the newly-built, government-controlled electric power plants. Much sugar is exported, along with tobacco, fruit, rum, and textiles. Many of the hillsides are used for farming, for there is little level land on the island. Soil erosion has been a problem as well as the wearing out of the soil from tobacco and repeated planting of other crops. The government has done much work in soil conservation.

An old Spanish fortress stands at the western end of San Juan, Puerto Rico.

Palm trees and other tropical growth line the beaches of American Samoa.

Puerto Rico was a poor and unhealthy place to live for many years. Today, it is an example of how much a good government can do to improve a land. Dense population still makes a great problem, but living conditions are far better than they were twenty years ago. The over-crowding has led many Puerto Ricans, under their right as American citizens, to go to the mainland cities to look for jobs.

What Pacific Islands are protected by the United States?

The United States, in order to have fueling stations for its ships at sea, looked to islands in the Pacific Ocean for places to set up naval bases. One such place is American *Samoa*, one of the Samoan Islands of the South Pacific. In 1900, the United States agreed to take this island under its protection in exchange for the right to set up a naval base there. Samoa became a *protectorate* of the United States.

The Samoan Islands are very colorful with their tropical growth and customs and dress of the people. The people are Polynesians, and look much like the first Hawaiians.

Wake Island, about halfway between Hawaii and Japan, is also a protectorate of the United States. It has been held by the United States since 1899.

At the close of World War II, the island of *Okinawa* also became an American protectorate. Japan surrendered it to the United States. The United States keeps Army and Air Force bases there and has complete rule over the island. According to the peace treaty, however, Okinawa may never become a state as Hawaii did or be given its independence as the Philippine Islands were.

The locks shown here are the first through which a ship going from the Pacific Ocean to the Atlantic Ocean would pass. The Pacific Ocean may be seen in the background.

Who controls the Panama Canal Zone?

You have already learned that the United States built the Panama Canal in land that belonged to another nation, the country of Panama. The agreement with the Republic of Panama still stands, with a few changes.

Today, the Panama Canal is managed by a United States government organization called the Panama Canal Company. The Panama Canal Company is in charge of the way the ships coming into the harbor are handled. It also owns a railroad that crosses Panama. It owns the houses and other buildings which are rented to people who work on the Canal. Telephone, water, electricity, and other community services are also provided by the company.

The towns in the Canal Zone, however, are under the government of the Republic of Panama. The entire Zone is under United States military protection. Ships of all countries may use the Canal in peacetime, but the United States has the right to limit use of the Canal in the case of war or threat of war.

Who owns the District of Columbia?

Long ago, when the first Thirteen States were choosing a capital for the new nation, there was some argument as to which state should be the location for the national capital.

The argument was finally settled when a district that would be part of no state at all was set up. This district would belong to all Americans throughout all the states.

The District of Columbia is the official seat of the United States government. It is a section of land on the eastern shore of the Potomac River, across from Virginia, and touching Maryland on three sides. George Washington, knowing the Potomac River well, chose the location after Congress requested that he select one. The Capitol was built on top of a low, broad hill, with a wide avenue leading from its main entrance.

The city was planned by a famous French engineer, Major *Pierre Charles L'Enfant*. It was he who saw how beautiful it would be possible to make the city. He urged Congress to "make no little plans." This early planning helped to give Americans a capital city of which they may well be proud.

The people of Washington have no voice in government, except to vote for President and Vice-President without having to return to their home states. This right was given them through an amendment to the Constitution of 1961. They have no representation in Congress.

Washington city government is directly under Congress. The federal government pays some of the city's expense, but taxes paid by the people who live there cover most of it.

Every American is interested in keeping Washington, D.C., beautiful, for it belongs to all.

Many people visit the Washington monument in the nation's capital city.

Congress meets in the Capitol, seen in the center of this picture.

The new Senate Office Building is among the many government buildings in Washington.

Words to Know

Aleut (ăl′ē̇ ōot) 350

crater (krā′tẽr) 353

Guam (gwŏm) 356

Honolulu (hŏ′nȯ lōō′lōō) 353

kayaks (kī′ăks) 350

Kenai (kē′nī) 352

Ketchikan (kĕch′ĭ kăn′) 351

Kilauea (kē′lou ā′ä) 353

Kodiak (kō′dĭ ăk) 350

Mariana (mâr′ĭ ăn′ȧ) 356

Mauna Loa (mou′nä lō′ä) 353

Oahu (ȯ ä′hōō) 353

Okinawa (ō′kĭ nä′wȧ) 359

Pierre Charles L'Enfant (pyâr chärlz läɴ′fȧɴ′) 361

Polynesians (pŏl′ĭ nē′shăns) 354

protectorate (prȯ tĕk′tẽr ĭt) 359

St. Croix (sānt kroi′) 357

Samoa (sȧ mō′ȧ) 359

Sitka (sĭt′kȧ) 351

typhoons (tī fōōnz′) 356

Yukon (yōō′kŏn) 351

Questions

1. Who is usually thought of as the discoverer of Hawaii?

2. What is the name of the Alaskan Indians? What are kayaks?

3. What use did Russia make of Alaska during the years that she claimed this land?

4. What natural resources are found in Alaska?

5. In what way is the land of Hawaii different from the land of any other state?

6. From where did the first settlers of the Hawaiian Islands come? What is the name given these people?

7. When did Hawaii become a state?

You See for Yourself

From books in your library, learn more about Captain James Cook and his famous voyage. Make a map showing his route and the places he stopped. How did the Hawaiians receive Cook and his men at first? Where and how did Cook die? How is his grave marked today?

Now You Know

The boundaries of the United States do not end with the original forty-eight states. The forty-ninth state, Alaska, lies in the far northwest corner of North America. It is our largest state in land area but has the smallest population of any American state. Its natural resources and its location near Asia make Alaska very important.

Hawaii, the only island state of the United States, entered the Union in 1959, just a few months after Alaska became a state. The federal government is the largest source of income, but the tourist and sugarcane and pineapple-growing industries are important.

The United States still holds two territories, Guam in the Pacific Ocean, and several of the Virgin Islands in the Caribbean. The United States has very important military bases on Guam. Puerto Rico, once a territory of the United States, is now self-governing, but the people there are still citizens of the United States. American Samoa, Wake Island, and Okinawa are Pacific islands under the protection of the United States.

The Panama Canal Zone is another distant region of great importance to the United States. The zone is under the military protection of the United States at all times, but the Republic of Panama governs the towns.

The District of Columbia lies on the mainland of the United States, but it is part of no state. The city of Washington, the federal capital, is in the District of Columbia.

You Talk It Over

You have read about several gold rushes during your study of the United States this year. What do you think would happen today if rich gold deposits were discovered in a new place? What risks does a person take when he joins in a gold rush?

Look at the Panama Canal Zone and the Virgin Islands on a map. Why could the Virgin Islands be important in the guarding of the Canal Zone? Why would it be harmful to the United States if an enemy destroyed the Panama Canal?

Puzzlers

List numbers one through twelve on a sheet of paper. Read the statements on this page. Write the letter of the picture beside the number of the statement that best describes the picture.

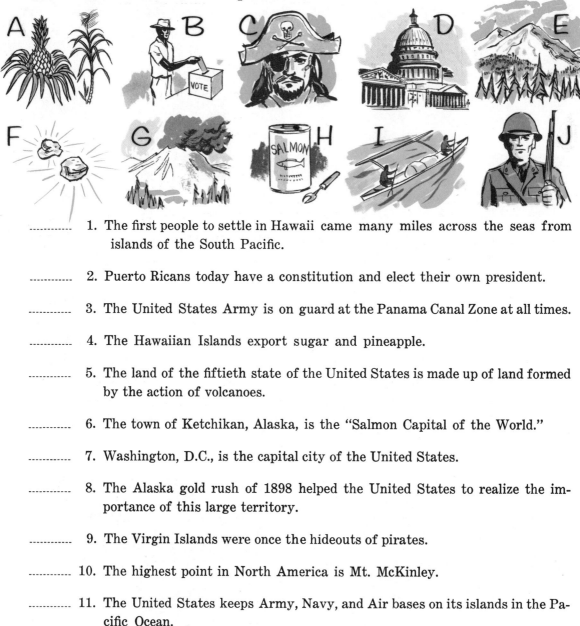

.... 1. The first people to settle in Hawaii came many miles across the seas from islands of the South Pacific.

.... 2. Puerto Ricans today have a constitution and elect their own president.

.... 3. The United States Army is on guard at the Panama Canal Zone at all times.

.... 4. The Hawaiian Islands export sugar and pineapple.

.... 5. The land of the fiftieth state of the United States is made up of land formed by the action of volcanoes.

.... 6. The town of Ketchikan, Alaska, is the "Salmon Capital of the World."

.... 7. Washington, D.C., is the capital city of the United States.

.... 8. The Alaska gold rush of 1898 helped the United States to realize the importance of this large territory.

.... 9. The Virgin Islands were once the hideouts of pirates.

.... 10. The highest point in North America is Mt. McKinley.

.... 11. The United States keeps Army, Navy, and Air bases on its islands in the Pacific Ocean.

.... 12. Hawaii continued under the rule of kings and queens for many years after outsiders began to settle there.

Unit Activities

You give a play

Choose members of your class to play the roles of Captain James Cook and his men. Write and act a play showing the adventures that he and his men had at different places they stopped. You may use large sheets of wrapping paper on which to draw a background for Alaska and Hawaii. Other pupils may play the parts of Aleut Indians and Hawaiians when Cook and his men arrive.

You write a story

Read some library resource books to learn about life in the early days of Alaska or Hawaii. Then use your imagination to write a story about a boy, a girl, or perhaps even an animal who lived in one of these states.

You learn about the Panama Canal

Find out as much as you can about how the locks of the Panama Canal raise and lower ships in the water to get them through the waterway. Place a toy boat in a basin of water. Take some of the water out of the basin and watch what happens to the boat. Then add water to the basin and watch what happens to the boat. Be able to tell how the Panama Canal locks are like the basin of water.

You make a report

Learn more about the growing of pineapple in Hawaii. Write a report and read it to the class. Tell how it is planted, cared for, how long it takes a crop to ripen, and how it is harvested.

365

13

You, a Citizen of Today

If you had been born in a log cabin on the frontier 150 years ago, you would have been a citizen of the United States, just as you are now. But the world into which you were born would have been much different from that in which you live today.

Families on the frontier each provided most of their own needs. They lived simple lives, wanting little more than just food, clothing and shelter. Almost everything they had was homemade, including their amusements. The things a family wanted but needed help in getting could usually be had through the community formed among the neighbors. Neighbors often worked together to help a family.

Children of today must study many subjects in school to help them grow up as wise citizens of the world.

367

Pioneer Americans. . .

built their own homes.

grew most of their food.

took care of their own health.

As years went by, the use of machinery came into American life. As a result, factories opened, with a need for workers trained to do each job and to operate each machine. Many men found that they could get more for their families by leaving the farm and working in a factory for wages. Those who stayed on the farms found it better to grow or raise just a few things to sell than to try to produce everything their families needed.

The United States was growing into a nation in which each wage earner learned a special skill.

Through working at this job, he could earn the money to buy the things his family needed, and many of the things they did not need badly, but wanted to have.

At the same time that factories began to turn out great numbers of products, there were new inventions in transportation and communication, bringing distant communities into closer touch with each other. People learned of new products other people had, and wanted them. Wage earners needed more money to buy things, and they formed labor unions, working together to get higher pay.

Today's Americans. . .

ACME CONSTRUCTION

hire companies to build their homes.

can buy food from all over the world in their grocery stores.

benefit from wonder drugs and advanced medical science.

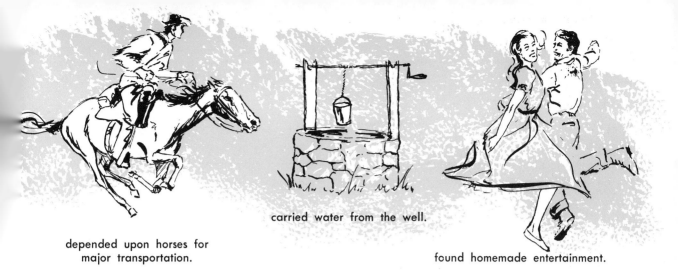

depended upon horses for
major transportation.

carried water from the well.

found homemade entertainment.

People wanted and were able to buy more and more kinds of goods and services. The American standard of living climbed upward. *Standard of living* means the degree to which people are able to get the things they need and want for themselves.

How business operates to meet the needs and wants of the people is called an *economic system*. The American economic sytem allows private individuals to own and operate businesses. This system has helped the people of the United States to reach the highest standard of living known in the history of the world.

At the same time that the standard of living was rising, each American came to need the goods and services of others in increasing amounts. When one person looks to another to supply a certain need, we say that person is *dependent* upon the other. When both persons look to each other for the special need the other can supply, we say the two persons are *interdependent*. The wide circle of dependence and interdependence in the United States today helps to keep our standard of living high. Each citizen, each community, and each state is important to all the others.

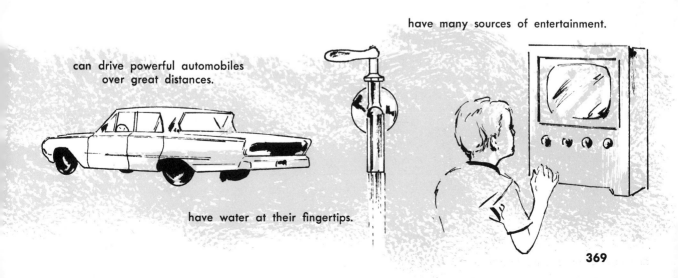

can drive powerful automobiles
over great distances.

have many sources of entertainment.

have water at their fingertips.

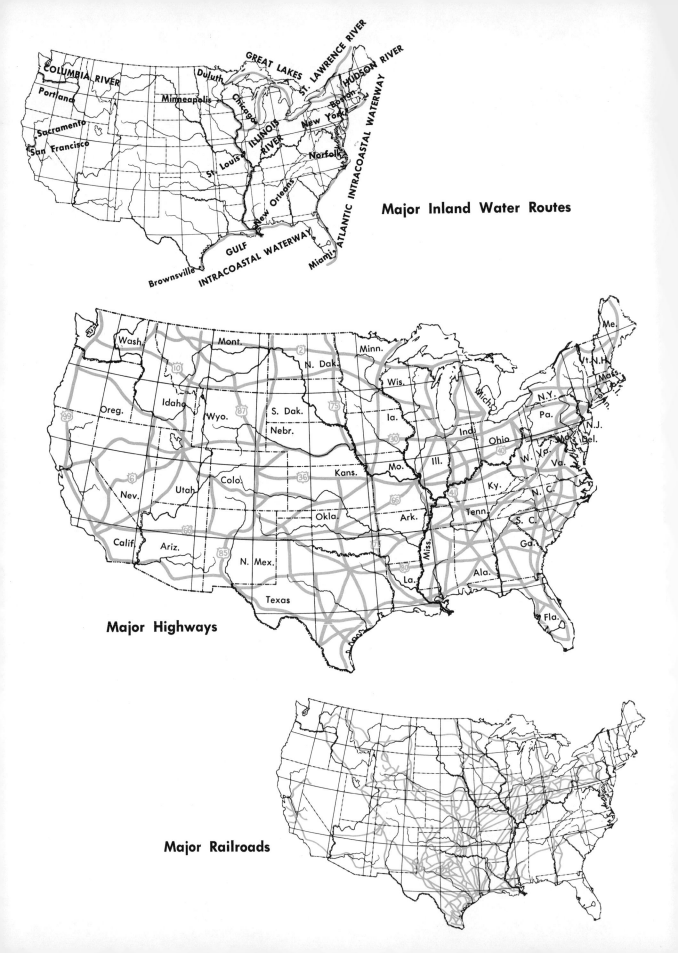

Major Inland Water Routes

COLUMBIA RIVER
Portland
Sacramento
San Francisco
Duluth
Minneapolis
Chicago
St. Louis
ILLINOIS RIVER
New Orleans
Brownsville
GULF INTRACOASTAL WATERWAY
Miami
ATLANTIC INTRACOASTAL WATERWAY
Norfolk
New York
Boston
HUDSON RIVER
ST. LAWRENCE RIVER
GREAT LAKES

Major Highways

Wash.
Oreg.
Calif.
Nev.
Idaho
Mont.
Utah
Ariz.
Wyo.
Colo.
N. Mex.
Texas
N. Dak.
S. Dak.
Nebr.
Kans.
Okla.
Minn.
Ia.
Mo.
Ark.
La.
Wis.
Ill.
Miss.
Ala.
Mich.
Ind.
Ohio
Ky.
Tenn.
Ga.
Fla.
N.Y.
Pa.
W. Va.
Va.
N. C.
S. C.
Me.
Vt.
N.H.
Mass.
Conn.
N.J.
Del.
Md.

Major Railroads

Millions of Telephones in the United States

(One system only)

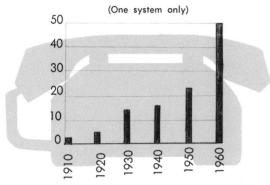

Millions of Television Sets in the United States

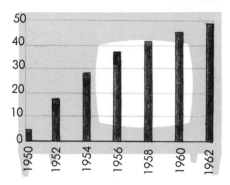

What are some of the networks that help make the states interdependent?

It would take far too much time and space to try to tell all the ways in which the states and the people that live in them are interdependent. The maps and graphs on these two pages show how the major systems of transportation and communication tie the nation together.

During the 1870's, the growing network of railroads began to show the problems as well as the advantages that would come with such improvements. Each state was making its own rules concerning the movement of goods and people, but these rules were often not obeyed. In 1887, the federal government set up the Interstate Commerce Commission to see to it that all states received fair treatment from the railroads that crossed through them.

As the networks that tied the states together grew, the work of the Interstate Commerce Commission became broader. Today the Commission is in charge of seeing that all federal laws dealing with trade between different states are obeyed. It may control rates and other trade practices of shipping by rail, water, truck, or bus. Gas and pipelines, too, are under its control. It is the work of the Commission to see that the public good is always served, and that small companies as well as large ones get good service and fair treatment in trade.

Defense

Agriculture

Commerce

Health, Education & Welfare

Justice

Labor

Treasury

Interior

State

Post Office

Federal Departments at Work in all States

How does government tie the states together?

Government, too, has become less simple than it was during pioneer days. Today, each state is part of a great network of government. Your state and community governments do much to give you a safe and healthy place in which to live. Yet much of this work is done under the help and sometimes the control of the federal government. The charts on this page will help you to understand some of the work of the federal government in our country.

When you are old enough to vote, you will be able to help choose the people in charge of the great network of government. You will want to do your part in seeing that the best people are chosen for office.

As a citizen, you will have rights that people of many other countries do not have. You will have the right to help make laws or help change them. At the same time, you will have the duty to obey the laws, even those you do not like, because they will be the laws wanted by the largest number of people who vote.

How are the nations of the world tied together?

Modern transportation and communication have tied the states of our country together. They have also brought the nations of the world into closer touch with each other.

It was a very great thing, back in 1866, when the first telegraph cable was stretched across the Atlantic. The cable was laid deep in the ocean by the crews of ships that carried great spools of the cable. The laying of such a cable had been tried four times, but each time the cable had broken. In 1866, under the leadership of an American named Cyrus Field, the first successful *transatlantic* cable was laid. Communication between America and Europe was cut to a matter of a few minutes.

Ninety years later, communication between nations took another great leap forward. In 1956, a transatlantic telephone cable went into service. A year later, a cable reached from the United States mainland to Hawaii. These cables made it possible to make overseas telephone calls much faster than ever before.

Before these cables were laid, such long-distance calls were made by using radio waves to connect distant telephone systems. This radio-telephone system makes it possible for ships at sea, and even automobiles on the highways to make telephone calls. The use of satellites such as Telstar makes it possible for us to communicate with overseas points by sight as well as by sound.

Air travel makes it possible for people to reach others all the way across the earth in a matter of hours. Many people whose homelands are far apart are meeting each other face to face through today's advanced transportation. With this closer contact, plus the continued trade that brings products of distant nations to our local stores, each American becomes also a citizen of the world as a whole.

The days when one nation could keep itself and its affairs apart from the rest of the world are gone. Each modern nation and person in that nation is in close touch with the rest of the world each and every day. Each nation knows at once the important events that take place within all the other nations of the world.

How do nations work together?

You have already learned of the work of Clara Barton in getting the United States to become a member of the world organization, the Red Cross. Red Cross workers today travel throughout the world, bringing help to people within all nations and trying to build up good feelings among the nations themselves.

There have been international laws to guide nations for many years. Many of these laws were obeyed just as a matter of custom over the years.

Members of the United Nations Court of Justice meet to hear sides in disputes among nations.

Other international laws have been written into treaties among different nations. These agreements deal with such things as how ships and airplanes may use the harbors and airfields of another, how the citizens of a country are to be treated while visiting a foreign country, or whether or not criminals must be sent back to countries from which they have escaped.

Many international laws have to do with war. There was a time when most nations agreed that churches, hospitals, and even whole cities which played no part in the fighting should not be attacked. Now that atomic bombs and guided missiles have come into use, it would be impossible to follow such laws. Nations everywhere know that the cost of a war in which such weapons were used would be very high.

The United Nations was set up at the close of World War II with the idea that the nations of the world would have a place to settle their differences through discussion and other peaceful methods. One part of the United Nations is an International Court of Justice, which hears both sides of a question when an argument arises between nations. The Court tries to settle the problem with fairness to both sides. Representatives from all nations, large or small, get a chance to speak in the interest of their country and its people. At the same time, each country is supposed to grow in the understanding of the problems faced by other nations.

There is still much to be done in the area of world understanding. The United States is still a young nation when compared with many of the world's nations. Yet it is a world leader in many ways. As a whole, the people of the United States live more comfortable lives than people in any other country of the world. This is largely because of the great strength of this nation in its vast natural resources, its huge farm production, and its manufactured products.

Despite its wealth, the United States is not free of the interdependence that exists among the nations of the world. American businessmen need to sell their products at markets in foreign nations, just as foreign nations must sell their goods here.

American businessmen, however, face problems in trading with other countries. Some of the goods produced in other lands can be sold at lower prices than the same type of goods produced in the United States. This is often due to the fact that people ask higher wages here, in order to keep our high standard of living. Wages paid are part of the cost of the finished goods. The selling price, because of our higher wages, often is higher than that of another nation.

An economic system of a nation grows stronger only when as many dollars come in as leave the nation. International trade is an important part of making the incoming dollars match the outgoing. How to balance the dollars calls for much planning on the part of American business and government leaders. They must work together, and with men from other nations, too.

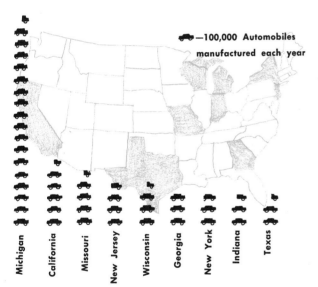

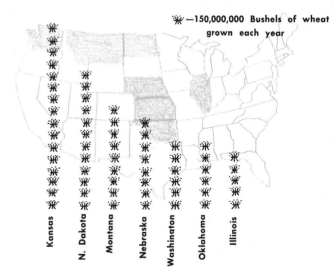

The United States—A World Leader in Production

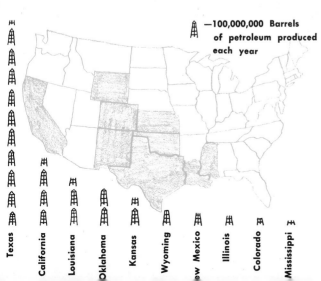

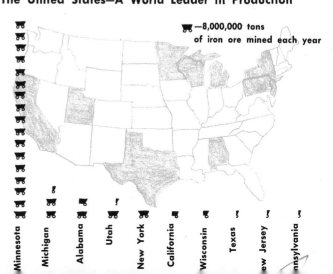

What work for better world understanding is being done?

World citizens everywhere, from the heart of Africa to the heart of the United States are trying to understand each other better. Each different nation brings from its past, from the days of little communication among nations, a collection of customs and ideas that often seem strange to people of different backgrounds. Yet when people from different nations learn to know each other well, they often find that behind the strangeness is a human being with feelings and wishes not much different from their own.

Perhaps *you* will be able to help in days to come. Many Americans now come into close contact with people of other nations. They travel abroad, go as students to live with a family in another land, work for the government or an industry in a foreign country, or go with the Peace Corps.

All who travel with the idea of learning from the people of other lands and of giving a little of themselves help to bring about better world understanding.

Words to Know

dependent (dė pĕn dĕnt) 369

economic system (ē′kŏ nŏm′ĭk sĭs′tĕm) 369

interdependent (ĭn′tēr dė pĕn′dĕnt) 369

Standard of living (stăn′dĕrd ŏv lĭv′ĭng) 369

transatlantic (trăns′ăt lăn′tĭk) 373

Questions

1. What is meant by the statement: "The states of the United States are interdependent"? Why were the pioneer communities not so interdependent as today's communities?

2. What is the work of the Interstate Commerce Commission? When and why was it set up?

3. What great advance in world communication was made in the year 1866? Under whose leadership was this accomplished?

4. What is the role of the International Court of Justice? Of what larger organization is it a part?

You See for Yourself

Learn more about the Peace Corps from encyclopedias or magazines. When was the organization set up? Who may join the Peace Corps? For how long does one work as a corpsman? What are some of the countries in which the Peace Corps is working? What are some of the kinds of work done by the Peace Corps?

Now You Know

The lives of United States citizens have changed greatly since the days of the pioneers. Through the years, the various regions of the United States and the people living in them have moved steadily toward increased interdependence. Today, all parts of the United States are linked by many different systems of transportation and communication. The work of a number of divisions within the federal government also helps to tie the country together.

The movement toward interdependence has not been limited to within our borders. Today's transportation and communication systems bring the citizens of countries all over the world into close touch with each other.

The trading of goods and products with other nations also brings about closer contacts between them. The government and business affairs of one nation are of interest and concern to many other nations, near and far. The nations of the world as well as our states are interdependent.

World interdependence makes it all the more important for the nations of the world to be able to live peaceably. The use of atomic weapons makes it almost a necessity. The United Nations is the biggest organization that works for world peace today. Yet private persons who travel in distant lands can do their part by being willing to learn from others and to extend kindness and understanding to others.

You Talk It Over

What part has trade played in the history of the world as you have studied it so far? Before you answer, you may want to recall the importance of trade to the Europeans of the 1400's. How did their interest in trade help to change the history of the world? In what ways was trade important to the American colonists?

What things other than goods and products can be gained through trade with other people?

If you were a tourist in a foreign country, what are some of the things you would want to find out about that country? What would you like others to know about the United States?

Glossary

The following system of indicating pronunciation is used by permission of the publishers of Webster's New International Dictionary, Second Edition, copyright, 1934, 1939, 1945, 1950, 1953, by G. & C. Merriam Co.

ā as in āle   ē as in ēve   ȯ as in ȯbey
â as in câre   ė as in ėvent   ô as in lôrd
ȧ as in chȧotic   ĕ as in ĕnd   ŏ as in ŏdd
ă as in ădd   ĕ as in silĕnt   oi as in oil
ă as in ăccount   ē as in makēr   ōō as in fōōd
ä as in ärm   ī as in īce   û as in ûnite
ȧ as in ȧsk   ĭ as in ĭll   ŭ as in ŭp
ȧ as in sofȧ   ō as in ōld   ŭ as in circŭs

advertising (ăd′vēr tīz′ĭng). The business of bringing products a manufacturer has for sale to the attention of buyers. 286

alkaline (ăl′kȧ lĭn). Having a salty nature. 340

amendments (ȧ mĕnd′mĕnts). Changes or additions that are included at the close of an original document. 156

apprentice (ă prĕn′tĭs). A person who works in a trade or profession with little or no pay until he has learned that particular craft. 101

arsenal (är′sė năl). A place at which war supplies are stored. 208

assembly line (ă sĕm′blĭ līn). An arrangement of workers and equipment in which each worker performs one certain step in the production of an item of manufacture. The product is completed when it reaches the end of the line. 255

bauxite (bôks′īt). A mixture of several minerals taken from the mine in an earthy mass. It is used in the making of aluminum. 303

bogs (bŏgz). A swampy area filled with decayed plant life. 287

borough (bûr′ō). One of the five political divisions of the New York City area. 282

brackish (brăk′ĭsh). Extremely salty. 340

breaking plow (brāk′ĭng plou). A heavy, strong plow needed to turn under grass-covered wilderness. 229

butte (būt). A steep-sided hill or cliff rising out of an otherwise level land area. 335

Capitol (kăp′ĭ tŏl). The building in Washington, D.C., in which members of Congress hold their meetings. 169

caravan (kăr′ȧ văn). A group of travelers passing through deserted or unfriendly territory. 47

channel (chăn′ĕl). The groove in the earth through which a river flows. 29

chart (chärt). A sorting of information into a special order for easier reading and understanding. 16

claim (klām). Government land which a person chooses to farm or mine for a certain length of time. At the end of that time the land becomes his. 228

colony (kŏl′ȯ nĭ). Land or territory dependent upon and more or less controlled by another country. 76

compass (kŭm′pȧs). Arrows or other lines drawn on or beside a map to show directions on the map. 12

conservation (kŏn′sēr vā′shŭn). Making wise use of natural resources through avoiding waste and preparing for future use. 303

corduroy (kôr′dŭ roi). A term used to describe early roads built by laying logs crosswise along the route. 198

cotton gin (kŏt″n jĭn). A machine used to separate the seeds from the fibers of the cotton plant. 159

crater (krā′tēr). The hole, often wide and deep, at the top of a volcano. 353

credit (krĕd′ĭt). An agreement between buyer and seller in which the buyer does not pay the seller the full price of an item at the time of purchase. Both agree on the time of full payment in the future. 264

dame school (dām skōōl). A colonial school for young boys and girls in which a housewife held classes in her home. 100

democracy (dė mŏk′rȧ sĭ). A form of government under which the people themselves have a voice in the making of laws and selection of officials to run the government. 157

densely populated (dĕns'lĭ pŏp'ů lăt ĕd). Inhabited by many people. 281

dependent (dê pĕn'dĕnt). Looking to another for supplying a want or need. 369

diagram (dī'å grăm). A drawing used to show the construction or the operation of something. 19

dictator (dĭk tā'tẽr). Someone who exercises complete control of a government and all the people living under it. 265

economic system (ē'kŏ nôm'ĭk sĭs tẽm). The way in which business operates to supply the needs and wants of the people. 369

erode (ê rōd'). Wear away, often by the action of wind or moving waters. 336

exports (ĕks'pōrts). Goods sent from a country, city, or other area to be sold away from that area. 225

federal government (fĕd'ẽr ăl gŭv'ẽrn mĕnt). That government which has jurisdiction throughout an entire country. 151

fertile (fûr'tĭl). Having the necessary minerals and other richness to allow the production of crops. 315

flatboats (flăt'bōts). Large flat-bottomed boats used in the early days of water transportation in the United States. 164

flint (flĭnt). An extremely hard kind of stone often used by the Indians in making arrowheads. 62

free state (frē stāt). A state in which slavery is against the law. 206

frontier (frŭn tẽr'). A border of a country or other area which faces an unsettled area. 126

generator (jĕn'ẽr ā'tẽr). A machine used to produce power, often electrical power. 284

glacier (glā'shẽr). A great sheet of ice and snow extending over a given area of land. 28

globe (glōb). Small form made to look like the earth. 10

graph (grȧf). A kind of diagram using specially indicated divisions to show relationships among facts. 17

harvesting (här'vĕst ĭng). The gathering of a crop from the field when it is fully ripened. 193

hornbook (hôrn'bʊ̄k). A small board on which the letters of the alphabet and other educational material was written. The board was protected by a thin layer of transparent "horn" taken from the horns of animals. 100

Ice Age (īs āj). A period during prehistoric times when large areas of the earth were covered by glaciers. 28

immigrants (ĭm'ĭ grănts). Persons coming from one country to live in another country. 224

impressment (ĭm'prĕs'mẽnt). Forcing into the service of a person or group of persons. 178

indentured (ĭn dĕn'tụrd). Obligated to serve another person for an agreed length of time. 102

indigo (ĭn'dĭ gō). A kind of plant from which blue indigo dye is made. 92

interdependent (ĭn'tẽr dê pĕn'dĕnt). Two or more parties, each of which looks to another to supply wants or needs. 369

irrigation (ĭr ĭ gā'shŭn). A man-made method for bringing water to dry lands so that the soil may produce crops. 38

jerky (jûr kĭ). Meat that has been sliced or stripped and then dried. 160

key (kē). A listing to explain the meaning of symbols used on a map. 15

laborers (lā'bẽr ẽrz). Persons making up the working force of a factory. 251

latitude (lăt'ĭ tŭd). Distance measured in degrees north and south of the earth's equator. 11

locks (lŏks). Man-made water stairway for ships going from one level of water to another. 196

longitude (lŏn'jĭ tŭd). Distances measured in degrees east and west of the prime meridian of the earth. 10

maize (māz). The Indians' name for the type of corn they raised in the New World. 86

manufacturing (măn'ů făk'tụr ĭng). The making of any item, either by hand or with the use of machinery. 158

market (mȧr'kẽt). A place at which buying and selling takes place. 169

map (măp). A drawing representing a portion of the earth's surface. 11

mesa (mā'sȧ). A type of rocky hill with a flat top and steeply-sloping sides. 299

militia (mĭ lĭsh'ȧ). A group of citizens trained in military procedures but called to duty only in emergencies. 135

minutemen (mĭn'ĭt mĕn). A group of American men who promised to be ready to fight the English on a minute's notice during the years just before the War for Independence. 134

missionaries (mĭsh'ŭn ẽr'ĭz). People whose work it is to help needy people in any way they can. Missionaries are often supported by churches. 79

natural resources (năt'ů răl rê'sōrs ĕs). Any plants, animals, minerals, or other materials found in nature for which man has a useful purpose. 223

navigation (năv'ĭ gā'shŭn). The science of steering a correct and true course, especially on the water or in the air. 47

pack train (păk trān). A number of animals used by man to carry goods from one place to another. 118

patriot (pā′trĭ ŭt). One who loves his country well and fights hard for all it represents. 137

plantation (plăn tā′shŭn). A large farm on which many of the daily needs of the workers are met within the limits of the plantation itself. 102

plowshare (plou′shâr). The blade, or that part of the plow that cuts into the earth. 192

population (pŏp′ụ lā′shŭn). The total number of persons living within any given area. 224

profit (prŏf′ĭt). Money left after all the expenses of a business have been paid. 170

projection (prō jĕk′shŭn). The particular method of changing the shapes of land and water areas of the earth that a mapmaker uses to show portions of the earth's curved surface on that map. 11

protectorate (prō tĕk′tĕr ĭt). A country or other area dependent upon another for any number of needs. 359

politics (pŏl′ĭ tĭks). The science of government or of running a government. 209

ratify (răt′ĭ fī). Accept or approve. 155

raw materials (rô mȧ tēr′ĭ ȧlz). Materials from which products are manufactured. 284

reaper (rēp′ēr). A type of farm machine used for cutting grain in the field. 193

represent (rĕp′rė̇ zĕnt′). To speak in behalf of another. 131

reservations (rĕz′ēr vā′shŭnz). Large areas of land owned by the federal government and set aside for the use of Indians. 235

reservoir (rĕz′ēr vwôr). Large body of water held behind a dam. 304

scale (skāl). The listing which indicates how much of the earth's surface is shown by a certain measure on a map. 12

section (sĕc′shŭn). One square mile of land. 153

sod (sŏd). The top layer of soil containing grass and its roots. 229

sodbuster (sŏd′bŭs′tēr). A name often given to settlers of the Great Plains regions during the 1800's. 229

source (sōrs). The point at which a river begins. 172

sparsely populated (spärs′lĭ pŏp′ụ lāt ĕd). Inhabited by few persons. 281

standard of living (stăn′dĕrd ŏv lĭv′ĭng). The degree to which people are able to get the things they want and need for themselves. 369

stock (stŏk). A share in a company or business. 263

stock market (stŏk mär′kĕt). A place where stocks are bought and sold. 263

tepee (tē′pēz). A tent-like dwelling of American Indians, made by covering a pole framework with animal skins. 45

textiles (tĕks′tīlz). Woven fabrics and/or items made from woven fabrics. 284

town meeting (toun mēt ĭng). A political practice begun by New England settlers in which all the citizens of the town met to decide local law. 84

towpath (tō′păth). A path along the bank of a river or canal and used by a team of work animals pulling a boat. 198

transatlantic (trăns′ăt lăn′tĭk). Reaching across the Atlantic Ocean. 373

tribe (trīb). A particular group of Indians that worked together in one way or another and followed a certain system of government. 30

trust (trŭst). One giant company made of several smaller ones in the same line of business. 251

tutor (tū′tēr). A private teacher hired to instruct only a few or even one pupil. 103

union (ūn′yŭn). An organization of laborers through which workers make their views known to management. 251

uranium (ụ rā′nĭ ŭm). An extremely rare element used as a source of atomic energy. 338

voyage (voi′ĭj). A journey by sea or water. 50

wigwam (wĭg′wŏm). A hut-like Indian dwelling made of grasses, or animal skins. 31

Index

A number in boldface type indicates a map on a page.

Texas, 63, 176

ACKNOWLEDGMENTS

Acknowledgment is made to the following agencies for permission to reproduce photographs:
Bettmann Archive, 256, 257
Chicago Historical Society, 100, 213, 244-247
Esther Henderson, 333, 335
Kaufmann & Fabry, 323
Shostal, Cover
United Press International, 63 (posed by actors re-enacting historical event), 265, 278, 279, 282, 283 top, 284-285, 290, 298, 320, 335 bottom, 342

Photographs appearing on the pages indicated here appear through the courtesy of the following:
City of Detroit, Title page
Mathilda Schirmer, 29
Ford Motor Company, 255, 319
Atomic Energy Commission, 266
National Aeronautics & Space Administration, 268-270
Ohio River Company, 271
Buffalo Chamber of Commerce, 283
Reading Company, 284
National Broadcasting Company, 286
Shade Tobacco Growers Agricultural Association, 287
Vermont Development Department, 289
State Planning & Development Commission, Concord, N.H., 289
Philadelphia City Representative, 291

U.S. Department of Agriculture, 296-297, 315, 333
Texas Highway Department, 303
Tennessee Valley Authority, 304
Oklahoma Planning & Resources Board, 298
Virginia Chamber of Commerce, 298
National Cotton Council, 306
North Dakota Travel Department, 312-313
Kansas Industrial Development Commission, 314
American Iron & Steel Institute, 315
Hotpoint, 317
Minnesota Vacation & Information Center, 318
Missouri Commerce Department, 324
U.S. Department of Interior, 330-331, 336, 343
National Park Service, 334
Climax Molybdenum Company, 337
Colorado Department of Public Relations, 339
Las Vegas News Bureau, 340
International Paper Company, 341
Hawaii Visitors Bureau, 348-349, 353
Pacific Area Travel Association, 352
Puerto Rico Information Service, 358
U.S. Defense Department, 359
Pan American Union, 360
Washington Visitors Bureau, 361
Toronto Board of Education, 366-367
United Nations, 374

Map Index